HOLY WRITINGS, SACRED TEXT

Also by John Barton
Published by Westminster John Knox Press

How the Bible Came to Be

Reading the Old Testament: Method in Bible Study
(Revised and Enlarged)

Holy Writings, Sacred Text

The Canon in Early Christianity

JOHN BARTON

Westminster John Knox Press
Louisville, Kentucky

Copyright © John Barton 1997

First published in Great Britain 1997
by Society for Promoting Christian Knowledge,
Holy Trinity Church, Marylebone Road, London NW1 4DU

Unless otherwise stated, the scripture quotations in this book
are from the Revised Standard Version of the Bible,
copyrighted 1973 by the Division of Christian Education
of the National Council of the Churches of Christ in the U.S.A.,
and are used by permission.

Cover design by Pam Poll

First American edition
Published by Westminster John Knox Press
Louisville, Kentucky

This book is printed on acid-free paper that meets the
American National Standards Institute Z39.48 standard. ⊛

PRINTED IN THE UNITED STATES OF AMERICA
98 99 00 01 02 03 04 05 06 07 — 10 9 8 7 6 5 4 3 2 1

Library of Congress Cataloging-in-Publication Data

Barton, John, date.
   [Spirit and the letter]
   Holy writings, sacred text : the canon in early Christianity /
John Barton. — 1st American ed.
      p.   cm.
   Originally published: The spirit and the letter. London : Society
for Promoting Christian Knowledge, 1997.
   Includes bibliographical references and indexes.
   ISBN 0-664-25778-X (alk. paper)
   1. Bible—Canon.   2. Bible—Evidences, authority, etc.   I. Title.
BS465.B36 1998
220.1′2—dc21   97-41413

For Mary and Katie

Contents

LIST OF ABBREVIATIONS

ABD	*The Anchor Bible Dictionary*, ed. D. N. Freedman, New York and London 1992
BETL	Bibliotheca ephemeridum theologicarum lovaniensium
BHTh	Beiträge zur historischen Theologie
CBQ	*Catholic Biblical Quarterly*
ET	English translation
HThR	*Harvard Theological Review*
HUCA	*Hebrew Union College Annual*
IDB	*The Interpreter's Dictionary of the Bible*, ed. G. A. Buttrick, Nashville 1962
JBL	*Journal of Biblical Literature*
JR	*Journal of Religion*
JSOT	*Journal for the Study of the Old Testament*
JTS	*Journal of Theological Studies*
LXX	Septuagint
MS	Monograph series
NTS	*New Testament Studies*
NT Suppl.	Supplements to *Novum Testamentum*
OS	Oudtestamentische Studiën
OTL	Old Testament Library
PG	*Patrologia Graeca*
SBL	Society of Biblical Literature
SJOT	*Scandinavian Journal of Theology*
SNTS	Society for New Testament Studies
TLZ	*Theologische Literaturzeitung*
TU	Texte und Untersuchungen
TZ	*Theologische Zeitschrift*
VT	*Vetus Testamentum*
VTS	Supplements to *Vetus Testamentum*
WA	*Weimarer Ausgabe* of the works of Luther
WUNT	Wissenschaftliche Untersuchungen zum Neuen Testament
ZAW	*Zeitschrift für die alttestamentliche Wissenschaft*
ZNW	*Zeitschrift für die neutestamentliche Wissenschaft*
ZThK	*Zeitschrift für Theologie und Kirche*

Preface

I BECAME INTERESTED in the biblical canon when working on two books in the 1980s. In *Reading the Old Testament*, a survey of the various methods used in biblical study, I had to engage with the work of Brevard S. Childs and his 'canonical approach'. This is a hermeneutic of the Bible which, though it includes a particular theory about the formation of the canon, focuses primarily on how we should read Scripture today. At the same time I was also working on *Oracles of God*, an analysis of how the 'prophetic' books of the Old Testament were interpreted in the Second Temple and New Testament periods, and for this I had to establish which books were then regarded as 'prophetic'. To my surprise, this turned out to involve complex issues to do with the formation of the Old Testament and its 'canonization'. Though I do not believe the historical and the hermeneutical questions are directly connected, nevertheless they have continued to rub together in my mind. Both relate to an overarching interest in the reception of biblical texts, in both ancient and modern times.

In addition, studying the Old Testament canon and coming to what I thought were some new conclusions about it led me to wonder whether similar questions might be asked of the New Testament, and so I have found myself venturing into New Testament studies and even patristics, much as I did in *Oracles of God*. The result is a book that deals with the canon of both Old and New Testaments, and their complex relationship with each other, but not in any exhaustive way: I have not even attempted to be comprehensive in my coverage, and I offer primarily some suggestions or food for thought, inviting the reader to consider some questions that the standard textbooks do not deal with.

This is a historical study. It is only indirectly a contribution to the current debate about the canon of Scripture, biblical authority, and hermeneutical theory. It is not that I think these matters unimportant. On the contrary, I think they are so important that they cannot be dealt with at the same time as conducting an investigation into the origins, and original significance, of the biblical canon. Readers critical of my historical conclusions will probably think that they derive from prior convictions about these other questions, and some of course will argue that historical enquiry always is driven by contemporary concerns in any case. I am under no illusion that my disclaimer will save me from either of these allegations—especially the second, which is not an accusation but a general theory about the sociology of knowledge. Without getting into a general discussion of whether 'objective' study is possible, and if so whether it is desirable, I think it is worth pointing out that the conclusions to which I come in this book do not seem to me to serve either a conservative or a liberal agenda as these are generally conceived, but point to shortcomings in both. At least, they do so if either liberal or conservative religious believers appeal to alleged historical facts in justifying their own attitudes to the canon. If they do not, then nothing in my work can either confirm or contradict them, because I nowhere say how Scripture *should* be regarded; only how it was in fact regarded at various points in the past. I believe my findings could be related to current concerns where these do involve hypotheses about the origins and development of the canon: but to do so would require another book.

Hebrew and Greek are transliterated here by a system which is much simpler and cruder than the standard scholarly systems but entirely adequate, I believe, for a book in which nothing hinges on replicating all the graphic features of the original texts. Those who know Greek and Hebrew will recognize the words easily enough. The only less-than-obvious convention is the use of (i) to indicate iota subscript in Greek.

The basis of *Holy Writings, Sacred Text* is my Hulsean Lectures, delivered in Cambridge in the Lent Term 1990. It is a pleasure to thank the Board of Management of the Hulsean Fund for electing me into the Lectureship, and to colleagues in Cambridge who made me so welcome when I delivered the Lectures.

The material has been extensively reworked since then, and drafts of various chapters have been given as papers and lectures to the Irish Biblical Association, the Divinity Faculty in the University of Aberdeen, the Religion in Antiquity Seminar and the Patristics Seminar in Oxford, the Theology Faculty Colloquium in Baylor University, Waco, Texas, and the Theology Society in the University College of North Wales, Bangor. For the many suggestions made by members of the audience on these occasions I am very grateful, and also to my hosts, Kevin Cathcart, William Johnstone, Maurice Wiles, Bill Bellinger, Gwilym Jones, and Catrin Williams.

Many friends and colleagues have given me advice and help with particular themes and problems, and I should like to thank in particular Ernest Nicholson, Martin Goodman, Jeremy Hughes, and Joanna Davson; and also Tal Goldfajn, who helped me to think about ideas of language and meaning in Jewish thought, an important theme in the book.

As always, thanks are also due to my wife, Mary, and our daughter, Katie, for much support and encouragement, and the book is dedicated to them both with love.

Everyone at SPCK has been helpful – and patient, for the book has been too many years in the making.

John Barton

～1～
The Origins of the Canon:
An Imaginary Problem?

> The discordant objects, not carefully placed for effect, had
> through time acquired a rightness of place.
>
> P. D. James. *Original Sin*, London 1994, p. 28

THE FORMATION OF the Christian Bible is a story with neither
beginning nor end. The first Christians already had a scripture,
inherited from Judaism, whose origins time has concealed; while
still today the edges of the biblical canon are blurred, with old
disputes about the 'deuterocanonical' books asleep perhaps, but
by no means dead. But no one would deny that there was a critical
period for the canonization of the New Testament portion of this
Bible. Its outer limits are marked by the life and teaching of Jesus,
and the series of fourth- and fifth-century conciliar decisons which
settled all but a few marginal uncertainties about the contents of
the New Testament. Though the evidence is scrappy, circumstantial, and often obscure, most of it has been known for the last two
centuries, and the basic texts are already to be found as an appendix
to the Hulsean Lectures of Christopher Wordsworth, delivered in
1848 and published in the same year.[1] Bruce M. Metzger's *The
Canon of the New Testament*[2] adds further material and a wealth of
secondary literature; but at its heart lie the same texts that Wordsworth discussed. These and a few other texts may well be called
canonical themselves, and no theory about the biblical canon has
any hope of success unless it finds a place for them. But though the
texts are necessary, they are plainly not sufficient; for there remains
little agreement on their interpretation.

Cross Purposes in the Study of the Canon

The question which scholars have been trying to answer about
the origins of the New Testament canon may be put as follows.

How and why did the Church come to accept as authoritative
Scripture a New Testament containing no more and no less
than twenty-seven books, and to place this alongside either the
Hebrew or the Greek Scriptures, renamed the 'Old Testament'?
To this question there have been in scholarly tradition three
principal answers, whose proponents chase each other eternally
around the unchanging texts just mentioned like the figures on
Keats' Grecian urn, never catching each other yet never abandoning the chase. My aim is not to join them, but to see if I
can discover why they never succeed in meeting; and (to antici-
pate) my suggestion will be that the question of the canon, as
just posed, is what in German is called a *Scheinfrage*, an illusory
question or pseudo-problem. It is not that there are no questions
of substance involved in it, but that (as usually understood) it
bundles together so many questions that apparently conflicting
'solutions' of it seldom in reality share any common ground on
which to meet and clash.[3] Rather than looking for an answer to
the 'question of the canon', we shall try to take it apart, and shall
find that its components form a deeply interesting set of inter-
related topics which are seldom treated systematically. Our
object will therefore be the modest one of defining the agenda
for discussion, rather than providing a set of answers. But when
we have done so, we may find that the question of the canon has
disappeared, and that the urn has broken in our hands.

1. A first proposed solution to the question of the canon is that the
growth of the New Testament canon happened spontaneously;
the early Church simply continued the Jewish tendency to write
and revere authoritative religious books. Although, it may be
said, the faith of the first Christians was rooted in a person
rather than in a book, yet the passage of time made it essential
for the story of that person's life and teaching to be committed
to writing; and once this had happened, the New Testament
canon should be seen as already present, at least in embryo. To
discover the details of the process we call 'canonization' is chiefly
a matter of investigating how the books of the New Testament
were *received* in the early Church. As soon as an early Christian
writer can be shown to cite or use the Gospel according to
Matthew, for example, we can say that we have evidence for the
canonicity of that Gospel.

The classic statement of this position is Theodor Zahn's massive *Geschichte des neutestamentlichen Kanons.*[4] Zahn made an exhaustive examination of New Testament citations in the Fathers, and concluded that there was already a Christian canon by the end of the first century. This does not necessarily mean that the Church entered the second century with every one of the present twenty-seven books already canonized; citations of the Pastorals, for example, or of the minor catholic epistles, do not become plentiful until somewhat later. But there was already, according to Zahn, a collection that we may without anachronism call the 'New Testament', even though he knew that this term did not itself become current until later. The essential point in Zahn's reconstruction is that the New Testament was a spontaneous creation of the first generations of Christians, not something forced on the Church by internal or external pressures. As such, it belonged to the earliest period of the Church, as citations and allusions from the Apostolic Fathers onwards made evident. This had already been argued in an earlier British contribution to the history of the canon, Westcott's *A General Survey of the History of the Canon of the New Testament.*[5] 'According to Westcott,' as Metzger observes,

> the formation of the canon was among the first instinctive acts of the Christian society, resting upon the general confession of the Churches and not upon independent opinions of its members. The canon was not the result of a series of contests; rather, canonical books were separated from others by the intuitive insight of the Church.[6]

Empirical evidence of all kinds is capable of either undergirding or undermining this position. For example, if there was an 'ecumenical edition' of Paul's letters (even one lacking Hebrews or the Pastorals) by the early second century,[7] then we should probably agree with Zahn that they were already well on the way to becoming 'scriptural' or 'canonical' for the Christians who received them. For to collect letters originally addressed to a series of different churches, each with its specific problems, and ensure that they are read in all the churches, is surely to say that they have just the kind of wider and more generalized value and reference which belongs to what we mean by 'Scripture'. But if, on the other hand, it could be shown that well into the second century there were writers who did not know, or who even rejected, major portions of our New Testament – as it is sometimes maintained that Justin did not know the Fourth Gospel[8] – that would weaken the case for so early a date for the incipient 'canon'. And of course very late datings for New Testament books, such as the Tübingen School's mid- or late-second-century date for John and Acts,[9] would equally make Zahn's early canon impossible to maintain. But Zahn himself had helped to demolish this possibility in any case, by showing the authenticity of the letters of Ignatius, with their allusions to passages in both works.[10]

What is less clear is that Zahn was really vulnerable to the main attack he actually received, that of Adolf von Harnack. In the sixth appendix to his *The Origin of The New Testament*[11] Harnack argued in effect that most of Zahn's meticulously compiled evidence was irrelevant to the question in hand. It showed only that (most of) the New Testament books were known and used in the early Church, not that they were scriptural or canonical. Harnack's objection points to something extremely important, a blurriness in the focus of Zahn's enquiry which made it seem more useful than it really was. Zahn drew little distinction between (a) using a book, (b) citing it as an authority, (c) regarding it as 'Scripture', and (d) assigning it a place in a restricted, official 'canon'.

But Harnack's attack on Zahn did little to clarify matters, since he himself failed to see quite how subtle the problem was. The four categories just mentioned are not discrete. They are points on a spectrum, and there are infinite gradations between them. Harnack writes as though there were a simple contrast between the citation of a work as important, and its acceptance as canonical Scripture – simple and opposed categories, at opposite ends of the range of possibilities. But the prior question is: had people in the late first century attained such conceptual clarity about the distinction between 'canonical' and 'non-canonical' in Harnack's sense? If they had not, then Zahn may well have been answering (and answering correctly) the only question it makes sense to ask for this early period. In strictly formal terms, Harnack would then have been quite correct to regard Zahn's early dating of the 'canon' as a failure; but in point of substance little would be changed. It would still be true that many New Testament books were held in very high regard by the end of the first century; we should simply have been put on our guard against using the term 'canon' to describe this phenomenon.

This brief discussion of one of the most important early modern disputes over the canon may help to give plausibility to the earlier hint that many questions in the study of the canon are matters of appearance rather than of substance: terminological controversies in which the antagonists talk past each other, though often with great skill and sophistication. That is not all there is to be said, not by far; Harnack and Zahn were not merely at cross purposes; but at cross purposes they certainly were.

2. Be that as it may, the distinction Harnack drew in his controversy with Zahn was to prove crucial for all subsequent study of the New Testament canon. Ever since Harnack it has been usual to see a critical difference between citations of (or allusions to) New Testament books pure and simple, and their citation *as Scripture*; and the present majority view of the formation of the Christian Bible owes more, perhaps, to this distinction, painstakingly applied by a long line of distinguished scholars, than to any other single discovery.

Westcott, in fact, had already used the following test: is a book cited as *graphē*, or with the introductory formula *gegraptai*?[12] Applying this test tended to produce a later date than Zahn's for the clear emergence of the canon – the mid-to-late second century. And this is the period that has now almost universally established itself as the critical one, with Justin Martyr at one end and Origen at the other. Since Harnack, it has become usual to see the preceding period as mere preparation – a time when not-yet-canonical writings circulated and were gradually accepted beyond the communities that produced them; and to see the time from Origen down to the eventual conciliar decisions about the limits of the canon as what A. C. Sundberg aptly calls a 'mopping-up exercise'.[13] The second century emerges as more important than the other two periods, because in it we find the essential issue on which the notion of 'canonicity' hinges being addressed articulately for the first time, and resolved more or less unambiguously. In asking whether or not a Christian book is cited as *graphē* – that is, in the same manner as the Old Testament – one is discovering whether or not the Church attributed to it the same status as the Old Testament.

Applying this criterion enables one to face in two directions at the same time. If a book is so cited, that means that it had 'scriptural' or 'canonical' status: so *at least* this book must have been part of a (semi-)official collection commanding general respect and on a par with the older scriptures of the Jews. If a book was not cited as *graphē*, then it must have been outside the collection; and hence we can begin to form some idea of what the collection contained *at most*. Once there is a criterion that will determine unambiguously both that certain books definitely were 'Scripture' and that others definitely were not, we can speak unequivocally of the existence of a canon, a *list*, where it is permissible 'neither to add nor to take away'.[14]

Central to Harnack's understanding of the second-century synthesis is this double movement of inclusion and exclusion. The fixing of the canon is no longer seen as a process of natural, almost unconscious growth, but as a work of deliberate selection. In Harnack's terminology, the *growth* of a body of Christian writings is a pre-canonical stage. One might see growth as the result of 'intrinsic' factors – the need for a written record to replace fast-disappearing memories of Jesus, the collection and dissemination of apostolic letters that could otherwise have been lost. But the drive to *selection* from this larger amorphous corpus of material was much more the result of 'extrinsic' constraints – first and foremost, the suppression of heresy.

> The heterodox often raised questions about the text, the authorship, and the meaning of biblical books because they wanted to get rid of unattractive doctrines. The problems they raised made it necessary for churches to create lists of the books accepted by the churches. Such lists very gradually turned into canons, or authoritative lists, of the books generally accepted.[15]

Thus we arrive at one of Harnack's most celebrated theses: that we owe our New Testament to the conflict with Marcion.

This thesis, which has been elaborated in a new context above all by Hans von Campenhausen, will be discussed in detail in the next chapter, and I shall say little about its merits here. It is important, however, to see its structural importance in Harnack's emphasis on the second century. Harnack argued that there were many forms the Christian Bible could have taken – seven possibilities are listed in the second appendix to *The Origin of the New Testament*, and we shall consider them, too, in the next chapter. The controversy with Marcion pushed the Church towards accepting the kind of canon Marcion had adopted, though with a different content.

Marcion forced the Church to make up its mind on the question
of what to *include* in the Bible. Marcion's Bible is said to have been
twofold, 'Gospel' (a mutilated version of Luke) plus 'Apostle' (an
expurgated version of the major Pauline epistles, with Galatians at
its head because of its polemic against 'judaizing'). This twofold
structure, Harnack claimed, lies at the root of the Church's canon
of dominical plus apostolic writings, and to counter Marcion
much more was included in each part than he had allowed: all
four Gospels, all of Paul's epistles, and other apostolic writings,
as well as Luke's second volume (Acts). But in a sense Marcion's
canon was tripartite, for (according to Tertullian) his own *Antitheses* were appended as a kind of anti-Old Testament. The
Church responded to this not by producing something like a
testimonia book, but by annexing the whole Old Testament – no
longer as an independent collection, but as part of a single Christian Bible. Thus Marcion did not only determine the shape of the
New Testament, but in a sense was responsible also for the idea
that the Old and New Testaments were not two separate collections, but parts of a single one. Harnack saw the anti-Marcionite
Christian Bible as the result of a quite deliberate and conscious
decision by (particularly) the Roman church. However much
work remained to be done on it, the decisive step was taken at
the time of the Marcionite crisis, and all else could very well be
described as mere 'mopping up'.

Though many modern scholars are sceptical of the importance
Harnack attached to Marcion,[16] it would be widely accepted that
he was roughly right about the period in which something recog-
nizable as our Christian Bible emerged, and that controversy with
heresy was a formative factor. Hans von Campenhausen[17] has extended Harnack's idea so as to encompass also the Montanist
crisis. In the process he helps to show how a single hypothesis –
the need to combat heresy – could account not only for the
Church's decision to include particular books in its Scriptures
but also for its decision to exclude others. This theory has the
effect of confirming the mid-second century as the decisive
moment at which *both* halves of the formula 'neither to add nor
to take away' became established, and hence the moment when
the canon in the true sense was born. Against Marcion, the
Church was impelled to decide that it could not spare certain
books from its Scriptures; against the Montanists, that others

(such as the Montanists' own prophecies) must not be included on any terms.[18]

Harry Gamble sums up the alleged Montanist influence on the formation of the canon as follows:

> First, since the prophetic oracles of Montanus and his followers were sometimes compiled in written form and cited as authoritative, the church had to disclaim these by specifying which writings did have authoritative value. Second, and more important, because Montanism asserted new and continuing revelation, the church was led to insist that inspired revelation was confined to an age now past – the age of Christ and the apostles – and that only such teachings as derived from that time had binding force . . . Thus, just as Marcion is often credited with conceiving the idea of a canon and forcing the church, in reaction to him, to enlarge the scope of its authoritative scripture, so Montanism can be viewed as later furnishing the opposite impetus to limit the scope of authoritative writings.[19]

Gamble himself is sceptical about the influence of Montanism on the formation of the canon, but it is interesting to note that Metzger still attaches considerable importance to it.[20] If there is a consensus about this, it is probably that Montanism, like Marcionism, was 'one factor among others' in edging the Church towards the canonization of its Scriptures. Above all, what has established itself as received wisdom is that the second century saw the first serious attempts to resolve the balancing-act that allowed both inclusive and exclusive tendencies their proper place, and thus began to make clear both the supreme authority of the books within the approved collection and the inferiority of those outside it. Most scholars see the sharper focus and definition of 'Scripture' or 'canon' which we owe to the work of Harnack and his followers as an unmitigated gain, even if the importance of second-century heresies in making the Church define the contents of the canon has been exaggerated.

3. Yet not everyone is happy with the second-century theory of the canon. The main dissenting voice in recent years has been that of A. C. Sundberg, whose studies of the canonization of the New Testament followed his major work of reassessment of the Old Testament canon.[21] Central to Sundberg's theories about both

Testaments is an insistence that the term 'canon' should be distinguished from the term 'Scripture'. In the case of the Old Testament, he argues that there were *scriptures* in Judaism from at least the fifth century BC, but no *canon* until well into the Christian era. 'Scriptures' are books which a community accepts as holy and authoritative – which may be an open-ended class; but a 'canon' is an exclusive list of the books which have such a status. As Metzger helpfully puts it, there is a difference between a collection of authoritative books and an authoritative collection of books.[22] It was not (Sundberg claims) until the second or third century AD *or* that Jews began to understand Scripture as a closed category to which no other books could be admitted.

The distinction can readily be illustrated from the alleged influence of Marcionism and Montanism, each of which bears on one of the two equal and opposite issues involved in 'canonization'. The development to which Marcionism is supposed to have given the impetus, that of including more in the New Testament than Marcion wished, could not on Sundberg's definition be regarded as part of 'canonization'. On the other hand, the alleged effect of Montanism was indeed to make Christians restrict their Scriptures by excluding certain books, and this would therefore count as incipient 'canonization'. Sundberg does not in fact share the view that Montanism had this effect, but if he did, he would allow the word 'canon' to be used in that connection, whereas for the alleged reaction to Marcion it would be wholly inappropriate.

The differences between the traditional Christian Old Testament, following the LXX, and the more restricted Hebrew Scriptures, reflect for Sundberg the fact that in the first century AD Scripture for both Jews and Christians was simply a 'wide religious literature without definite bounds'.[23] The respective Greek and Hebrew canons of the Old Testament reflect later decisions by Christians and Jews respectively. Sundberg's theories about the Old Testament canon proved to have two implications for the student of the New Testament canon.

(i) If we believe that the Old Testament canon of Scripture was delimited only after a very long development in which its scriptural status had come gradually to be acknowledged, we shall be predisposed to think that something similar might have happened in the case of the New Testament. Perhaps Harnack did not go far enough when he suggested that the canon came into being as late as the second century. To speak of 'canonicity', it is necessary to show that certain texts were consciously and deliberately excluded and, more, that the resulting collection of 'canonical' texts had an official status; and this, Sundberg believes, cannot be shown anything like as early as this.

The one supposedly second-century text that purports to give an official listing of biblical books is the Muratorian Fragment, but Sundberg argues that this has been wrongly dated. So far from being a late-second-century Roman list, it should be regarded as a fourth-century text from the Eastern church. Sundberg has carried few scholars with him in this, no doubt partly because there has been a feeling that the later dating is all too convenient for his theoretical position. But the most recent discussion of the Fragment, by Geoffrey M. Hahneman, has shown that Sundberg had much more evidence on his side than is generally realized, and has argued forcefully for the late dating.[24] Hahneman's arguments seem to me generally convincing. But, as we shall see later, even an early date for the Fragment does not necessarily do much harm to Sundberg's theories. It might fairly be said that he has simply been more consistent and logical than Harnack in distinguishing the growth of Scripture from the closing of the canon. If 'canon' is defined as tightly as he prefers to define it, it is hard to find clear evidence for it much before the late fourth century – especially if one tries to be true to the Church's own use of the word *kanōn*, since by general consent Athanasius' Festal Letter 39 of 367 is the first unequivocal evidence for the use of the word to mean a fixed list of biblical texts.

INT

(ii) If Sundberg is right about the fixing of the Old Testament canon, this has a direct effect on the argument from citation formulas such as *hōs gegraptai* with quotations from *New* Testament books. In the second century, he holds, the use of such a formula with a quotation from what we now know as the *Old* Testament did not imply that the book quoted formed part of an exclusive, authoritative corpus, since there was as yet no such thing. Accordingly, the fact that New Testament quotations are sometimes introduced by this formula cannot be used to show that New Testament books were 'canonical'. 'The Christian church did not receive a canon of scripture but scripture on its way to a definite canon in Judaism. And it was not until the third century and after that the church came to struggle with the problem of defining its Old Testament for itself.' Consequently, 'the comparison of the citations of Christian literature with Old Testament citations cannot establish canonicity for Christian writings.'[25]

It is not only, as others have pointed out, that the citation of a New Testament text even with a formula such as *gegraptai* need not necessarily imply recognition of it as a Scripture, in that the formula may be used in error (for example, under the misapprehension through a memory-slip that the passage being quoted comes from the Old Testament). Nor is it merely (as Sundberg himself suggests) that too much is being read into *gegraptai* or *graphē* anyway, and they are really not technical terms. It is that the authoritative texts which could appropriately be cited as 'Scripture' or 'that which stands written' were not yet felt to form a closed corpus to which nothing might be added. The point can be well illustrated from Theophilus' *ad Autolycum*. Here indeed the Fourth Gospel is cited as *graphē*. But little can be proved from this; for Theophilus (2:36) cites sayings of the Sibyl in the same breath as utterances of the Old Testament prophets, and probably regarded them also as *graphē* – which for him seems to mean any text which was composed under prophetic inspiration. If such texts are to be called 'canonical', then Theophilus' 'canon' contains, potentially, all inspired utterances from every human culture. There is no denying that he ascribes a high status to John (and Paul), putting them on a par with other prophetic texts; but it is wholly misleading to talk of his 'canon', an anachronism of the worst kind.

As Sundberg puts it, 'In the first centuries, no other criterion than inspiration, poured out freely upon the church, was required for a Christian writing to be regarded as scripture (Iren. Haer. III. xxi.3–4).'[26] Indeed, Harnack had said something similar: 'It is firmly established that this collection of inspired writings [sc. the New Testament] is a remainder-product – for once upon a time everything that a Christian wrote for edification counted as inspired.'[27] But Harnack thought this was already changing in the second century; Sundberg believes it lasted well into the fourth.[28]

It has, I hope, by now become apparent how far the disagreements among the three positions I have outlined are disagreements about the definition of terms, rather than about matters of substance. It should be obvious that much in the progressively later dating of 'canonization' from Zahn through Harnack to Sundberg is generated simply by an ever-increasing narrowness of definition for the

term 'canon'. There has been a great deal of discussion of the ety-
mology and use of the term 'canon', authoritatively summarized
by Metzger in an appendix to his recent study.[29] Controversy cen-
tres on whether its eventual use to refer to Scripture in Christian
writers rests on the sense 'authoritative rule' – so that the 'canon' is
originally the same as the 'rule of faith', but comes by extension to
be those books in which the rule of faith is authoritatively communicated; or on the sense 'fixed list' (as in the so-called 'Alexan-
drian canon' of generally approved secular authors[30]). Whichever
is historically the case (and critical opinion seems on the whole to
favour the latter), modern scholars plainly equivocate when they
use the term. Even if we leave aside the use of 'canon' without the
article to refer to the final *Gestalt* of the Bible (as in the work of B.
S. Childs),[31] we may clearly identify a scholarly tradition which
speaks of texts as 'canonical' if they are widely received as possessing authority, and another which reserves the term for those texts
which, after a process of sifting and evaluation, have been approved and stand on a limited list.

If we use the term in the first sense, we are likely to endorse
Zahn's assessment, at least in outline, and argue that most of our
New Testament was canonical by the early second century: most
of these books were recognized as texts that Christians should take
seriously, and to which authority was ascribed. If we adopt the
second definition, we cannot date 'canonization' much before
the fourth century, and Athanasius' Festal Letter 39, which is the
first text in which Scriptures are explicitly said to be 'of' or 'not of'
the 'canon', becomes the earliest concrete evidence for it. If we
decided that we ought to use the term 'canon' only in a sense
that is attested historically, we should therefore have a choice between Zahn and Sundberg. Either Scripture could be said to be
canonical already by the early second century, in that Christian
writers were already ascribing authority to it then; or it did not
become canonical till the time of Athanasius, since that is when
the idea of a fixed list first emerged. The position adopted by Harnack, von Campenhausen and a broad consensus of other scholars
suffers from the disadvantage that it corresponds to no historically
attested use of the term 'canon'. But whichever solution we opt
for, it makes – and this is the essential point – scarcely any difference. Metzger notes this in relation to the controversy between
Zahn and Harnack, but it applies equally to all three of the positions we have outlined:

Harnack understood the New Testament canon as a collection of books that possessed authority because they were regarded as holy Scripture. . . . Accordingly he placed the rise of the New Testament at the close of the second century. Zahn, on the other hand, equally understood it as a collection of books possessing authority, but he did not insist that this authority should be based on the thesis that 'the New Testament is holy Scripture'. He could, therefore, speak of the existence of a New Testament 'canon' a hundred years earlier than Harnack could. The actual facts were hardly touched by the controversy.[32]

We might add, 'Sundberg understands the canon as a collection of books possessing unique authority, a collection from which all doubtful elements have been purged away and which is defined by an authoritative list. Accordingly he places the rise of the New Testament canon in the mid-fourth century. But the actual facts are hardly touched by his arguments.'

Precisely similar problems arise in discussing the Old Testament canon, as I have tried to show in my book *Oracles of God*.[33] There, scholars range from those who see the Old Testament as essentially complete in the fourth or third century BC, to those who would argue that its canon was still 'open' well into the Christian era – Sundberg, as we saw above, believes that Jews and Christians 'closed' their Old Testament canon independently, and that neither the Greek nor the Hebrew Old Testament was 'canonical' before about the third century AD.

Yet there too the differences are in many ways at a terminological level. S. Z. Leiman, a proponent of the very early dating, defines a canonical book as 'a book accepted by Jews as authoritative for religious practice and/or doctrine, and whose authority is binding upon the Jewish people for all generations'.[34] Sundberg, on the other hand, distinguishes 'scripture' as 'religious literature that is in some sense authoritative' from 'canon' as 'a closed collection of scripture'.[35] It is obvious that this definition will produce a later dating. But it is not clear that much of substance is changed. There is undeniably a different atmosphere in the work of these two scholars: Leiman creates an impression that Jewish Scripture is venerable and trustworthy and has always been thought so, Sundberg that it is shifting and doubtful and that not very much depends upon it. In the same way, in the sphere of New Testament studies, Zahn is much more likely to appeal to conservative Chris-

tians than Sundberg or even Harnack. But the difference is nearly
all at this rather emotive level, and our understanding of how various texts came to be seen as part of 'the Bible' is not materially
affected whichever solution we adopt.

The Use of Scripture

Our discussion may seem by now to have run into the sand. I have
tried to move, by apparently logical stages, towards a conclusion
which surely cannot be true: that there is really no disagreement on
the question of the canon. Well, as I have already hinted, I do in
fact believe that there are real (and major) disagreements between
scholars on the questions to which the shorthand term 'canonization' has conventionally been attached. But it was important to
show that these disagreements do not lie where they appear to lie.

Where should we go from here? A possible way forward has
been suggested in a recent book by an Austrian statistician,
Franz Stuhlhofer.[36] Stuhlhofer argues that an underlying flaw in
traditional discussion of the canon is the use of a 'two-class' model,
according to which books are either canonical or not. This has
forced scholars to ask false (because anachronistic) 'yes or no'
questions about the canonical status of books. So long as we ask
only 'was this book canonical or not in this or that period?' we
presuppose that 'canonical' was something that books could be;
and our definition of it becomes a critical ingredient in the probable answer.

The sterility of the resulting discussion arises (so Stuhlhofer
believes) because the question is inappropriate to the material
being examined. Given their diverse definitions of 'canon',
almost all the scholars we have discussed are in a sense right in
their conclusions: (a) New Testament books did have considerable
authority in the late first and early second centuries, just as Zahn
thought; (b) they were added to, though not indiscriminately, in
the second to third centuries, as Harnack and von Campenhausen
believe; and (c) it is only from the fourth century onwards that we
find authoritative rulings about their exact compass.

But in another sense practically all the scholars are also wrong.
For (a) no one in the first century yet had the idea that the inchoate
New Testament would one day form a fixed, single book; (b) in
the 'formative period' identified by Harnack and von Campenhausen most of the books were already agreed by all, though there was

as yet very little opposition to including others; and (c) when fourth-century Fathers and councils attempted to regulate the 'canon', they were doing little more than codifying what was already almost universally accepted. This strongly suggests that most of the really interesting questions have somehow got lost in the web of words, and that the term 'canon' has merely darkened counsel.

It is worth asking whether other traditional questions about the canon may prove on inspection to be equally pseudo-questions. Stuhlhofer suggests that disagreement over whether canonization was a process of growth or of selection is similarly a matter primarily of terms. Obviously if one adopts Sundberg's definition of 'canon', then canonization is a process of selection: 'canonization' is the name (*our* name) for the cumulative effect of decisions that various books should be excluded, the hardening up of rulings against the acceptance of *antilegomena*. Just as obviously, on Zahn's definition canonization was a matter of growth. In each case, 'growth' or 'selection' is the process the two scholars have chosen respectively to discuss, and they have opted to call it 'canonization'. When, on the other hand, von Campenhausen sees the second-century developments as evidence that canonization involved *both* growth (e.g. inclusion of more books than Marcion was prepared to accept) *and* selection (refusal to accept Montanist claims that more books should be admitted), this is not really a disagreement with either of the more 'extreme' positions: it is just that von Campenhausen is prepared to use the word 'canonization' to do duty for both processes. All are in fact agreed that we owe the present New Testament both to the inclusion of books (otherwise it would not exist at all) and to the exclusion of books (otherwise it would have gone on growing indefinitely). Apparent disagreement is generated entirely by the introduction of the terms 'canon' and 'canonization'. Modern scholars are of course perfectly entitled to use these terms as they wish, but need to recognize the danger of building the conclusions into the premisses if they want to use them in discriminating among different historical reconstructions.

Stuhlhofer correctly (I believe) diagnoses what has gone wrong here as a tendency to interpret over-teleologically, as though those who brought about a certain historical state of affairs already had the end in mind from the beginning:

As with all processes that ended in an outcome which is still valid in the present, we as historians are in danger of judging matters with too much regard to the present. This danger is well known from the history of the natural sciences, but also (for example) from the history of the papacy. One is inclined to retroject current states of affairs or points of view into earlier times; and even when one recognizes that the present state of affairs was not yet a reality then, one is fixated onesidedly on the question how far the then state of affairs was still different from the present one, or alternatively how close it already was. Thus, we say, the scientist did not yet know, or did already know, what we know today; the Bishop of Rome was already recognized, or not yet recognized, as pope in the modern sense; and ecclesiastical writers did not yet have, or did already have, our present-day canon. History is being seen as a linear process: people of earlier times already had the same goal as us, but were simply not yet so close to it. But in reality past times often had quite different questions to ask, and quite different goals, from later ones, so that we fail to understand the past if we try to grasp historical sources by using modern categories of thought. For instance, we fail to understand the early history of the canon if, with each author we consider, we ask whether he reckoned this or that book as part of 'the canon' or 'the New Testament'; if we do that we are applying a division which emerged later to an earlier time, as if it were a matter of course that people could only live with such a two-category distinction (i.e. with the clearest possible delineation of a canon).[37]

Stuhlhofer has tried to establish some more useful categories by asking, statistically, about the intensity of citation and use of biblical books in the early Church. In this he is doing no more than Harnack himself had attempted in *Bible Reading in the Early Church*: 'The question *in what sense* the collection of writings known as the New Testament was regarded as a *Canon* of religion is not decided by saying that it was regarded as canonical, but can only be answered by finding out what use was actually made of this collection.'[38]

Stuhlhofer argues that at no time during the patristic age does a twofold classification of books into 'canonical' and 'non-canonical' correspond to what can be established about their use. The important question is not *whether* particular books were cited, but *how often* they were cited. And here it is misleading to quantify the use of a book as though all books were of equal size. If we do that we shall conclude, for example, that the shorter Pauline epistles must have been less important than the longer ones, because there are fewer examples of citation in the Fathers. What should be assessed is how much a book is quoted in relation to how often it ought to be quoted if all 'canonical' books were to be quoted *proportionately to their size*. When this statistical method is applied to the data provided (for example) by the *Biblia Patristica*, a clear pattern emerges which requires us to classify books into *three* rather than two classes. There are books cited substantially more frequently than one would expect, if all parts of the (later) New Testament had been equally important; books cited substantially less often than should be the case on that assumption; and books which are either scarcely cited at all or are cited only for purposes of rejection. (This corresponds in principle to the theoretical position as set out by Origen and Eusebius, which thinks not of 'canonical' and 'non-canonical' books, but of books definitely accepted (*homologoumena*), books definitely rejected (*notha*), and a third category of disputed books (*antilegomena*).[39] But the actual distribution of the books is not the same as theirs.)

The picture that emerges is surprisingly clear. From the Apostolic Fathers onwards, the Synoptic Gospels (especially Matthew), the Fourth Gospel, and the major Pauline epistles are cited very much more often than one would predict, if one supposed that the whole of the New Testament we now have was equally 'canonical' or important. Correspondingly, the rest of the New Testament (including Acts) is manifestly much less important.[40] The third category, books scarcely cited at all, contains most of those which later decisions and decrees affirm to be non-canonical; even in the earliest period none of them is cited even so often as the books of the second class.[41] All this is illustrated with a wealth of statistical information which it is hard for the non-specialist to evaluate, but which seems to me to move discussion of 'the canon' on to a new level of precision.

The formation of the New Testament, as Stuhlhofer understands it, involved three phases, which correspond approximately to our three (supposedly inconsistent) theories, and which show that all the scholars so far discussed really are, as we have suggested, correct in what they affirm even if mistaken in their rejection of each other.

1. In the first stage, which was complete astonishingly early, the great central core of the present New Testament was already being treated as the main authoritative source for Christians. There is little to suggest that there were any serious controversies about the Synoptics, John,[42] or the major Pauline epistles. As C. H. Dodd put it in his inaugural lecture in Cambridge in 1936: 'It is certain that the early Church . . . believed that the inmost secret of its life was variously expressed in the propositions, "The Kingdom of God is at hand" [Synoptics] – "If any man is in Christ there is a new creation" [Paul] – "The Logos was made flesh and dwelt among us" [John].'[43]

It is true that there are few references to these books as *graphē*, but it is also true that they are referred to more (proportionately to their bulk) than the Old Testament, by most writers from the Apostolic Fathers onwards. It is only in the third century that citations of the Old and New Testament begin to level out. This is perhaps the really surprising conclusion to which Stuhlhofer's statistics lead: that the core of the New Testament mattered more to the Church of the first two centuries than the Old, if we are to judge by its actual *use* of the texts. Stuhlhofer is not the only scholar to have noticed this in individual cases – Metzger, for example,[44] notes that Justin seems to regard the Gospels as in practice more important than the Old Testament, in his description of the liturgical use of these texts in First Apology 67:3–5. But Stuhlhofer shows that the point can be generalized, and applies to the great bulk of early Christian writers known to us. The figures are quite arresting: in the Apostolic Fathers, the New Testament is used the following times *more often* than the Old (with figures adjusted for the relative lengths of the two collections):[45]

Shepherd	5.5
2 Clement	5.5
Ignatius	5 to 50
Didache	12
Polycarp	27

The figures are approximate, and will vary with different editors' assessment of what counts as a 'use' of biblical texts (hence the wild discrepancy over Ignatius), which is a matter of judgement in which a statistician cannot get involved. But it is hardly to be supposed that the truth in each case lies in the opposite direction!

The Old Testament (LXX) is about 3.73 times longer than the New Testament, so that every case listed above represents a consistently greater *absolute* number of New Testament citations than of Old Testament ones – a statistic easy to confirm impressionistically simply by reading the Apostolic Fathers with a mind attuned to the possibility of biblical citations and use.

Indeed, there is good reason to think that many early Christian writers did not possess a complete Old Testament (not surprisingly if Sundberg is right about its comparatively late 'canonization'). This leads Stuhlhofer to a conclusion which shows just how inadequate the traditional test of scriptural status (citation as *graphē*) is:

> We see here a paradox. The early Church cited the Old Testament as 'Scripture', but to begin with tended to possess it only in a fragmentary form. The New Testament, on the other hand, was widely available and was used much more heavily, but it was not yet cited as 'Scripture'.[46]

On this account Zahn, if anything, underestimated the extent to which New Testament Scripture already existed and was regarded as 'canonical' in his sense by the early second century.

Citations of apocryphal gospels and of other books that were later excluded from the canon do not begin to compete with the frequency of citation of the basic core. But Acts, the shorter catholic epistles, some minor Paulines, and Revelation clearly fall into an intermediate class. And a few works that would eventually sink into the third class appear with them – for example, the *Shepherd*. At this stage, therefore, it would be quite mistaken to say that the canon was fixed, since its edges were still quite fuzzy; yet it would be equally mistaken to say that 'there was no Christian Scripture other than the Old Testament' – for much of the core already had as high a status as it would ever have.

2. In the second and early third centuries, as already mentioned, there is a levelling out: books in the second class begin to be cited relatively more often, and Old and New Testament seem to have a more equal status. But it is still the case that a threefold classification is needed to do justice to the statistics. There is not a clear distinction between books in the New Testament and books outside it: rather, there are (a) much-cited books and (b) little-cited

books, plus (c) books whose use is deplored or which are explicitly said to be usable only for special purposes, such as the instruction of catechumens (this is the Muratorian Fragment's view of the *Shepherd*). The extent to which the first class was stable is shown, for example, by the fact that virtually no one ever suggests demoting books from it. The statistics of citation in the second century provide little evidence for disputes about 'the canon'. Everyone used much the same Scriptures as the essential core, and controversies, such as there were, concentrated on the edges of what would later be the canon: on questions such as whether particular books were to be rejected altogether or allowed a subordinate place, whether there were one, two, or three genuine Johannine epistles, or whether Hebrews was really Pauline and hence *as* authoritative as the letters that certainly were.

On the one hand, there were almost no disputes about the core, which had long since ceased to grow – in this sense Harnack's second-century date for the growth of the canon is too late. On the other hand, no one yet thought of Scripture as forming a closed collection – in this sense it is too early. As Stuhlhofer says, one sometimes gets the impression from scholars that everyone in the second century had something we could call a 'New Testament', but was coy about disclosing precisely what it contained – hence the very sketchy character of the evidence. In fact there was no such idea, no simple 'canonical' versus 'non-canonical' distinction. Christian writers knew of some books everyone accepted (and we know for certain which these were) and of others that belonged on a kind of (as yet unformalized) Index – again, mostly known to us. In between was a grey area. But books from this area were cited much less frequently than those in the core anyway, and it does not make sense to say either that they were, or that they were not, 'canonical'.

Nevertheless, we may say that the line of interpretation from Harnack to von Campenhausen is vindicated as correct in its central assertion that the second century saw the Old and New Testaments placed more on a level and their contents treated more uniformly. Writers increasingly feel the need to appeal to authoritative books; and when they do so, more of what we now think of as the Bible forms the basis of their citations.

3. Thirdly, Sundberg's main contention also finds some support from Stuhlhofer's statistics. It is indeed only in the fourth century

that rulings about the fringes of the canon become firm. But here again there is a paradox. Athanasius' Festal Letter 39 appears for the first time to fix exactly the books we now have as 'of the canon'. Yet in this very document the old threefold division re-sserts itself. Alongside the canonical books and those definitely rejected, the *Shepherd* and the *Didache* (along with the deuteroca-nonical books of the Old Testament such as Wisdom) are assigned a semi-canonical position for use in catechesis. And this indeed remained the formal position until the sharper decisions of the Reformation and Counter–Reformation, and it is still the tradi-tional Anglican and Lutheran position on the 'Apocrypha' of the Old Testament.

Thus we may say that an authoritative corpus already existed even earlier than Zahn thought, but that it was still not firmly defined even as late as Sundberg claims. And in every period, undercutting the apparent development of a 'canon', there is an underlying threefold division in the status of the books Christians read and cited, which remains remarkably constant throughout and makes one suspect that the idea of 'development' may be something of an illusion anyway.

Stuhlhofer's book, brief as it is, seems to me to have advanced the study of the canon considerably. His statistical tables open the way for much further work. His recognition that there have *in practice* been three classes of book for Christianity from the earliest time for which we have records, irrespective of the *theoretical* posi-tions writers have adopted or the terminology they have used, seems to me fundamentally important for any fresh theory about 'canonization' that might be developed in the future.

Stuhlhofer seems to suggest that a three-class system is practi-cally inherent in any religion that uses sacred texts at all; and at the same time that it is very unlikely to be recognized when adherents of such a religion try to define or describe overtly the relationship they actually have to these texts:

There is always a tension between the existence of several classes of text and an unambiguous canon (= two classes, either/or). Let us assume that multiple classes exist – for exam-ple, three classes, in which the middle class consists of books which may be read privately, but not publicly in church. But this is a labile state of affairs; for either a given book is good – so why should it not be read in church? – or it is bad – so why may it even be read privately? This labile state will easily tip over in one direction or the other. . . . If, on the other hand, a two-class system prevails, *in practice* some books will be taken more seriously than others, perhaps as more productive for dogma, or as easier to understand, or as better expressing what is held to be important (Luther's criterion of 'what promotes Christ') – so that in the end gradations come to prevail even within the 'canon'.[47]

This suggests a further reason for the conflicting interpretations which scholars place on the evidence from the early Church. If we ask about the actual use and citation of texts, and so discover which books were in practice important for Christians, we are almost bound to arrive at a threefold division. Some books were used a great deal; others were used a little; others were hardly used at all or were quoted only to show how wrong they were. Of course, only empirical data can tell us *which* books fell into each category; the fact that very few books actually moved from one category to another is one of the very important factual discoveries of Stuhlhofer's work. But if we ask how these writers described their attitude to the texts they used, we are much more likely to find an either/or mentality, because in each case a writer would need to take up a definite position. Even so, we do in fact find a (surprisingly) widespread recognition of a threefold division (*Dreiklassigkeit*) in the sources.[48]

There is, in any case, seldom any way of telling how representative of wider movements were those occasional attempts at ruling on 'canonicity' that have come down to us from the first few centuries. On the whole the danger that we shall overestimate their importance is probably greater than that we shall overlook them, since if we are on the hunt for evidence about canonization such attempts will always tend to assume an exaggerated importance – so that if we are to allow ourselves a bias at all, it should probably be a compensating one in favour of being particularly sensitive to evidence for three (or more) classes.

Be that as it may, a failure to distinguish between implicit and explicit evidence on attitudes to Scripture is likely to blur our focus. And this is exactly what has happened in the study of the canon. Scholars have simply *added together* the evidence of citation and that from explicit lists of sacred books as though one could supplement or correct the other. They have failed to see that the 'canon' people use when not attending to questions about scriptural authority is hardly ever the same as the 'canon' they explicitly acknowledge when answering a question about it. The word 'canon' can perfectly reasonably be used for either; but to use it for both at the same time more or less guarantees that no useful conclusions can be drawn. Yet this is just the method scholarship has usually adopted: to see a smooth progression from the use of a given biblical book to its inclusion in an official or semi-official list of sacred books, and to argue that these are successive stages in its 'canonization'. The whole conceptual basis of this way of proceeding is, if Stuhlhofer is correct, radically flawed.

It should be clear, though this is not our main concern at present, that similar insights could be applied to the study of the Old Testament canon. Here almost everyone would agree that the 'core', the Pentateuch, was formed and acknowledged very early. Just as with Stuhlhofer's core New Testament, so with the Torah, there is hardly any evidence that its authority was ever in dispute; and that means that, if we choose to say that it was 'canonical', we shall immediately have to add that it was never 'canonized' – a paradoxical way of speaking which here, too, suggests that the term 'canon' obscures more than it clarifies. In the case of the Old Testament, too, the very early recognition of most of the books that would eventually be included (in some cases, soon after they were written, e.g. Daniel) stands alongside a very late date for the formal decision about exactly which among the less important books should be 'in' or 'out'.[49] To say that 'canonization' in this formal sense did not happen until well into the Christian era does not mean that until then it was an open question whether the 'central' books were authoritative. On the contrary, such controversy as there may have been affected only the very margins of the 'canon', not its core. That is why in a sense 'conservatives' like Leiman and 'radicals' like Sundberg are both correct. But when that has been said, the (perhaps more interesting) question of which books mattered most to Jews and Christians has not been touched.

In both Judaism and Christianity it is clear that there was also a 'canon' in the 'implicit' sense just described – a group of books which were really functional for the religion, rather than merely officially approved in theory. The historical books, for example, never seem to have been in the least controversial, yet neither Jews nor Christians ever used them much in their writings – they stand in this respect in much the same position as Acts for early Christian writers: undoubtedly 'authoritative', scarcely ever used. This may sometimes be explicable on the grounds that not all scriptural or potentially scriptural books were available to particular communities, as I speculated (rashly) that the synagogue at Nazareth may have possessed only the Torah, Isaiah, and the Psalms,[50] but there are other equally possible explanations: certain books may be what Stuhlhofer calls *ergiebiger* – have a greater yield – for the particular purpose an author has in mind, or be better known to his intended readers and therefore more convincing as a basis for agreement. (Thus it may be argued that Justin's *Dialogue with Trypho* uses the Old Testament far more than the New because the subject-matter of the *Dialogue* makes this essential, and the opponent does not recognize the New Testament in any case. Little if anything can be concluded about Justin's own 'canon' of Scripture from a work composed with such a specific purpose.)

Growth and Limitation – Separate Processes

Let us experiment, then, with the following way of describing the formation of the Christian Bible. I said at the outset that it was 'a story with neither beginning nor end'; but in reality it is two stories, and the attempt to mix the two has been the source of most of our confusions and controversies.

1. The first story is of the growth and acceptance of various Christian writings as possessing authority for the nascent Christian Church, alongside and in some relation to the Scriptures of Judaism (not precisely defined). None of the arguments, such as Sundberg's, about the late date of ecclesiastical rulings on the compass of Christian Scripture has any bearing at all on our dating of this development in Christianity, and in particular they do not at all call into question the contention, well supported by the evidence, that it happened very early in the life of the Church. Indeed, Sundberg himself recognizes this, saying (very much in the manner of Zahn) that the growth of Scripture was an early and largely unconscious process. It may have been influenced by the fact that Judaism, for all that its 'canon' was still fluid, was already very clearly a 'religion of the book'.

The fact that in early authors such as the Apostolic Fathers New Testament writings are seldom referred to as *graphē* is neither here nor there.[51] The effective authority implied in the way such authors cite texts from what would become the New Testament, and especially from the 'core' (the Synoptics, John, and Paul), shows that in practice these books already had a very high, indeed unchallenged, status for the Christian community. Theophilus of Antioch, for example, does not cite New Testament texts with the formula *gegraptai*, yet he can write, 'Concerning the justice of which the law spoke, the teaching of the prophets and the gospel is consistent with it because all the inspired men made utterances by means of the one Spirit of God.'[52] Thus the New Testament writers are not to be distinguished from those of the Old; both equally speak by the divine Spirit.

It is commonly asserted that the books of the New Testament were not written to be 'Scripture', but this is not equally true of all parts, unless we understand 'Scripture' very narrowly. Philemon was not written to be Scripture; but the Fourth Gospel may be a different matter. Its Prologue makes it seem in effect a Christian Genesis; and, like the other Gospels, it seems to set itself the task of telling the authoritative version of the story of Jesus in a way that will command the assent of all believers.[53] Matthew, similarly, has often been described as a kind of Christian Pentateuch.[54] So long as we think of the formation of the Christian Bible as the growth of authoritative Christian writings, leaving aside the question of the formal definition and delimitation of Scripture as belonging to a different story, it is hard to resist the conclusion that the Gospels were intended from the first as the supreme religious writings of the Christians. If that is accepted, it scarcely seems to matter very much whether or not we say that they were 'Scripture': their status as the most important books in the world was assured. If they were not *graphē*, then the *graphē* had been surpassed by them; phenomenologically, they were Scripture, having the kind of authority and standing for Christians that holy books do have for the religions to which they belong. And the fact that they came to be interpreted allegorically – accorded the ancient equivalent of a 'close reading' – is further evidence of this.[55].

The formation of the core of this Christian 'Scripture' was virtually complete, as Stuhlhofer has shown (and as Zahn had already argued), at a surprisingly early period. The Gospels and Paul are already in practice the most important authority by the time of the Apostolic Fathers; and this pattern never changes from then on.

External evidence which ought to be allowed its full weight

here is that assembled by Roberts and Skeat in *The Birth of the Codex*.[56] From the earliest papyri of the New Testament, the Christians' preference for a distinctive form, the codex, is already clear. Hand in hand with this goes the practice of writing the so-called *nomina sacra* in abbreviated form, as though the Church were inventing its own distinctive variant on Jewish reverence for the scroll and the carefully written Divine Name. I shall deal with these matters in their own right later. But they are mentioned here because, although they tend to confirm that the Christian writings were not seen as exactly the same kind of thing as Jewish Scripture,[57] they nevertheless formed a quite special kind of literature to which great authority was ascribed and which was treated with (newly devised) forms of reverence. The recent work of David Trobisch[58] also calls attention to the striking uniformity among New Testament texts in the early manuscript tradition. The apparently unproblematic character of the status of these (comparatively recent) Christian books is much more surprising than it initially appears to us, who are used to the idea of a 'New Testament', and it does not at all suggest a lengthy period of tentative acceptance leading eventually to 'canonization', but a very rapid attribution of supreme authority. In that sense the Church entered the second century with a core New Testament already enjoying 'scriptural' status, and never found any reason to change it.

At the other end of the time-scale, books outside the central core continued to accumulate and to acquire varying degrees of authority for many centuries, more or less unaffected by the 'decisions' about the canon which have bulked so large in scholarly discussion. Many books both inside and outside our present New Testament enjoyed prestige and religious authority, not in any way on a par with the core, but clearly greater than that of books in general or, of course, of those that the Church actually rejected. These are the books which form Stuhlhofer's second class: Acts, the minor catholic epistles, Revelation, the *Shepherd*, the *Didache*, and in due course acts of martyrs, conciliar decrees, and other miscellaneous works. These may be called 'canonical' in something like the sense that we may call the Mishnah and the Talmud canonical in Judaism. When people are *asked* which books are in their Scriptures, a clear decision is needed, and Christians eventually would come to say that Acts was 'in' and the *Didache* 'out', just as Jews would deny that the Mishnah is 'Scripture'.

But so long as we are asking about the effective religious authority, then although such books do not begin to compete with the central core (Gospels + Paul for Christians, Torah for Jews), they are clearly not in the same category either as rejected books or as just any book one might happen to come upon. They form a penumbra around the basic texts, which fades off indefinitely. As we have seen, even in the classic text for the 'closing' of the New Testament canon, Athanasius' Festal Letter 39, the existence of such a penumbra is explicitly acknowledged. Neither Jewish nor Christian Scripture has ever had the hard edges of the Qur'an in this respect. The effective 'canon' is a fluid one, though its core is constant from the earliest times.

2. The second story is that of Christian attempts to list and define which books should count as Scripture. This does not come at the end of a process which begins with the uninhibited growth of scriptures, as on the developmental models we have been discussing. It is already to be found at least as early as Tertullian, as Harnack showed, for he presupposes that the idea of the Church ruling certain books as 'not to be read' was no novelty. Christians possessed the idea, at least, of an 'Index' from quite early times; the conciliar decisions of the fourth and fifth centuries were not a fresh departure. Tertullian is quite familiar with the idea of 'banning' books: see, for example, *de cultu feminarum* 1:3, *de anima* 2, and *de pudicitia* 10 and 20. Long before Tertullian, the Pauline corpus already contained a proscription of spurious letters, in 2 Thessalonians 2.2 (probably itself a spurious letter, but attack is the best means of defence).

Most of the 'classic' texts relating to the canon are of course evidence for a tradition of listing and seeking to identify exactly which books should be read in the Church and which should not. Sundberg is correct in thinking that it was only in the fourth century that a consensus emerged about the details of this, and even this did not prevent continuing disputes at the margins of the canon for many years to come. But one should not therefore think that an *interest* in identifying which books belonged in the Bible was new in the fourth century. So far as the Old Testament is concerned, it is not till Jerome and Augustine that we find sharp controversy over the respective merits of the longer Greek and shorter Hebrew canons; but already in the second century Melito had gone (or says he had) on his famous fact-finding trip to Palestine to discover which books were accepted by the Jews.

The mistake commonly made in discussions of the canon is, I believe, a failure to see the comparatively abstract and theoretical character of this kind of interest. Notoriously, even those Fathers who rule most firmly on the limits of Scripture do not reflect this in their own citations – Jerome went on using the longer, Greek Old Testament after his controversy with Augustine, just as he had before. More attention, perhaps, should be paid to the question of what we may call the *Sitz im Leben* of such patristic discussions of the compass of Christian Scripture. They are seldom part of an attempt to regulate which books Christians might or might not use, as though this were a matter of general doubt and difficulty. In cases where there genuinely was doubt, patristic listings often allow the doubt to remain. Thus Origen discusses theories about the provenance of Hebrews;[59] and Eusebius (who explicitly recognizes three categories of book, *homologoumena*, *antilegomena*, and *notha*) notes that Revelation is among the agreed books, though some doubt it, and says that 'some have counted also the Gospel of the Hebrews' among the spurious books, though others take it as one of the genuine writings 'of the new covenant'. James, Jude, 2 Peter, and 2 and 3 John are all 'disputed'. Thus exactly where rulings are needed, none is offered.[60]

The context of canonical lists is often an apologetic one: to show how genuine and how carefully sifted is the limited range of Scripture that the Church accepts, and how free it is from all error and inconsistency. This is no different from Josephus' defence of Jewish Scripture in *contra Apionem*:

> We do not possess myriads of inconsistent books, conflicting with each other. Our books, those which are justly accredited, are but two and twenty. . . . Although such long ages have now passed, no one has ventured either to add, or to remove, or to alter a syllable.[61]

For such arguments, the facts of the case need not be exactly as stated; at any event there is no need to suppose that people at large shared the writer's own concern to delimit Scripture so exactly. It would not do for such discussions to be *wildly* out of line with general practice – but then it is quite clear that they are not, for they all share the common core of texts we know to have been uncontroversial. It is only at the margins that patristic 'canons' have anything new to tell us, and it precisely here that we cannot be at all confident that they reflect practice rather than theory.[62]

Besides apologetics, such listings may also be designed to rule out heretical books – such is almost certainly the case with most synodical decisions. Here again, the listing of the books received by all orthodox Christians is not 'canonization' in the sense of a decision: the whole point is to list what is believed to have been (or can plausibly be presented as having been) received *semper, ubique, et ab omnibus* (always, everywhere, and by everyone), through the natural consent of all the faithful. The aim of the exclusions is to anathematize certain specific books favoured by particular groups, books which were in any case on the margins of 'canonicity'.

> The fact that there was something like an 'Index' does not mean that the Church already had a strictly delimited number of 'canonical' books. Nor was such a thing necessary: to rule out 'heretics' it was generally enough to place their main works on the Index and at the same time to emphasize the authority of the books which had been accepted from the beginning (Matthew, Paul ...). That was enough to accomplish a clear demarcation against all 'heretical' groups.[63]

The 'approved' books are not being selected from a potentially very much larger list, but simply recalled from immemorial tradition – 'canonized' only in the sense in which saints are 'canonized', that is, acknowledged to be (already) rightly held in reverence by the consensus of the faithful. The aim is not to draw a line around these books, as though no others could *conceivably* be comparable, but rather to say of certain other, specified books that they at least do *not* measure up to those long received in the Church.

Thus synodical decisions concentrate on exclusion rather than inclusion, simply leaving the central core as they find it and denying that it may be extended in certain directions. As Harnack pointed out, in the Muratorian Fragment the 'canon' is said to be closed in practice, since all approved books must come from the apostolic age (hence the exclusion of the *Shepherd*). But it is not closed in principle, for any newly discovered apostolic writing would presumably qualify for inclusion – just as (I have argued[64]) Josephus' canon was also open in principle, though in fact only twenty-two books had ever been found that could meet the entry requirements.

The two stories – the growth of Scripture, and the attempts at listing its contents – of course interacted. What is listed is, as we have seen, very substantially what was used and cited, though with the extremely important proviso that it by no means reflects the relative weight attached to different books. And as time went by, writers began to make more use of previously unimportant books simply because they did appear in official lists, and use of books declared 'apocryphal' began to decline. Nevertheless the two processes, though they affect each other, are not two aspects of a linear development, as I hope to have shown. This has one particularly important corollary.

I argued above that proponents of all three of the now standard interpretations of the history of the canon could be seen to have right on their side, provided that one defined 'canon' in such a way that it would generate their respective conclusions. By using the insights of Stuhlhofer's work, I went on to suggest that much of what might interest us in the growth and delimitation of Scripture concerns questions which to some extent bypass the points at issue between our three groups of scholars. Hence the impression that there is much more agreement than there seems to be, and that the areas of dispute are really quite small, was on the whole confirmed. I tried to unravel some of the confusions in much modern discussion, and to show that there were three periods in the formation of the Christian Bible more or less corresponding to the three (allegedly incompatible) positions: that is how one can explain the aparent conflicts in the evidence.

However, Stuhlhofer has made it much easier to defend this interpretation in the case of the first and third theories (Zahn and Sundberg) than in that of the second (Harnack and von Campenhausen). Both Zahn and Sundberg have the merit that they are really talking about only one of the two processes, even though they use the blanket term 'canonization' for it. The second century, however, was established by Harnack as the centrepiece for all theories of the canon, and it is this that has commanded the majority opinion of scholars. Yet it is exactly here that separating the elements of theory and practice tends most to undermine the consensus. For what this reveals is that the *growth* of Christian Scripture made its greatest advances in the first century, though it continued and never entirely ceased thereafter; while for the tendency to *list* 'official' books, the most important period was the late third to fourth century, even though such moves were not a novelty and went back in embryo almost to the beginnings. Either way, the second century fails to establish itself as the critical period.

It is only by joining together the two distinct developments we have outlined that the second century can be made to appear so crucial – for by then the early tendency to acknowledge a common core had fully established itself, and on the other hand the wish to draw up comprehensive lists of approved books was already under way. But these two things do not add up to a creative period: rather, one is the results of 'decisions' (or rather passive acceptances) which in essence were taken some years before, and the other represents the beginnings of a tendency that had not yet come into its own. On these grounds it seems probable that Harnack was wrong to ascribe such creative significance to the second century. But if so, then we should probably also reassess his emphasis on the importance of Marcion (and von Campenhausen's on the allegedly complementary influence of Montanism). In the next chapter I will offer some reflections on this problem.

The Development of the Canon and
Modern Debates

Thus we have in some ways confirmed the hypothesis that the question of the canon, as commonly posed, is something of a pseudo-problem. But I have tried to show that very major historical issues do none the less lie beneath the surface, and that some of them can be resolved. Empirical evidence suggests that there was a Christian Bible, in fact if not in name, from very early times, perhaps even before some of the books that ultimately found their way into it (the Pastorals, 2 Peter?) were written. There is also good reason to think that conscious decisions about the outer limits of the Bible were not reached till well into the fourth century, if then, and we know that large parts of the Christian Church retained significantly different lists until many years later still. Whether we summarize all this by saying that 'the canon' is an early or a late development is largely a matter of choice. What is important is that we recognize *both* truths, and do not try to escape from one by holding fast to the other.

The broad consensus that all the really important developments occurred in the second century fudges this, and in the process enables 'liberals' and 'conservatives' in the Church and in the scholarly world to dodge issues which they ought, respectively, to face more squarely. Something close to our New Testament had enormous importance and authority for Christians even before the conflicts with Marcionites or Montanists: it is not a late development of secondary importance. If, therefore, one wishes to maintain a rather 'liberal' position, arguing (as I myself have done) that Christians are not in origin a 'people of the Book',[65] one will have to allow oneself to be challenged by this recognition, and not seek to evade it. As we shall see, it then becomes very important to ask exactly how these authoritative books were understood, and in what precisely their authority consisted – questions which so far have remained wholly untouched, but which will concern us later.

On the other hand, there is little succour here for the conservative position that exactly our present New Testament, no more and no less, was the authority for the early Church, for its edges were extremely fuzzy for much longer than even the comfortable consensus allows. And since lists bear no exact relation to what may be called the 'effective' canon of most Christian writers, traditional insistence that references to deuterocanonical or apocryphal books in the Fathers are not meant to imply that they are being quoted 'as Scripture' needs to be given up; for most of the patristic period such terms are more or less meaningless and anachronistic. Stuhlhofer's evidence for the threefold division (*Dreiklassigkeit*) of books in the early Church drives a coach and horses through most of the 'either/or' questions which conservatives expect the history of the canon to answer. Thus our modest aim of showing that scholars are merely at cross purposes has perhaps in practice resulted in a worthwhile modification of received opinions.

A Fresh Agenda

In concluding this chapter, let me try to indicate the sorts of question it leaves on the agenda for 'canon studies'.

First, one effect of our conclusions so far has been to leave an aching void in exactly the place where people generally think all the creative work was done: from about the mid-second to the early fourth century. If Christian Scripture arrived very early on the scene, but its formal definition as an authoritative collection came much later, how were these books, collectively, understood in the intervening period? It is worth quoting Harnack again: 'The question *in what sense* the collection of writings known as the New Testament was regarded as a *Canon* of religion is not decided by saying that it was regarded as canonical, but can only be answered by finding out what use was actually made of this collection.'[66] By 'use' he here meant 'private' use; but the point can be generalized. So far we have spoken simply of biblical writings as 'authoritative' for the Church, and (following Stuhlhofer) have tended to equate authoritative *status* with intensive *use*. This I believe to be justified; but it leaves open many (some would say, almost all the really interesting) questions. *How* are such books cited, and what is supposed to follow from the citation? Looking for formulas such as *hōs gegraptai*, though they provide only a very crude and unsatisfactory test, was a serious attempt to engage with these questions. People wanted to know not just whether books were cited, but what they were cited *as*.

Rather than appealing to formulas, I shall try to approach the matter by asking about the actual intentions of a few authors as these emerge from the whole drift of what they write. One important issue this raises, which will form the theme of chapters 3 and 4, is how far the words of the Gospels in particular were understood to be inherently oral tradition of the words of Jesus and the apostles, even though they are actually being quoted from a written document. Justin and Irenaeus are particularly important witnesses here. This will lead us into a more general consideration of the oral/written distinction in Christian and Jewish understandings of Scripture – a complex problem with no simple solution, especially because, once again, theory and practice may not match. Writers may claim that their authority is Jesus himself (as Ignatius did, for example), but in fact it may be clear to us that it was the Jesus of one particular Gospel, and it may be correct therefore to say that this Gospel was their effective 'canon'. Conversely, it may be asserted that 'Scripture' is the ultimate authority, yet words of Jesus (in some cases perhaps even *agrapha*) may turn out to have the power to overrule 'what is written'. To say that the New Testament had canonical authority is only the beginning of any account of what might be going on in such complicated cases – which are, in fact, the norm rather than the exception.

A second group of questions has to do with the meaning of Scripture, considered as a written text. Some Christian writers seem to cite texts atomistically, others with regard for their context; and 'context' here may mean context within a single book, or as part of a larger collection – 'the Gospels' as a fourfold canon, or 'the Pauline epistles' as a whole. The so-called 'canonical method' in modern biblical studies has highlighted the possibility, and the alleged importance, for modern believers, of seeing the canon itself as a 'locus of meaning',[67] but little work has been done on ancient anticipations of this approach, if any. So far we have been treating the listing of books as on the whole an external matter, having little effect on how they were actually read and used, but this assumption ought to be tested empirically. It could in theory be the case that canonical listings preserve important hermeneutical principles. Collecting books together is potentially an interpretative process. Once again, all this is ignored if one simply asks whether given books were or were not 'canonical'.

In chapter 5 I shall examine some attitudes towards the form and contents of composite 'works' such as the Bible in the ancient world, and hope to show some interesting divergences between Christian and Jewish ideas. If the 'oral/written' question is a matter of asking how far what was authoritative was the 'gist' or content of the New Testament irrespective of the exact verbal or graphic form which gave the reader access to it, here the opposite question is to be asked: how far was it the exact graphic detail of the text that was 'canonical', even apart from the events, words, and ideas registered in it? Such questions are seldom satisfactorily answered in the literature; and for much of the time they are not even asked.

Marcion Revisited

No one puts new wine into old wineskins; if he does, the wine
will burst the skins, and the wine is lost, and so are the skins;
but new wine is for fresh skins.

Mark 2.22

THE DEVELOPMENT OF the Christian Bible has traditionally been
seen as a linear process: first growth, then attribution of authority,
then delimitation. In chapter 1 I proposed instead that the first and
third of these steps are better understood as independent of each
other. There was already a sense that some books were 'non-scriptural' (delimitation) in the period when the 'canon' was still in
principle wide open (growth); conversely, even in the fourth century, when questions about the limits of Scripture held the centre
of the stage, people remained open to newly recognized 'ancient
scriptures'. It has been a mistake to see inclusion and exclusion as
successive stages in a single process of 'canonization'. One consequence of my argument has been to modify sharply the now conventional view of the second century as the decisive period for the
formation of the canon – in other words, the period when inclusion gave way to exclusion. Most of the present Christian Bible
was already 'Scripture' before the mid-second century, while on
the other hand decisions about its exact boundaries still lay in the
future.

Plainly this can only be maintained at the cost of abandoning
the heritage of Harnack – continued in recent times by von Campenhausen – who saw the second century as crucial. The corner-
stone of this theory was the place of Marcion as the one who
invented the idea of a New Testament and forced the Church, by
way of reaction, to adopt one of its own. And so I think I need to
give some alternative account of Marcion, and of his place in the
history of the canon.[1]

The Alleged Importance of Marcion

Harnack said that 'the Catholic New Testament beat the Marcionite Bible; but this New Testament is an anti-Marcionite creation on a Marcionite basis'.[2] Similarly, von Campenhausen writes, 'The idea and the reality of a Christian Bible were the work of Marcion, and the Church which rejected his work, so far from being ahead of him in this field, from a formal point of view simply followed his example.'[3]

The recent consensus is more moderate, but still allows him an important place. It is well summed up by Metzger:

> It is nearer to the truth to regard Marcion's canon as accelerating the process of fixing the Church's canon, a process that had already begun in the first half of the second century. It was in opposition to Marcion's criticism that the Church first became fully conscious of its inheritance of apostolic writings. As Grant aptly puts it, 'Marcion forced more orthodox Christians to examine their own presuppositions and to state more clearly what they already believed.'[4]

In this modification of Harnack's position, it is still suggested that it is because of Marcion that the second-century Church became self-conscious about its 'canon'. It had to make a deliberate decision to the effect that more books belonged to the *instrumentum* (as Tertullian called it) than Marcion wished to insist, and that these books enjoyed an authority equal to those of the Old Testament – but not an authority of such a kind as to abrogate the older collection, as Marcion wished to argue.

Thus the question of the canon became *overt* for the first time through Marcion, particularly in its 'inclusive' aspect. Instead of merely accepting the books of the Old Testament and the growing corpus of Gospels and epistles passively, the Church was forced by Marcion's rejection of the Old Testament and draconian revisions of the Christian books to make up its own mind and give definite rulings in defence of the material Marcion was seeking to suppress. As C. H. Cosgrove puts it, in an important article to which we shall return, Marcion forced the Church to think also about the *reasons* for canonicity. It had to begin to develop some criteria besides mere tradition for accepting certain books rather than others – for example, the idea of apostolic authority as guaranteeing the authenticity of records of Jesus or his teaching. 'The Great Church ultimately followed Marcion's ideas of apostolic authority.'[5] A similar emphasis characterized John Knox's work of 1942: 'The structural principle of Marcion's canon became the organizing idea of the catholic New Testament. Here is the fundamental fact in the relation of Marcion and the canon . . . Marcion is primarily responsible for the idea of the New Testament.'[6]

In this chapter I shall argue that even in this modified form Harnack's thesis about Marcion has obscured more than it has clarified in the history of the canon. This requires me to give both an alternative account of the second-century developments in the growth and delimitation of Scripture, and also an alternative account of the work of Marcion himself. In neither case shall I be suggesting what would be patently absurd, that Harnack and von Campenhausen have totally misunderstood either Marcion or the second-century Church; only that his importance has been exaggerated. As already argued, the development of the Christian Bible was a much more 'natural' development than Harnack supposed; and though Marcion represents a significant episode in it in some ways, in others it simply passed him by. Indeed, I shall argue that Marcion can be understood better as a conservative, overtaken by events, than as the radical innovator of Harnack's theory.

A basic account of the respects in which Marcion's 'canon' was supposedly influential in leading the Church to fix its own is provided by Harry Gamble:

> Marcion supposedly provided the structural principle of Gospel–Apostle on which the catholic canon is built; Marcion's use of the letters of Paul is seen as the cause of the prominence of Paul in the canon of the church (which could not afford to honor Paul less than Marcion had); and the church was compelled to compensate Marcion's one-sided emphasis on Paul by incorporating a larger and more diverse number of apostolic writings.[7]

As Gamble argues, none of these points is very convincing. It is particularly hard to see how the need to *include* more than Marcion did can logically have led to a decision to 'fix' the canon, if by this is meant to close the list, that is, to *exclude* books from it. A more natural reaction to Marcion would have been to insist that the 'canon' was not limited to a small range of books but encompassed a larger, perhaps open-ended, collection. The appeal to 'the Lord and the Apostle' certainly preceded Marcion; the collection of the Pauline epistles was already under way before his time; and citations of Paul as an authority form a continuous tradition from the Apostolic Fathers onwards, unaffected by the Marcionite controversy.

Stuhlhofer has helpfully isolated two symmetrical aspects of Marcion's actual lack of influence on the canon, pointing out, first, that many of his distinctive preoccupations were not followed by the Church at large at all, and, secondly, that the Church's canon has many features not anticipated in his work.[8]

1. Marcion was supposedly the first to decide that Christian Scripture ought to have limits: one Gospel (an expurgated Luke) and ten Pauline epistles. One might naturally suppose, therefore, that Harnack was correct in saying that, since the Church also eventually decided on a limited corpus of texts as its Scripture, and no one before Marcion had had such an idea, it erected 'an anti-Marcionite creation on a Marcionite basis'. There are, however, two problems about this.

(i) Marcion's Bible was a critical reconstruction. He assembled the scriptures which the Church at large was currently using, and by applying a critical intelligence to them he decided which parts deserved this status, and which should be rejected. In this he did not regard his own judgement as infallible, and later Marcionites felt free to amplify his 'canon' – for example, by the addition of the Pastoral epistles, which they judged genuine, and by supplementing the text of his Gospel from other traditions. Marcion's 'canon' is a first attempt at establishing just which books can be seen as a true expression of the gospel which Marcion taught: it is a canon arrived at by a kind of *Sachkritik*. There is very little evidence that the Church at large ever followed this method to arrive at its own canon. On the contrary, canonization was usually the codification of already long-accepted use. Origen speaks for many of the Fathers when he defends the canonical Scriptures by quoting Proverbs 22.28: 'Remove not the ancient landmark which your fathers have set.'[9]

The 'criteria of canonicity', as studied for example by Isidor Frank,[10] seldom include a testing of the Scriptures against credal or other doctrinal traditions. Rather, the books are accepted from tradition or rejected on the grounds that their antiquity or apostolic origin is suspect. Books which are accepted are then 'shown' to be also orthodox, and those rejected are not infrequently held to be heretical. But we can hardly ever show that the real ground for acceptance or rejection was a doctrinal test.[11] The Muratorian Fragment, for example, excludes the *Shepherd* on the grounds that it was written *nuperrime temporibus nostris*; and whether we take this to mean 'recently, in our own day' or 'in post-apostolic times',[12] the criterion has to do with antiquity, not with content. Thus the Church did not really follow Marcion's example; the similarity is much more apparent than real. Furthermore, as we have seen, it is important to distinguish between the exclusion of *particular* books (which was already happening in the second century, and independently of Marcion – cf. Tertullian's comment that certain books have been rejected by a council[13]) from the drawing of a decisive line under the books within the canon. The latter is not definitely attested before the fourth century, and it is only this which would offer a true parallel to Marcion's procedure. But it is plain that by the time it happened, it cannot have been as a result of his influence.

(ii) It is somewhat misleading to say that Marcion was the first to fix the boundaries of the 'Christian Bible', and that therefore the Church must have been following his example when it did the same, even though its canon was larger. For this overlooks the utterly crucial difference that Marcion's 'canon' excluded the Old Testament, a course of action which the Church in no sense imitated. Probably Harnack's thinking here runs as follows: For the Church the Bible was the Old Testament, and what would become the 'New Testament' had as yet no 'scriptural' status (it was not cited as *graphē* or with the formula *hōs gegraptai*, and so on). Marcion, because he rejected the Old Testament, was thus left with a Christianity that had *no* Scriptures at all. Therefore he supplied the deficiency by elevating his canon of Gospel + Apostle to the status the Old Testament had for orthodox Christians. This was the decisive breakthrough which led the Church in its turn to promote the New Testament books to this higher 'scriptural' status. Thus the Church can be seen as the heir of Marcion, even though the New Testament canon it adopted was a different one from his.

But there are many problems in seeing matters in this way. It is not at all clear that the status Marcion attributed to his 'canon' was the same as the status attributed by the Church to the Old Testament; nor that the Church had previously attributed no such status to the Christian writings that would form the New Testament. Rather, as we have seen, Christian writers before Marcion tended anyway to cite New Testament texts more often than Old Testament ones,[14] with every sign that they regarded them as extremely authoritative. This had already led to questions about how such authority was related to that of the older Scriptures. Marcion's solution of these questions – the wholesale deletion of the Old Testament – was novel, but it did not mean that the Old Testament was replaced with the New, as though the New had not previously existed; it meant rather that only part of 'Scripture' was left in place. The Church as a whole in no sense followed this example.

One can only extract Harnack's conclusion about Marcion's importance by very greatly underplaying the authority which the 'New Testament' books already possessed for the Church, and by failing to see the critical difference between fixing the canon of the New Testament as a second part of the Christian Bible, and establishing it as the only Scripture. In fact it might even be argued that, so far from Marcion's Bible replacing the existing Old Testament Scripture with a New Testament, Marcion actually abolished the category of 'Scripture' altogether. His Gospel + Apostle is presented more as reliable ancient documents than as 'Holy Scripture' – one of the respects, I shall argue, in which he was a conservative.[15] But in that case the parallel with what the Church eventually did in canonizing its Scriptures is even less close than Harnack thought.

2. Thus there was little in Marcion's work that the Church imitated, despite superficial appearances to the contrary. Stuhlhofer goes on to argue that there is, equally, much in the history of the canon for which no Marcionite precedent can be found. For example:

(i) By the end of the second century there are terms for what we now call the 'New Testament'; there is no evidence that Marcion had a name for his 'canon'. Some have thought that Melito's expression 'the scriptures of the old covenant' implies that he would have referred to the New Testament writings as 'of the new covenant', though this cannot be more than a conjecture. This point is perhaps a small one, but is not trivial.

(ii) The collection of the four Gospels probably (as Harnack himself thought) goes back before Marcion. Even if it does not, it is clear that this is one development in which Marcion, with his single, critically reconstructed, Gospel, can have played no part.

(iii) The citation of the New Testament as *graphē* is found occasionally before Marcion.[16] But in any case there is no evidence that its occurrence grows in frequency immediately after the Marcionite controversy, nor that Marcion had any part in causing it. We do not know whether Marcion himself used any particular citation formula in his own writings; though it might reasonably be surmised, following my suggestion above that Marcion saw his 'Bible' as a collection of historically authentic documents rather than as 'Scripture', that he is somewhat less likely than ecclesiastical writers to have cited it as *graphē*. In so far as ancient usage (still current in Irenaeus) preferred to refer to what 'the Lord' or 'the Apostle' teaches rather than to use *hōs gegraptai* for New Testament citations, Marcion is if anything more likely to have followed rather than changed this usage, given his own insistence that (for example) the Gospel was not a holy ancient writing but the very words of Jesus himself.

(iv) The Church soon came to regard the text of the New Testament, like that of the Old, as fixed and unalterable, and to practise allegorical exegesis of it – in the ancient world, one of the marks of a 'scriptural' text (and one to which we shall return). Marcion strongly rejected allegorization, and did not think of the text of his 'Bible' as fixed. It was the result of his own scholarly 'research' into the traditions about Jesus and Paul, and was open to further correction in the light of additional investigation. This way of thinking did not influence the Church at all.

(v) There may have been a Pauline corpus before Marcion, though this is speculative. If the arguments of Young Kyu Kim, dating P^{46} to the late first century, are sound, then Paul's epistles existed *as a collection* before Marcion.[17] But Kim's work has not met with general acceptance from textual critics. J. J. Clabeaux[18] argues that Marcion attests many pre-Marcionite readings in Paul which show that there must have been a Pauline corpus before him. But it seems to me that his arguments show at best that the individual letters are pre-Marcionite, and *may* have formed a corpus.

The hypothesis that Marcion influenced or accelerated the development of the canon is predicated on the idea that in the second century there was a dramatic change in the way the Church read and received New Testament books, for which some explanation is required. On the contrary, as Stuhlhofer puts it:

If we think of the countless continuities in early Christian use of the New Testament books, we are impressed by the 'deep silence, for observers from later generations, in which the canon came into existence' (Franz Overbeck). It is a history quite without any revolutions. All the essentials are there from the beginning, and the tiny changes occur so gradually that no one notices them.[19]

Marcion as a Traditionalist

How then should Marcion be understood? I should like to point to two ways in which he was more a traditionalist than an innovator, before going on to suggest where his originality really lay.

1. Our starting-point might be a fact about Marcion which was already pointed out by Harnack, but which at first glance is extremely surprising. Marcion of course rejected the Old Testament, and this was indeed the main charge against him from Tertullian onwards: that he had sundered the creator-God who spoke in the old Scriptures from the God revealed in Jesus. But this does not mean that Marcion thought the Old Testament inaccurate or a pack of lies; far from it. He simply took it for granted that the creator-God did indeed utter the words of which it is composed, and also that everything he said in it was entirely true. 'The Jewish Scriptures represent a true revelation of the Creator, but they do not speak of or for the God whom alone Christians ought to worship.' 'Marcion did not repudiate the Old Testament in the sense of regarding it as altogether evil; it was a valid revelation of the Creator's deity.'[20] Furthermore, he rejected all allegorizing interpretations: the Old Testament Scriptures are not just true, but *literally* true. Marcion's rejection of allegory – *mē dein allēgorein tēn graphēn* – is entirely of a piece with his rejection of the older Scriptures as superseded. Once they are read without the veil of allegory to come between their natural sense and the Christian reader, their incompatibility with Christianity immediately becomes apparent.

The paradoxical consequence is that Marcion's interpretations are generally rather close to traditional Jewish readings of the Old Testament. He held, for example, that the Messiah predicted in the prophets was an earthly, purely human, royal figure who was still to come; his role would be to act as a saviour of the Jewish people from their earthly enemies, just as Isaiah and Jeremiah foretold.

He had nothing to do with Jesus, the heavenly Saviour of the redeemed in every nation. Other supposedly 'messianic' texts were not such at all. They referred to actual Jewish rulers of the past, such as Hezekiah, and they had already been fulfilled in the history recounted in the historical books of the Old Testament. The old Scriptures were, in fact, a Jewish book through and through, but they were a wholly reliable and trustworthy Jewish book. Whereas Marcion thought that the Gospels and epistles had been extensively interpolated by false 'judaizing' apostles, he apparently saw no flaws in the Old Testament record at all, but treated it as the infallible utterances of the God of the Jews.[21] His 'rejection' of it was thus not in any sense an attack on its veracity or reliability; it stemmed from trying to take its exact form, as the revealed word of the creator of the world, very seriously indeed. It was simply that the God Christians worshipped was distinct from, and superior to, that creator figure.

On the traditional interpretation of Marcion this attitude to the Old Testament is hard to accommodate. The conventional view is that Marcion rejected the texts which for other Christians were the only Scriptures, the Old Testament, and so had to elevate the status of (what would become) the New Testament to take their place. But in fact Marcion's understanding of the Old Testament makes sense only if he shared the belief of all Christians that it did indeed consist of divine oracles. It never occurs to him to argue that no god really spoke through these books, or that they were spurious human inventions. His whole way of presenting the gospel takes for granted the self-evident status of the Old Testament, though of course by way of antithesis instead of 'completion' or 'fulfilment'. At the same time he seems to have regarded the 'New Testament' not at all as a 'scriptural' text, inspired by God and so sacrosanct, but much more as a collection of historically important documents from which the truth about Jesus and about the true 'Pauline' gospel could be discovered – once they had been properly edited, and cleansed of later accretions.

Thus Marcion seems to have been a kind of fundamentalist about the Old Testament, which he 'rejected', but a critical historian when it came to the New Testament, which he 'accepted'. He did not replace the Old Testament with the New in the sense that he attributed to the New Testament the same kind of status that the Old Testament had traditionally possessed for Christians. He left the Old Testament intact as inspired Scripture, though now as the Scripture of a discarded religion; and he derived his own new religion from a New Testament understood not at all as an alternative 'Scripture', but as a collection of authentic historical records.

Now the respective attitudes to the Old and New Testaments are – if we leave aside the element of evaluation – very similar to those which are supposed to have prevailed in the Church generally in the late first and early second centuries. According to the consensus view, the Old Testament Scriptures were usually seen as uniquely the *graphē*, the holy and authoritative text for Christians; the New Testament writings did not yet have this status. My own argument has been that this consensus view is in some respects misleading, and that the attribution of 'scriptural' status to the New Testament is earlier than the date at which what is usually regarded as the crucial evidence for it (citation as *graphē* or with the formula *hōs gegraptai*) first occurs. But we must not exaggerate: of course there *was* a period when only the Old Testament was Scripture; for example, this was clearly still so for Paul. The evidence I discussed in chapter 1 points us to the conclusion that the New Testament was 'authoritative' earlier than Harnack supposed. But it does not begin to touch on the theories about this authority which Christian writers consciously adopted, which may well have been (indeed, almost certainly were) often at variance with the testimony of their own *use* of these texts. And at this level we should certainly find that writers well into the second century evince a different attitude to Old and New Testament texts. To put it simply, the words of the Old Testament are assumed to be spoken by God because they are in the sacred books; the words of Jesus or Paul are authoritative because of who spoke them, and for that reason it is fitting to treasure and safeguard the books in which they appear. The practical difference this makes to readers of the two Testaments is extremely slight, but the theoretical difference, once questions of 'Bible' and 'canon' come to be overtly discussed, is considerable.

Marcion belongs squarely in this period of the development of the canon. He shares the universal Christian assumption that the Old Testament contains divinely inspired words (even though he thinks the god who inspired them an inferior being). He also shares the belief that the words spoken by Jesus have a unique and inherent authority which does not derive from the books in which they stand recorded, but which should certainly lead Christians to be concerned to get them recorded, and recorded accurately. Marcion knows what Jesus taught from the 'tradition'. On the basis of that tradition he is in a position to emend the Gospel(s) and render them more accurate. Orthodox Christians regarded the gospel texts in much the same light in this period. As Ellen Flesseman-van Leer puts it: 'People knew what the gospel message was, and no one asked *how* they knew. The Church as a whole knew what had happened, and also knew its meaning, because it was constantly recounted and proclaimed.'[22]

In practice it was probably from a written Gospel that most Christians by the second century came to know what this tradition was – though of course from a Gospel as interpreted in their local community, in preaching and liturgy and catechesis. The same is no doubt true for Marcion. But he did not himself see the tradition about Jesus as having reached him through a Gospel; rather, like Paul, he had received it 'not from man' but from the Lord. In its light he was able, not infallibly but with good hope of success, to revise the 'Gospel' text and purify it of what was alien to the true tradition. To handle the Old Testament text in the same way would have been quite unacceptable for him: these were ancient divine oracles, not susceptible of correction. In all this Marcion is a true child of his time or even, one might say, a conservative. So far from inventing the 'New Testament' as a superior source of authority to the Old, Marcion maintains the old conventions according to which there is only one *graphē*, the Old Testament, and a Jesus/Paul tradition knowable by Christians even without any written New Testament Scriptures. Marcion's innovation does not lie in his creation of a New Testament. The movement that would lead inexorably towards one was already well under way before him; while the theory that would make it part of a 'Christian Bible' – the same sort of thing as the Old Testament – had not yet arrived; and, when it did, it owed nothing to him.

2. Once we have seen the possibility of regarding Marcion as a conservative, we may begin to notice other ways in which he seems more like a throwback than an innovator. What of his insistence that there was only one true Gospel, the book which Paul referred to as 'my gospel'? Marcion was of course anachronistic in thinking that Paul meant to refer to a written gospel-*book* (though Eusebius (*Ecclesiastical History* 3:4) took the expression in the same

way, and also thought it meant Luke).[23] But in believing that
Christians ought to use a single, definitive version of the life and
teaching of Jesus he may not have been so novel as he seems.

Harnack, in one part of his theory that has been widely questioned, argued that the four-Gospel canon already existed in Marcion's day, and that he was deliberately rejecting it. Even if this is an
anachronism, there is good reason to think that all four Gospels
were known and used in Marcion's day, and indeed he himself
appears to have drawn on all of them – his followers at any rate
did so, since they are supposed to have supplemented his 'Luke'
from Mark and Matthew and to have engaged in polemic against
certain incidents in John, such as the wedding at Cana. The passage
which Tertullian reports as the beginning of Marcion's Gospel
('anno quintodecimo principatus Tiberii proposuit eum *descendisse
in civitatem Galilaeae Capharnaum, uti de caelo creatoris*, in quod de suo
ante descenderat'; 'he alleges that in the fifteenth year of the princi-
pate of Tiberius he [Jesus] descended to Capernaum, a city of
Galilee, as from the heaven of the creator into which he had previously descended from his own realm') may owe something to the
Fourth Gospel as well as to Marcion's own 'docetic' Christology.
But this does not imply that other Christians were already regarding the four Gospels as forming a fixed collection or 'canon'.
(Indeed, Harnack's own argument would be strengthened if one
supposed that no one before Marcion had had any idea that the
corpus of gospel material should be limited at all, and that Marcion
was making the first attempt to separate 'authentic' from 'inauthen-
tic' traditions about Jesus.) Might it not be said that the true anticipation of Marcion lies not in any putative earlier *collections* of
Gospels, but in the writing of the Gospels themselves? Baur had
suggested this before Harnack, though Harnack himself is critical
of it: 'The most one can say is that Marcion elevated into the
principle of his criticism what Luke and Matthew had been bold
enough to do to Q and Mark in isolated cases.'[24]

We might go further than this, however. Whatever the motives
of Mark or even Matthew, the purpose of the third Gospel as
stated in its prologue does seem to envisage a supersession of
other Gospels: 'Luke' is providing the definitive version of the
story, to replace earlier and more imperfect versions. In taking
Luke as his standard Gospel, Marcion may have seemed to himself
merely to be restoring it to its original intention – as the best account so far of the events of salvation – and suppressing both the

adulterated version of it which he had known from his youth and all other 'spurious' Gospels, such as Mark, Matthew, and John. What Marcion intended is surely not so far from what Luke had intended. One might indeed argue with H. Merkel that every Gospel is an attempt to solve the problem of the inconsistency of the extant written and oral traditions about Jesus and to suppress its predecessors.[25] The idea that the Gospels supplement each other, perhaps from different points of view (as in Clement of Alexandria's famous description of the Fourth Gospel as a 'spiritual' version of the same story as the Synoptics), is a hermeneutical device that commends itself once the Church has come to accept that all four Gospels are canonical, but not one that can have operated when each was actually being compiled. In the case of John, one might go further and argue not only that it was intended to suppress all the Synoptics, but even that it was meant to replace the Old Testament Scripture with a superior Christian Bible, a kind of new Genesis (hence its beginning: *en archē(i)*. . .). In that case its intention would be very close to Marcion's.

Harnack suggested that the Fourth Evangelist was even bolder than Marcion, for he invents new historical incidents and speeches – he is not, like Marcion, seeking to correct and restore, but actually to create:

> He too [sc. John] stands on the basis of a given archival stratum, the first three Gospels, and handles this underlying material very freely indeed, leaving things out, rearranging, and making detailed corrections, just as Marcion does. And he too subjects all the material to a negative and productive dogmatic criticism; but in this he proceeds in a much bolder way than Marcion, not only developing long speeches, but probably also inventing completely new historical situations.[26]

The Fourth Evangelist himself did not leave us any accounts of what he thought he was doing, and nor do we know for sure what earlier Gospels he had at his disposal. We have to deduce his intentions from the words of the 'narrator' in the Gospel itself, and this person, as modern literary theory has reminded us, is not simply to be equated with the actual writer. Nevertheless, it is not far-fetched to see him as a revisionist, improving on older materials; and in this he is not so different from Marcion.

Thus we might see Marcion as an 'evangelist' out of his time. The days had passed when one could do what Luke or John had done, and seek to correct the existing Gospels – a further sign, if such were needed, that they were already well on the way to possessing 'canonical' or 'scriptural' status without any help from Marcion who, if he could, would actually have arrested, rather than hastened, this process.[27]

If Marcion had predecessors, in the persons of the evangelists themselves, he had at least one successor: Tatian.[28] It is perhaps no accident that one of Tatian's (lost) works was apparently called *Problemata*, and dealt with discrepancies between the Gospels or perhaps between the Old and New Testaments, much as did Marcion's *Antitheses*. Tatian like Marcion regarded the existing Gospels not as sacred texts but as historical sources: 'Tatian . . . like Justin regards the Gospels as historical accounts of a life of Jesus; from this historical point of view he was bound to come up against the frequent contradictions in what the evangelists have to say.'[29] (We shall return to Justin later.) Accordingly, he harmonized to produce a definitive account of what 'must have' happened. The *Diatessaron*, woven out of the Gospels we now have,[30] together, probably, with some material from 'non-canonical' gospels and some *agrapha*, was still in use in the Syrian churches in the time of Theodoret at the end of the fifth century.[31] Even after these churches fell into line, so far as their official 'canon' was concerned, it remained an important text – an acceptable gospel-harmony for many Christians.

Thus Marcion stands in an honourable line, in which he is neither an innovator nor a reactionary. There was one influential strand of thought in the Church, from the New Testament period itself down to the end of the patristic age, which believed Christians should possess and use a single definitive account of the life and teachings of the Lord. The production of our present New Testament represents the defeat of his view; and Marcion is one of those it swept away. The New Testament is not an 'anti-Marcionite creation on a Marcionite basis'; it is the result of the church's allowing Scripture to form by natural (and untidy) growth, rather than by the kind of consistent and rational criticism of which Marcion was an exponent.

Alongside his 'Gospel' Marcion canonized an *Apostolikon*, a collection of those of Paul's epistles deemed by him to be authentic (because doctrinally 'sound'). Harnack argued that it is to this move that we owe our New Testament, in which 'the Lord' and 'the Apostle(s)' have equal status. As Stuhlhofer has pointed out, one major problem about this is that we do not know for sure that Marcion did accord *equal* status to his two 'canonical' books. Indeed, if he really thought that the Gospel he had restored was the book to which Paul was referring when he talked of 'my gospel', one might logically suppose that he thought it had superior authority to Paul's own teachings, even though both were to be seen as absolutely binding on Christians. Be that as it may, we may ask whether Marcion was really being so innovative in developing a 'bi-partite' canon of Gospel and epistles. It has often been pointed out that many early Christian writers speak of the dual authority of 'the Lord' and 'the Apostle'. True as this is, it does not necessarily overturn Harnack's point, since such references do not seem to envisage two written collections in quite the way Marcion understood them: they can be interpreted as references to two sources of essentially oral tradition.

A stronger counter-example might be provided by a text such as the *Didache*. The date of the *Didache* is still disputed, with English-speaking scholars tending to favour a mid to late second century date, and continental scholarship continuing to defend the late first century and so placing it before the writing of some of the later books of the New Testament.[32] In either case, however, we may see in it a significant parallel to Marcion's *Apostolikon*. The final authority for the author of the *Didache* is the words of Jesus: the Lord's Prayer, for example, is to be recited *hōs ekeleusen ho kurios en tō(i) euangeliō(i) autou* (as the Lord commanded in gospel) (8:2), where *euangelion* could well mean a written Gospel (perhaps Matthew); 9:5 cites a word of Jesus with the formula *hōs errethē*. There is no doubt that the *Didache* was intended to be the authoritative handbook for Christian practice in the churches for which it was written, probably in Syria, and most likely it was meant to stand alongside a Gospel (Matthew?) as the official apostolic commentary on the words of the Lord himself. Frank suggests that a close parallel would be the relationship of the Mishnah to the Torah, and speculates that the *Didache* is the work of a Christian academy designed to correspond to the rabbinic academy at Jamnia – probably much the same kind of institution as Stendahl's 'school of St Matthew', maybe indeed that very school.[33] An alternative model might be the relationship of the 'Prophets' (or the

'Prophets and Writings') to the Torah in rabbinic Judaism: Matthew + *Didache* could then be an early Christian equivalent of Law + Prophets.

In any case the parallel with Marcion's Bible is close and instructive. Harnack describes the writing of the *Didache* as an example of one of his various models for Scripture which the Church might have adopted but veered away from: 'a systematized "Teaching of the Lord" administered by the "Twelve Apostles" of the character of the "Apostolic Canons, Constitutions, etc.", which also included "Injunctions of the Lord", side by side with the Old Testament and the Gospel'.[34] He tellingly observes that in a certain sense this model did in fact establish itself, and remains normative in the Catholic Church in the form of 'Scripture + Tradition'. Nevertheless, in exactly the form described by him it did not survive. We may well see Matthew + the *Didache* and Marcion's Gospel + Apostolikon as early, and unsuccessful, examples of the genre. Texts such as the *Epistle of the Apostles* probably represent other failed attempts in this direction. The eventual shape of the New Testament does in a loose way show the influence of these developments; but it does not owe anything specific to Marcion, who in this respect stands, again, in an older tradition.

A further highly characteristic feature of Marcion's system was the near-'canonization' of his own book, the *Antitheses*. We must be on our guard against the anti-Marcionite zeal of writers such as Tertullian, who may be deliberately blackening Marcion's character when they tell us that he elevated his own work to a status akin to that of Scripture. The fact that his followers held his work in such high regard need not imply that he himself meant it to become a sacred text. Nevertheless, it does appear to have been Marcion's intention that his book should provide the authoritative key to reading his Bible, and Tertullian tells us that the Marcionites had it *in summo instrumento* – perhaps in effect to be loosely rendered 'as an Introduction to the New Testament' rather than (egotistically) 'at the head of Scripture'.[35] As Harnack put it, 'Marcion's Gospel and *Apostolikon* were after all only half-comprehensible in their intentions, unless accompanied by the explanation offered by the *Antitheses*; from the beginning the latter had to accompany them.'[36] In a certain sense, after all, Marcion's 'canon' was parasitic upon the existing sacred books of the Church – another reason for denying him the creative role assigned to him by Harnack: one needed to know the larger corpus of Gospels and epistles as a kind of counter-text to Marcion's briefer 'canon', and also to be familiar with the Old Testament which he had excluded. The *Antitheses* then explain the omissions, the incongruities which *his* Bible had succeeded in eliminating.

For Marcion's gospel is the good news that mankind has been freed from the thrall of the Old Testament god; and unless one knows this (proscribed!) text, and knows also why it is wrong, one cannot properly welcome the gospel message. Thus the *Antitheses* are an essential part of the texts Marcion wished his followers to read, and Harnack was surely correct to say that they were effectively a *credal* document for the Marcionites: 'Finally, the work was meant to be not only a literary supplement ("dos") to the Gospel and a guarantee ("patrocinium") of it, but also a work regulative for the community – its credal book.'[37] Thus in Marcion's opinion the Church needed both parts of his expurgated 'Bible', the Gospel and the Apostle, but it also needed authoritative directions on how to interpret them. In particular it needed to be told how to relate them to the scriptures of the Jews which the wider Church (wrongly, as he believed) continued to accept. The correct way to relate them was, of course, antithetically. The *Antitheses* thus provided the essential content of Marcionite faith by way of an interpretation of Scripture. Harnack shows that it contained, in all probability, an introductory section providing a brief account of the essential gospel message (deliverance through Christ from the Jewish creator-god), followed by a reasoned discussion, pericope by pericope, of the Gospel and the Apostle, showing how these texts exemplified the underlying gospel message, and how they differed from the Old Testament. In the process, hermeneutical rules were provided for reading both the Christian Scriptures and the Old Testament, the chief one being the rule against allegorical interpretation – necessary in order to prevent the reader from engaging in types of exegesis that would succeed in reconciling Old and New Testament texts.

Clearly there was nothing quite like this in content in the early Church; at almost every point it differs from the Scriptures which the Church came to adopt. Purely formally, however, it is much more closely related to both earlier and later developments than we might at first think. Marcion's *Antitheses* argued for dissonance between the Old and New Testaments on the basis of non-allegorical exegesis, and no one else, so far as we know, did that. But plenty of writers argued for their congruence, on the basis of allegorical interpretation. The exegetical part of the *Antitheses*, as far as we can judge, was just the mirror-image of the *Epistle of Barnabas*, Melito's *Paschal Homily*, or Justin's *Dialogue with Trypho*. Harnack himself made this point, for he suggested that Marcion's work corresponded (antithetically) to another of his 'possible Bibles', no. 7: 'A book of the synthesis or concordance of prophecy and fulfilment in reference to Jesus Christ, the Apostles, and the Church, standing side by side with the Old Testament.'[38]

Such works, of which the *Dialogue* is the outstanding example, show Christians how to read the Old Testament in order to grasp its congruence with Christ; Marcion simply shows us how to read it if we want to grasp its dissonance. Formally, the task is much the same.

As to the general introduction which Harnack believed to have stood before the detailed exegetical part of the *Antitheses*, this resembles nothing so much as what Irenaeus calls the 'canon of truth': the basic, quasi-credal formulation of the essence of Christian doctrine in the light of which Scripture is to be read, and of which he gives a more extended treatment in his *Demonstration*. There was nothing original or unusual in Marcion's assumption that Scripture alone was insufficient, and that it needed a basic doctrinal matrix within which to be heard. This is the practically universal conviction of Christian writers in the patristic age, for whom the all-sufficiency of the Bible on its own would have seemed a very strange notion. Of course Marcion's doctrinal framework was a highly heterodox one; but the underlying conception of a work which would provide a doctrinal 'key to the Scriptures' was absolutely normal. Harnack thinks that a book showing the congruence of prophecy with Christ could easily have taken the place which the New Testament came eventually to fill, if anyone had produced a good enough example of it, and there is not much doubt that for some Christian communities books of *testimonia* were more or less 'canonical'. As it is, however, the Church received the canon of Gospels and epistles, and works like the *Dialogue* did not attain canonical status. Marcion thus represents a stage which the Church passed through but left behind: again a conservative rather than a reforming figure. 'The Marcionite Church,' wrote Harnack, 'is itself a witness of the importance for the Church of proving the concordance, and that it was well within the limits of possibility that a work of this kind with *canonical* prestige should have been produced.' But Marcion's work was clearly parasitic upon this tendency, as observed above; it is hard to see that he can have been its cause.

The Rejection of Allegory and the Ascendancy of the New Testament

What then was new in Marcion's system, and did it have any effect on subsequent developments in the Church's attitude to the Bible?

1. It seems to me that one really unusual feature in Marcion is his rejection of allegorical interpretation, a point which (though always acknowledged) is not made much of in traditional accounts of his work.[39] With the hindsight afforded by an experience of modern biblical criticism, which has in many ways been founded on a return to a 'literal' reading of the Bible, one is naturally tempted to reconstruct the following pattern of thinking in the early Church: the Old Testament appears to contain teachings at variance with some of what is taught in the New Testament; but the Old Testament is Scripture, and so cannot conflict with what is known in Christ; therefore the Old Testament must be read allegorically. Marcion's rejection of allegory would then mean simply that having noticed the contradictions, he refused to reconcile them by going down this route, and consequently arrived at the conclusion that the Old Testament must be wrong. On this interpretation of events, everyone *began* by reading the Old Testament 'literally' or in its 'natural' sense; orthodox Christians, recoiling from the conclusions to which this led them, decided that the natural sense must be abandoned, while Marcion and his followers (in this like modern biblical critics) preferred to say that the text they were reading 'literally' was simply non-Christian and that *it* should accordingly be abandoned.

But there is a flaw here. A preference for allegorical reading was not something forced on the Church by the demonstrable incompatibility with Christianity of the Old Testament, read literally. It was a way of reading Scripture inherited both from Judaism and from pagan religious tradition, and it was soon applied to the New Testament texts just as to the Old. Allegory may originally have been the solution of a difficulty, but for many people in the ancient world it had become the 'natural' way to approach sacred texts.

Indeed, we might say that an aptitude to be interpreted allegorically was part and parcel of sacredness in texts. When pagans rejected the allegorical meanings Christians found in their Scriptures, it was not usually on the grounds that this was not the 'natural sense' of the text – this, of course, was agreed by all. It was on the grounds that the texts were not sacred, and hence were not suitable for an allegorical reading. Once grant that a text is sacred, and no further justification is needed for reading it allegorically.

This assumption can be clearly seen from Origen's *contra Celsum*. Origen says that the Egyptians hold to absurd myths, yet 'if they relate this mythology, they are believed to be concealing philosophy in obscurities and mysteries; but if Moses wrote for a whole nation and left them histories and laws, his words are considered to be empty myths not even capable of being interpreted allegorically';[40] 'not even Celsus asserts that only vulgar people have been converted by the gospel to follow the religion of Jesus; for he admits that *among them are some moderate, reasonable, and intelligent people who readily interpret allegorically*';[41] 'Numenius the Pythagorean . . . had a greater desire than Celsus . . . to examine our own writings in a scholarly way, and was led to regard them as books which are to be interpreted allegorically and which are not foolish.'[42]

The harmony an allegorical reading produced (or assumed) between the Old Testament and the Christian faith proved unacceptable to Marcion because he was *already* convinced that the God of the Jews, the creator-god, was irreconcilable with the God in whom Christians believed. Consequently he concluded that there must be something wrong with a hermeneutic that glossed over this tension, and so came to reject the allegorical method. He sought a hermeneutic that would ensure that the Old Testament should be read so as to support his interpretation of it as anti-Christian; and 'literalism' commended itself for the purpose.

To put it another way: Marcion's prior conviction that the Old Testament was not 'Scripture' for a Christian led him to read it in the ways that non-scriptural texts were read, that is, non-allegorically. Like contemporary Jewish insistence on the literal meaning of Scripture, Marcion's literalism was a polemical doctrine, designed to rule out Christian interpretations. And it is there, I believe, in the emphasis on reading literally the Old Testament books whose authority he rejected, that his originality should be located – there, rather than in any influence for good or ill on the formation of the canon of the *New* Testament.

2. Perhaps it is there, too, that his subsequent influence can be seen. In their major study of sacred books in antiquity Leipoldt and Morenz made the interesting observation that the public reading of the Old Testament in the Christian Church seems to have been much less common in the first century than we tend to assume.[43] Jewish Christians will of course have continued the synagogue practice of scriptural lections – though the early history of this system is by no means clear, and reading Scripture may have been a less important part of Jewish liturgy than is usually assumed.[44] But Gentile Christians may well not have introduced the custom from the beginning. Was the Old Testament, for example, read in the worship of the Corinthian church? One would not guess it from 1 Corinthians 14. As we have seen, Stuhlhofer's statistics support the conclusion that in many early Christian writers the practical importance of the Old Testament was minimal, however little this should be taken to imply hostility to it. Leipoldt and Morenz go on to propose that it may have been in order to combat Marcionism that really extensive public lections from the Old Testament were introduced in Gentile churches, and then chiefly for the benefit of those fairly advanced in the faith.

For catechumens, as we know from even so late a writer as Athanasius, non-canonical Christian books were probably deemed more useful reading – this is the role in which the *Shepherd* survived for so long. When Jerome, later still, is advising converts on where to begin their Bible reading, he suggests that one should begin, not with the parts of the Old Testament on which Christian apologists had concentrated (such as the prophets), but with the wisdom books – good, sound ethical instruction – before turning to the Gospels second and the apostolic writings third; only after that can the prophets and Pentateuch be approached, and the Song of Songs last of all, 'lest, if someone reads it at the beginning, he fails to understand that what is concealed in the carnal words is the marriage-feast of the *spiritual* nuptials, and so is injured'.[45] For the beginner, therefore, the effective 'canon' would be the New Testament and wisdom books. Perhaps we have here the explanation for the Muratorian Fragment's inclusion of the Wisdom of Solomon with the books of the New Testament.

None of this means that the 'real' canon excluded the bulk of the Old Testament; as usual, much depends on our definition of 'canon'. But it is striking that, whereas (for example) increased use of Paul, which Harnack's Marcion hypothesis would predict for the immediately post-Marcion period, cannot be established from the statistics, increased use of the Old Testament can. And this may well help to confirm that it was Marcion's rejection of the Old Testament that caused the Church to adjust its own practice to remind people just how wrong Marcion was. The New Testament is not a fruit of controversy over Marcion; the Old Testament, understood as a book which Christians must attend to deliberately and consciously rather than as the taken-for-granted background of all thinking and praying, is. It was, after all, for his rejection of the Old Testament that Marcion was remembered, not for his part in creating the New.

3. We might press a little further and suggest that an insistence on allegorical interpretation, as opposed to its unquestioning acceptance, is also a product of the Marcionite question. Here the evidence will be hard to evaluate; for how can we tell whether a writer is practising allegorical exegesis unselfconsciously, or making an issue of it? But I think there are a few cases where this distinction definitely can be maintained.

One of the most interesting of them is Justin's *Dialogue with Trypho*. There is now an extensive literature on the intended audience for this work. Ostensibly, of course, it is written to confute 'the Jews'; but appearances may deceive. C. H. Cosgrove has argued, to my mind convincingly, that the real audience is a Christian one, with Trypho representing an imaginary opponent introduced to help Christians clarify their own minds on matters which, while in theory at dispute between themselves and the Jews, had been internalized as matters of controversy within the Church itself. Cosgrove proposes that the situation really in mind in the *Dialogue* is that of a church divided by opposing forces, 'judaizers' on one side and Marcionites on the other; as we have seen, in certain important respects, most notably in their rejection of allegorizing exegesis, these may have been brothers beneath the skin. The sense of the Church as the new Israel, writes Cosgrove, 'created a profound need for self-definition in terms of the Old Testament and an *internal* urgency for the meeting of Jewish objections to Christianity'.[46]

Von Campenhausen, indeed, contends that most controversies with 'Jews' in early Christianity, for example in the Fourth Gospel, are really expressions of quarrels over 'judaizing' within the Church: 'We are forced, therefore, to assume that John's target is not the Jews but his own Christian contemporaries.'[47] Miriam Taylor has argued in the same vein that 'the Jews' in early Christian writers are essentially *symbolic* figures, encapsulating the Church's own internal need to come to terms with the Jewish heritage it had imperfectly internalized. By a thorough examination of patristic treatises against the Jews she demonstrates that they seldom rest on a real social engagement with Judaism, but generally use 'Jews' as a foil for inner-Christian debates.[48] Again, P. F. Beatrice argues that the anti-Jewish polemic in Barnabas is likewise really intra-ecclesial, part of a Christian debate on the meaning of the covenant.[49]

To return specifically to Justin: there are a number of hints in the *Dialogue* that the real audience is Christian: the striking call to worship, addressed to 'all nations', in 29:1 (cf. also 24:3); and in 47 a long discussion of whether Christians who observe the Law can be saved – surely intended for 'judaizers' rather than for Jews. Above all, as von Campenhausen points out, Judaism is to be reprehended according to Justin because, by its *literal* observance of legal provisions in the Old Testament, it gives encouragement to those Christians who themselves want to understand the Law literally *because they wish to be justified in rejecting* it as unworthy of the God revealed in Jesus. This point surely must be aimed at Marcion or his like. 'The Jews may justly be reproached that by their external interpretation of the ordinances they encouraged the drawing of false conclusions, which turn "those who have no understanding", that is, the heretics, against the law God has given.'[50] The internal threat is the real anxiety here; as Cosgrove well puts it:

> The apology draws the outer world into its own inner circle for judgment as a way for the group to make sure of itself. The ostensibly centrifugal cast of apologetic literature may function as a mere foil for this more pressing internal process of self-identification; the dialogue with the outsider may represent no more than internal monologue.[51]

Thus, perhaps, it is Marcion, the viper in the Church's own bosom, who is symbolized by the straw man of 'Trypho',[52] the Jewish rabbi who in one sense represents all that Marcion most hated but in another is the very personification of his own 'low', literalistic, anti-allegorical interpretation of the Old Testament. It was Marcion, not the Jews, who led Christians like Justin to defend an allegorical reading of the Old Testament as the only way to save it for Christianity – which in turn was the only way to prevent Christianity turning into a Jesus-cult divorced from the theology of creation.

In Justin what had been the instinctive, received, traditional way of reading the old Scriptures becomes polemical and defensive. The issue is no longer really how to proclaim Christ through the prophetic texts, but how to prevent the proclamation of Christ from causing these texts to be abolished. It is Marcion's decanonization of the Old Testament, exposing it to the possibility of being read literally, and so of being seen not to support Christian belief, that is the great enemy. Justin's frantic attempts to show that all Old Testament texts, however unpromising, really point to Christ is a valiant rescue bid to win back these books for the Church, and so to undermine the heresy that would deprive the Church of the creator as the God and Father of Jesus Christ. Marcion emphatically did not cause the Church to have a New Testament; he did cause it to have an 'Old Testament', that is, to correlate the old Scriptures with its (already more or less formed) collection of Christian books and declare them to be its equal – rather than thinking of them as a book, either absorbed into the books of the new covenant and so hardly needing to be read any longer in its own right, or superseded and displaced, as Marcion taught.[53]

To say that Marcion 'caused the Church to have an "Old Testament" ' is not meant to imply that without him the Church would have drifted into the position he was trying to force upon it, of rejecting or losing the books we call the Old Testament altogether; only that without him it might have understood the status of these books differently. In a sense, indeed, the status of the Old Testament is assured even in Marcion's own system, where these books form the necessary 'counter-text' to the New Testament. One cannot understand his New Testament without the *Antitheses*, and one cannot understand the *Antitheses* without knowing the Old Testament, even though one knows it only in order to know that it is wrong. Marcion's Bible excludes the Old

Testament, but it requires the presence of an Old-Testament-shaped hole in order to make sense. So taken for granted were the old Scriptures that a Christian scheme of thought which simply ignored them was virtually unthinkable; they are present, either as light or shade, for everyone. The overwhelming impression one gets from reading the Christian literature of the second century is of the massive passivity of the Church in relation to its Scriptures. Where the Old Testament is concerned, we can only agree with Wrede:

> From a historical point of view it would be altogether unsatisfactory [even] to say that the Jewish Old Testament – as a whole or in part – continued in force for the Christians as if its recognition implied some kind of previous reflection, and as if the possession of this heavenly and infallible book were not in the eyes of the Christians one of the most striking commendations of the new religion.[54]

In the case of the New Testament, Marcion was already too late in trying to reduce the Gospels from four to one. Though Irenaeus might produce reasons to justify a four-Gospel 'canon', their very speciousness points to the truth that by then people simply 'knew' that Matthew, Mark, Luke, and John were holy books, and it was much too late to do anything about that, however inconvenient and cumbersome these four books were in comparison with a single consistent narrative. It is this truth that Zahn, for all his anachronism in the use of the word 'canon', was on to, and that Harnack somehow failed to give him credit for. The single most important cause of the existence of the complex, untidy, and unplanned character of the Christian Bible is the Church's deep instinct for preserving what was traditional, summed up definitively by Origen: 'Remove not the ancient landmark which your fathers have set.'[55]

No other reason for accepting books as canonical or scriptural even approaches in importance the argument that they have always been so accepted. And, as we have seen, apart from the very fringes of the canon, both Old and New Testaments were already in this sense 'ancient landmarks' by the mid-second century. Books were included in the 'canon' because they always had been, and were excluded because they had never been included; *decisions* to include or exclude are of quite marginal importance.

Just as Marcionism was not the cause of inclusion, so Montanism, it seems to me, was not the cause of exclusion.[56] Tertullian, according to Harnack, thought that the Montanist 'scriptures' should be added to the *instrumentum* of the Church. But in this Harnack was probably mistaken, at least in supposing that the Montanist texts were thought of as scriptural in the same sense as the books of the New Testament. As von Campenhausen comments, 'Nowhere do we hear that these writings were described as a "new Gospel", were cited as "scripture", or were combined as a third section with the old bible to form a new Montanist canon.'[57] Recent scholarship has tended to play down the importance of Montanism in leading to a 'closed' canon. And indeed the argument from tradition would have undermined any attempt in Montanism to regard the prophecies of Montanus and his followers as 'canonical'; for they were not 'ancient', and did not claim to be. And by the mid-second century that was already a distinguishing mark of Scripture. Recent works might be inspired and might be authoritative, but they were by definition not 'Scripture'.

I suggested above that Marcion should be seen as conservative in most things, but original in his opposition to allegory as a hermeneutical approach to the Old Testament. It is possible to argue that in this he fits quite well into a development that may be observed more generally in the second-century Church, where an older allegorizing method of appropriating the Scriptures was tending to give way to a greater consciousness of the difference between Old Testament and New and a consequent willingness to use the New to launch a critique of the Old. Christians had been able to read the Old Testament as a Christian book because they had instinctively treated it allegorically. If allegory is avoided, then the lack of fit between Old Testament and New soon becomes apparent. But the sense that the New Testament is a holy book, something like what the Old Testament had been for the Jews, makes it possible to live with this awareness, for a Christian can treat the New Testament as having (at least in the respects in which the two Testaments differ) replaced or superseded the old.

Here Harnack seems to me to have seen very clearly. In Appendix II to *The Origin of the New Testament* he discusses the consequences of the fact that Christians did not develop a Scripture consisting of 'a collection of late Jewish and Christian prophetic-messianic or prophetic-hortatory books inserted in the Old Testament – thus an expanded and corrected Old Testament'. This would have been the logical outcome of the approach adopted in the Pseudo-Clementines, where Christians corrected and adapted the Old Testament to make it more clearly Christian. If this had sustained itself, Harnack wrote,

> the distinction between the New and the Old Covenant would not have come to clear expression, rather most that is distinctive in the Old Testament would have been obliterated by means of allegorical interpretation. The same considerations would apply to the 'ius divinum.' The laws of the Old Testament and the new Christian laws, if such had, indeed, taken form within the enlarged Canon, would have become indiscriminately confused seeing that the former would have been spiritualised where necessary. *The New Testament, on the contrary, had the significance, which cannot be too highly valued, that it enabled the Church to set certain limits to the allegorical method of interpretation as applied to the Old Testament, and thus to give a fair opportunity for an historical understanding of the Old Testament.*[58]

If Harnock was correct in this, we are forced to a conclusion which runs counter to the common assumption that Christians *increasingly* allegorized the Old Testament in the interests of retaining it as part of their Scriptures.[59] On the contrary, we should have to say that allegorizing was the natural method from the earliest times, and represents no more than continuity with Jewish exegesis; all that differed were the actual meanings which the allegorical method 'discovered' in the text. But as time went by, and Christians came to have their own authoritative collection of Scriptures which taught directly, and not by allegory, the substance of the new faith, the need to use the Old Testament as a vehicle of Christian instruction was reduced. Accordingly its status was somewhat diminished, and it became less liable to allegorization, the characteristic mark of a holy text in the ancient world. Then its surface meanings became more evident, and Christians began to criticize them in the light of the faith taught in the New Testament. Allegory only becomes standard again once the status of Old and New Testaments has evened out, and they have come to be seen as equal parts of a single Christian Bible, all parts of which are sacred and therefore candidates for allegorization. The acceptance of the texts that would become the New Testament destabilized the Old, and made it seem – temporarily – fair game for the kind of criticism that people in the ancient world did not apply to sacred books. Marcion rode on the crest of this wave and tried to abolish the Old Testament as a Christian book altogether. But he was not unique; the growing status of the New Testament had led others to criticize the Old and de-allegorize it. These movements, and the shift from allegorization to criticism of the old Scriptures, are important evidence for the enhanced prestige the *New* Testament was acquiring in this period.

✋3✋
Two Testaments, One Bible

For my part, my records are Jesus Christ; for me, the sacrosanct records are his cross and death and resurrection, and
the faith that comes through him.

Ignatius, *To the Philadelphians* 8

MODERN CHRISTIANS HAVE inherited a Bible divided into two
sections, the Old and New Testaments. It is obvious that there
must have been a time when this was not yet the case; when 'Scripture' meant what we call the Old Testament. It is therefore interesting to ask when and how this situation came to be replaced by
the one we know now. Books on the canon have generally made
that their theme, and they have usually pointed to the second century AD as the approximate point of transition.

Our investigation has left much in this consensus view undis-
turbed, but it has questioned the neatness of the usual solution, re-
evaluated the place of Marcion in the process, and pointed to the
very early date at which many of the books that form our New
Testament already enjoyed a high status. I have tried to suggest,
however, that many of the standard questions and answers about
the canon have a certain two-dimensional character. They tend to
assume that the notion of 'Scripture' was well-defined for all early
Christians, and the only question was whether given books did or
did not belong within it. We have already seen that this is to over-
simplify. In attributing the same (or less, or more) authority to the
Old or the New Testament, people in the first Christian centuries
were not necessarily working with a univocal definition of Scripture, or of scriptural authority. The Old and New Testaments did
eventually come to constitute 'the Bible'. But the two Testaments
were not always treated as two examples of the same genre; sometimes they were regarded as two very different *kinds* of work. The
Old and New Testaments were in a state of disequilibrium, as

Christians struggled to relate their respective claims as the highest
authority. Only when these discords have been resolved can we
truly speak of a single 'Christian Bible'.

But the resolution of the flux has little connection with the decision to treat this or that individual book as 'Scripture', and
equally little to do with definitive rulings on the contents of the
'canon'. It is a matter of perception: not *whether* particular texts are
authoritative, but *how* their authority is felt to be related to the
authority of other texts. And in the second century at least it is
difficult to find development where this issue is concerned. In
this chapter we shall look at five interconnected issues: the relation
of old and new in Scripture; the 'argument from prophecy'; the
perception of the Old Testament as a Christian book; the idea
that the New Testament is an *aide-mémoire* for the communication
of the gospel; and the relation of oral and written tradition. In each
case we shall find a bewildering variety of views. In some cases it is
possible to trace a direction in the development of thought – not
always the direction we would expect; but in others all that can
safely be said is that early Christian thinking had many strands.

aid to the memory

Old and New

In chapter 1 I tried to suggest that there is a certain blandness in the
scholarly consensus about the origins of the Christian Bible. The
common view is that the first Christians ascribed full scriptural
authority to the Old Testament. Christian writings – Gospels
and epistles – gradually circulated and acquired an ever-growing
status until, in time, they came to be recognized as on a par with
the older Scriptures. Finally, decisions were taken about the outer
limits of the combined two-Testament canon.

On the contrary, I argued, the statistics of citation suggest a
rather different picture. The central importance of most of the
writings that would come to form the New Testament is already
established in the early second century, by the time of the Apostolic Fathers, and all but a very few Old Testament books (such as
Isaiah or the Psalms) already play second fiddle to the Christians'
own writings. Indeed, it is not until the third century that citations
begin to level out as between the two Testaments. All the indications are that the New Testament became almost instantly more
important than the Old for the nascent Church, and that this introduced a disequilibrium which – if Marcion had had his way –

could easily have led to a considered demotion of the Old Testament. However, plans to abolish the Old Testament were tainted with gnosticism. In insisting on the identity of God the creator and God the redeemer, orthodox Christians found themselves necessarily committed to the Old Testament, which they restored to a more central role. Thus the status of the two Testaments approached equality by the end of the third century.

This approach, based on observing the intensity with which early Christian writers actually *used* Old and New Testament books, seems to contradict the datum on which so much study of the canon has been based: the fact (and it is a fact) that Christians in the first two centuries seldom cite New Testament books as *graphē*, or with the formula *gegraptai*, 'it is written'. The paradoxical result is well captured by Franz Stuhlhofer's comment, already quoted:

> We see here a paradox. The early Church cited the Old Testament as 'Scripture', but to begin with tended to possess it only in a fragmentary form. The New Testament, on the other hand, was widely available and was used much more heavily, but it was not yet cited as 'Scripture'.[1]

It is this paradox to which the usual consensus fails to do justice. For how could works which were only beginning to be felt as 'canonical' so outstrip in importance the Scriptures so long acknowledged as the supreme authority by Jews and still universally referred to as *graphē* by Christians? The answer must lie in some change in the evaluation of the old and the new in the Church.

For Christians as for Jews and, indeed, for pagans, the idea of 'Scripture' inherently contained the idea of age and venerability. Passivity was the major factor in the reception of certain books as holy, and this depends on attributing a high value to the past. What is old is more reliable than what is new. This was such a widespread attitude in the ancient world that it is not surprising Christians should have adopted it. Leipoldt and Morenz say, 'People not infrequently require scriptures to belong to hoary antiquity. People in the ancient world, if they are pious, do not value novelty . . . it is remote antiquity that is the age of the gods and heroes.'[2]

This attitude persisted of course in the Middle Ages, indeed perhaps down to the Enlightenment. As the medievalist A. J.

Minnis puts it, 'To be old was to be good; the best writers were the more ancient. The converse often seems to have been true: if a work was good, its medieval readers were disposed to think it was old.'[3] Where modern authors would regard the suggestion that they had derived their ideas from older works as an accusation of plagiarism, medieval writers often strenuously denied their own originality in order to confer the authority of the past on what they had written: Chaucer, for example, falsely claims to be using old sources when he is in fact composing freely.[4] The present always carries less import than the past.

Now the 'canonization' of Christian Scripture can be seen – usually has been seen – from this point of view, as a smooth development from the reception of older Jewish Scripture. As Gospels and epistles became older, they acquired authority and were simply grafted on to the existing old documents. One can certainly see such a process at work, for example, in the way 2 Peter treats the Pauline epistles as old texts which (unsurprisingly) share the obscurity and difficulty of 'the other scriptures' (3.16): 'There are some things in them hard to understand, which the ignorant and unstable twist to their own destruction, as they do the other scriptures.' One can see it too in the general acceptance by the third century of the four Gospels, despite their mutual inconsistency, as ancient and venerable works which could not therefore be changed. If they contained 'difficulties', that was only what one would expect from old, 'scriptural' material. It was an invitation to a style of exegesis that would reconcile the apparent discrepancies – just as allegorical interpretation could show the inner consistency in the Old Testament.

The Muratorian Fragment certainly thinks along these lines. For this writer, the New Testament Scriptures, like the Old, belong to a special epoch. The Fragment says that the *Shepherd* was composed by Hermas *nuperrime temporibus nostris*, 'very recently, in our own days'. Traditionally this has been taken to mean that the *Shepherd* is more or less contemporary with the writer of the Fragment – one of the arguments for dating the Fragment early. It is possible, on the other hand, to take it more vaguely, as meaning, 'in these latter times, not in the apostolic age'.[5] But in either case, to give this as a reason why the *Shepherd* cannot be canonical is to bear witness to the belief that canonical Scripture comes from the past. It belongs to a period which is now closed. Accordingly, the text goes on to say, the *Shepherd* 'should indeed be read, but it cannot be read publicly to the people in church either among the prophets, whose number is complete, or among the apostles'.[6]

But though undoubtedly Christianity developed along these lines, in the way normal to ancient 'book religions', the fact that most of its Scriptures came to be accepted as authoritative so early suggests that in the very beginning it was going down a rather different path. The Gospels were received as, in practice, even more important than the Jewish Scriptures *before* they were old enough to have a natural aura of sacred antiquity. Paul's epistles were preserved and collected while Paul was still a comparatively recent memory. Revelation, which despite some doubts in the East was none the less widely accepted as an inspired book from early times, was not a pseudepigraphical 'ancient prophecy' like Enoch or even Daniel, but the record of a vision accorded to a 'modern' prophet. (Even if the work is in fact pseudonymous, it is virtually unique in not being projected back into deep antiquity, but attributed to a contemporary figure.) This attitude, so unusual in the ancient world, presumably has something to do with the early Christian conviction that a new and unprecedented era had arrived with Jesus and the apostolic Church. Newness was no longer a sign of inferiority but a mark of authenticity. This sense that old 'Scripture', holy and unalterable as it is, has nevertheless been surpassed by a new revelation which does not yet have an ancient scripture of its own, may account for some of the paradoxes in Christian attitudes to Scripture.[7] And it may ultimately be the reason why the simple black-and-white question whether given books are or are not 'canonical' is so unsatisfactory.

The first Christians had books about Jesus and his first disciples, and they used them as authoritative sources of information about the central events of salvation. These events dwarfed, in their minds, anything in the holy books they had taken over from Judaism. But they did not yet regard the written records of these events as 'ancient scriptures' in the same sense as the 'Old Testament'. The old test which tries to establish whether books are cited as 'Scripture', *graphē*, is thus a test of something important, despite its inadequacy for the task it is usually applied to. For the practical question of how important and authoritative particular books were for early Christian communities, it fails to help, precisely because the most important books were those that as yet were *not* 'Scripture' – the books which gave Christians access to the deeds and teaching of the Lord and of his authoritative first interpreters. These books were more important than 'Scripture', and to cite them as *graphē* might have diminished rather than enhanced them. They did not gradually increase in stature until they could be seen as equal with the Old Testament; rather, the evidence of their circulation and use shows that for the first few generations the contents of these books had a status *greater* than that of the Old Testament. But, just for this reason, once they did come to be cited as *graphē* in exactly the same sense as the Old Testament a Rubicon had been crossed. They too were now 'old books', and holy for that reason, instead of new books whose newness was the guarantee of their authenticity as witnesses to a new revelation.

The moment when Christianity ceased to be novel and became a system for transmitting a *depositum* is one of the most significant moments in its history. The New Testament contains documents that surely post-date this moment – the Pastorals, 2 Peter. *Früh-katholizismus*, 'early Catholicism', is now no doubt a dated term, but it did capture something of this sense that Christianity at some point turned into a 'normal' ancient religion, respecting the authorities of the past rather than the freshness of the present. And one of the most significant indicators of this change is that the New Testament came to be treated as like the Old. But this is not (from the perspective of an earlier Christian attitude) the promotion of the New Testament to a higher status, its 'canonization'. It is more like a diminution: the loss of the sense that prophecy has revived and the present is the sphere of God's fresh activity, and its replacement with that reverence for the past which was the hallmark of the ancient religious mind.

The Argument from Prophecy

There is another way of mapping early Christian thinking about Scripture, and that is to analyse the so-called 'argument from prophecy' – the assertion, universal in early Christian writers, that Jesus Christ is the fulfilment of the promises made in the Old Testament. It would be generally agreed that this was an extremely important part of early Christian thought. It can even be argued – though this is probably an exaggeration – that it was an important factor in the Christian Church's selection of the books that form its (longer) Old Testament. A rather extreme position of this kind was maintained by Jepsen, who suggested that the contents of the Christian Old Testament (in effect the LXX canon) were fixed by deciding which of the available 'sacred writings' of Judaism pointed to Christ, and therfore could be regarded as the 'Old Testament'.[8] Sundberg was attracted by this theory, since his reconstruction of the canonization process as distinct in Judaism and Christianity required him to provide some reason why Christians opted for the longer canon.[9] More recently, a similar theory has been made of central importance for biblical theology by Hartmut Gese.[10]

In fact it is hard or even impossible to show that there was a deliberate decision to adopt the Greek canon. It can scarcely be said that the additional books point more obviously to Christ than those of the Hebrew canon; indeed, citations of the deutero-canonical books are (as Stuhlhofer shows) quite marginal in early Christian writers. Only the Wisdom of Solomon approaches in importance the central books of the Hebrew canon (it was a special favourite of Athanasius, who thought it should *not* be reckoned in the canon!). Almost all the messianic prophecies which early Christians claimed had been fulfilled in Christ are to be found within the Hebrew Scriptures. In any case, so much of traditional Christian arguments from Old Testament to New depends on various strained forms of exegesis, and so little on a literal reading, that it is hard to know how one would establish that certain books 'really' pointed to Christ more than others. The theory that the Old Testament books are those which find fulfilment in the New is in practice prescriptive rather than descriptive: it is the statement of a hermeneutical rule about how Old and New Testaments are to be read. It is not an empirical observation about the contents of the Old Testament.

Probably then we should not see the contents of the Old and New Testaments as arrived at by a process of evaluation so conscious as theories of this sort imply. Accepted use was almost everything. But – and this is my point – what was not a principle of selection was none the less an important principle for interpreting and making sense of the received texts. The *effective* canon for many early Christian writers was in practice determined by the concentration of what were taken to be Christological prophecies in certain books. If Isaiah and the Psalms heavily predominate in Christian use, that may be because these books had early been felt to contain a wealth of texts which pointed to Jesus as Messiah. A conservative attachment to the Scriptures in their existing form arrested the development that could (as Harnack saw) have led to the replacement of the Old Testament with a selection of *testimonia*, though testimony-books did exist and had a significant role for some. But the mentality behind such books was the mentality with which the Scriptures themselves were being approached anyway. These were the texts that supported Christian claims about Jesus. Without the prophetic witness, the authority of Christ would have been less secure. As Frank Kermode perceptively puts it, 'The entire Jewish Bible was to be sacrificed to the validation of the historicity of the gospels; yet its whole authority was needed to establish that historicity.'[11]

The 'argument from prophecy' presupposes the authority of the Old Testament, and reasons as follows: if Jesus can be shown to be the one the prophets foretold, then his authority is thereby vindicated. It is important to see that this line of thinking works best within a Jewish context, where the authority of the old scriptures is taken for granted. For a Jewish Christian, not everything in the Old Testament needs to have a prophetic or messianic significance, since the old Law remains in force and is seen as a true revelation of God. The Old Testament is a given. The crucial question from this point of view is whether belief in Jesus as the Messiah is compatible with this self-evidently authoritative collection of books. The argument from prophecy seeks to show that it is, and maintains indeed that 'all the promises of God find their Yes in him. That is why we utter the Amen through him, to the glory of God' (2 Cor. 1.20).

To a modern reader the force of the argument from prophecy may seem greatly diminished by the fact that it often requires the alleged 'prophecies' to be read in a far from natural sense. How can the authority of the Old Testament be invoked to show that Jesus is the promised Messiah, we ask, if the prophetic texts have to be read in strained and unnatural senses before any correspondence between them and him can be demonstrated? Gershom Scholem reproached Paul with having thus wrested the Scriptures from their natural sense in order to support his new-fangled system of beliefs:

Paul had a mystical experience which he interpreted in such a way that it shattered the traditional authority.... A purely mystical exegesis of the old words replaced the original frame and provided the foundation of the new authority which he felt called upon to establish. . . . In a manner of speaking, Paul read the Old Testament 'against the grain'. The incredible violence with which he did so shows not only how incompatible his experience was with the meaning of the old books, but also how determined he was to preserve, if only by purely mystical exegeses, his bond with the sacred text.[12]

But this is an essentially modern perception of the matter. Of course, most of the interpretations of Old Testament prophecy we find in writers such as Paul would not have occurred to anyone as the natural meaning of the texts, if they had not already been convinced that Jesus was the fulfilment of whatever holy texts there might be. But this does not necessarily mean that they were guilty of a kind of double-think in maintaining that this is what the texts really meant. 'Purely mystical exegesis' of scriptural texts was not invented by Paul; it was the common coin of the ancient world. Once one grants that holy texts are liable to contain hidden and mysterious meanings, there is no reason why the interpretations given by Paul or the evangelists should not be the right ones. Thus the argument from prophecy, ramshackle as it may look to us, was quite capable of being a serious form of argument in the ancient context, and one – this is my point at present – which genuinely regards the authority of the Old Testament as the datum on the basis of which the authenticity of the new revelation brought by Jesus can be established.

But a significant change occurred, certainly no later than the early second century. Harnack thought it was characteristic of the Gentile churches; and this may well be right, since it is easily explained in terms of the necessarily different attitude towards the Old Testament which these churches adopted, by contrast with their Jewish counterparts. For Gentile Christians, the Old Testament was not the self-evident bedrock of religious authority. They acquired the old scriptures at the same time as they adopted faith in Christ; and probably in practice most of them only ever came to know well certain core passages – Genesis 1, some Psalms, messianic *testimonia* from Isaiah, and so on. This does not mean that other parts of the Old Testament were not regarded as 'canonical' in principle. But they were accepted as such only as part of a package, and it was not seriously thought that most Christians would read or take much interest in them. What mattered were the central passages, and these mattered *because* they pointed to Christ, who was believed in as the redeemer on the strength of the Christian kerygma, not primarily because an already known Scripture had been found to make more sense if read in the light of him.

The argument from prophecy thereby ceased to be a way of showing that Jesus was the continuation and only valid fulfilment of the religion, Judaism, which was already believed to be the one true revelation of God. Instead, it became a way of showing that the Scriptures of Judaism ought to be accepted by Christians, too, since (however obscurely) they witnessed to the one in whom Christians *already* believed in any case.

For the history of the biblical canon this is a momentous shift. It implies that the contents of the New Testament have become the datum, that the authority of the Old Testament depends on that of the New. Von Campenhausen argues, surely rightly, that this shift has already occurred for Justin:

> With this historical scheme of prophecy and fulfilment Justin gives a place of central importance to a concept which in Ptolemaeus had receded completely into the background. This concept derives from earlier Christian tradition; but now characteristically its purpose has been altered. Now the aim is not so much to demonstrate the validity of faith in Christ from the Scripture as conversely to re-establish the threatened authority of Scripture in the light of Christ.[13]

This tends to confirm Cosgrove's argument that Justin's motive is at least partly anti-Marcionite. Because the argument from prophecy is at home, in principle and in origin, in polemical debates with Jews, Justin's discussion partner needs to be presented as a rabbi. But in reality the argument of the *Dialogue* has little force against Jews. Its object is to show that, since it is to Jesus that Old Testament prophecies point, the Old Testament should be regarded by Christians as an authoritative book.

That Justin uses the argument from prophecy in this way has to be argued, though it is (I believe) very likely.[14] When we turn to Tertullian's *adversus Marcionem* the point is incontestable. Especially in Book 4, §§ 9 and 10, Tertullian uses the point-by-point correspondence between the New Testament records about Jesus and the prophecies of the Old Testament to argue that the Old Testament must, therefore, be a revelation of the same God as the Father of Jesus, and cannot be regarded as the work of an alien god. Tertullian shows considerable ingenuity in finding texts in the Old Testament which he can present as predictions of the life of Christ. In 4:9:2 he asks how we could reject the Old Testament once we have heard that Jesus told his disciples 'I will make you fishers of men'; for in Jeremiah 16.16 it says, 'I will send fishermen to catch them': *hoc enim dicto intellectum illis suggerebat adimpletae prophetiae, se eum esse, qui per Hieremiam pronuntiaverat: ecce ego mittam piscatores multos, et piscabuntur illos, homines scilicet* ('in saying this he was suggesting to them the understanding of fulfilled prophecy, that it was he who had foretold through Jeremiah, "I will send many fishermen, and they will fish them, that is, men"'). He tries to show, *ad hominem*, that even what Marcion has allowed to remain in the Gospel depends on and fulfils Old Testament prophecies. In changing Simon's name to Peter, Jesus was 'fulfilling' God's renamings of Abraham and Jacob (4:13:5); in allowing rich women to minister to him, he was fufilling Isaiah 32:9 ('Rise up, you women who are at ease'). He concludes (4:43:9): *misereor tibi, Marcion: frustra laborasti. Christus enim Jesus in evangelio tuo meus est* ('I pity you, Marcion; you have laboured in vain. For the Christ Jesus in your gospel is my Christ Jesus'). By fulfilling the prophecies, Jesus is not vindicated himself, for he needs no vindication; it is the prophets who are vindicated by him. As the Pseudo-Clementines put it: 'Jesus is not to be believed because the prophets foretold him, but rather the prophets are to be believed to be true prophets, because Christ bore witness to them.'[15]

Now if we are trying to establish at what point the New Testament became 'Scripture' in the early Church, this shift may be much more significant than the transition to using citation formulas (such as *hōs gegraptai*) with New Testament texts. For in Tertullian, and arguably also in Justin, the authority of the gospel accounts is taken for granted as the absolute starting-point for Christians. No longer is the Old Testament the norm of a scriptural book; the Old Testament now needs to be justified by showing its correspondence with the New. The authority of at least some New Testament writings is *agreed common ground* between Marcion and the orthodox. On the basis of those writings a discussion of the status of the Old Testament can proceed. The change of direction in the argument from prophecy is thus one important index of the growing status of the *New* Testament, and one which has perhaps not received the attention it deserves.[16]

After thus lurching from a concern with the validity of the New

Testament revelation to a desire to vindicate the Old Testament Scriptures, the argument from prophecy eventually settled into a sort of equilibrium. The argument came to work as it were in both directions at once. It became an invitation to contemplate the divine *plan* in which the old and the new dispensations are in harmony. For this, it does not matter in which direction the argument runs – whether to show that the old scriptures validate Christ, or to vindicate the old scriptures by pointing out that Christ is their fulfilment and validation. I would hazard the guess that the eventual symmetrical pattern of prophecy and fulfilment was a factor in the development of a Christian Bible consisting of two Testaments, apparently of equal status.

This results in a position where neither the New Testament is validated by the Old nor the Old by the New, but the providence and wisdom of God are proved by the congruence between the two, by the fact that the written revelation of God forms a coherent and self-consistent whole. This is a development one would expect to find in association with the need for Christian apologetics. I do not think it can be found explicitly in the Apologists, but it underlies some of Justin's argumentation in the *Dialogue with Trypho*: for example, he accommodates his wording of the passion narrative to that of the prophecies it is supposed to fulfil. Thus in *Dialogue* 101.3 he inserts 'they twisted their lips' (*ta cheilē diestrephon*) to the description of those who mocked Christ on the cross, because Psalm 22.7 uses this expression, though it does not occur in any of the gospel accounts of the passion.[17]

The Old Testament as a Christian Book

If we now go back to the time when the Old and New Testaments had not yet become commensurate parts of a single Bible, but were still seen as two rather different types of material, we find an odd dichotomy – odd at least from a later perspective. In the very early days it was possible to tell the story of Jesus and to report his sayings almost without any reference to the Old Testament Scriptures. (If Harnack was right, the Gospel according to Mark represents an extremely primitive phase when the passion narrative stood on its own, with no perceived need for demonstrations that it 'fulfilled' any older scriptures; only with Matthew does this need come to be felt.) But one reason why this was possible is the status the Old Testament text was felt to have. It was assumed

without argument by Christians that the Old Testament books
contain a Christian meaning – that it was indeed for the sake of
Christians that these books were written.

Paul interestingly exemplifies this double tendency. Although
he reports the common early Christian belief that Christ died and
rose 'in accordance with the scriptures' (1 Cor. 15.3–4), there is
little use of the argument from prophecy. But this does not mean
that he treats the Old Testament 'on its own terms', as though it
simply continued in force with the senses that Jewish exegesis
found in it. On the contrary, everything in it is to be interpreted
from a Christian standpoint – in this sense Scholem was quite right
to accuse Paul of reading it 'against the grain'. We do not find in
Paul any sense of *distance* between the Old Testament and the
Christian reader, which needs to be bridged by arguing that the
Christian dispensation 'fulfils' the older one. Rather, Christ was
already present in the world of the Old Testament, and all along
its real meaning was a Christological one. The rock that followed
the Israelites through the wilderness 'was Christ' (1 Cor. 10.4);
everything was recorded 'for our instruction, upon whom the
end of the ages has come' (1 Cor. 10.11).

Two second-century texts in which such an attitude clearly survives are the Epistle of Barnabas, and Melito's Paschal Homily. In
both texts the Old Testament already contains the Christian
gospel. For Barnabas, even the creation narrative in Genesis is
not really about the original creation of the world, but about the
new creation in Christ:

> When [God] turned us into new men by the remission of our
> sins, it made us into men of a wholly different stamp – having so
> completely the souls of little children that it seemed as though
> he had created us all over again. It is with reference to *our*
> refashioning that Scripture makes him say to his Son, 'Let us
> make man in our own image and likeness; and let them rule
> over the beasts of the earth, and the fowls of the air, and the
> fishes of the sea'; adding, as he contemplated the beauty of *our*
> fashioning, 'Increase, and multiply, and fill the earth.'[18]

For Melito, the narrative about the paschal lamb is a veiled and
allegorical description of the passion of Christ. It is not that one
should read it *alongside* the passion or resurrection narratives of the
Gospels, as a more modern Christian might do, seeing it as

prefiguring Christ; properly understood it is already an account of what Christ did and suffered. The Old Testament is not, as in the argument from prophecy, a proof of the reliability of the New Testament witness; it virtually is a New Testament itself, once it is read through properly enlightened, that is, Christian eyes.[19]

This may well be part of the explanation of two otherwise puzzling phenomena in early Christian literature. First, there are writers whose lists of Old and New Testament books assign writings to, as we would see it, the 'wrong' Testament. The most notorious case is the *Shepherd* of Hermas. Its possible inclusion in the Old Testament is opposed in the Muratorian Fragment, but on the grounds that the Old Testament is closed (not, for example, on the grounds that the *Shepherd* is a Christian book). But it still appears bound up with the Old Testament books even in some medieval manuscripts.[20]

Secondly, early Christians often propose 'corrections' of Old Testament texts in order to make them more clearly Christian, or Christological. A Christian thinker who wishes to see Old Testament stories or prophecies as foreshadowing Christ, and hence as belonging to an imperfect stage in divine revelation, is not embarrassed to find that some texts seem to have little overt Christological content: this is not suprising, and anyway various interpretative devices are available to extract a Christian meaning from the text. But sometimes in very early works we find proposals to emend the text, on the grounds that it must originally have been more clearly Christian in content. One of the most famous examples is Justin's accusation (*Dialogue* 73) that the Jews have tampered with Psalm 96.10, which originally said that the Lord reigned 'from the tree' (*apo xulou*) – in fact a Christian interpolation, but one which survived in Christian tradition into the Middle Ages and still appears in the Passiontide hymn 'Vexilla regis':

> impleta sunt quae concinit
> David fideli carmine
> dicendo nationibus
> 'regnavit a ligno Deus'.

('The things that David sang about in his faithful psalm are now fulfilled; as he said to the nations, "God has reigned from the tree".')

For such writers, Christ was already speaking in the Old Testament before the incarnation, and would have said nothing there incompatible with what he would afterwards say through the earthly Jesus;[21] consequently Christians were ideally placed, and had a positive duty, to correct the record of his pre-incarnational utterances so as to restore the Old Testament to the truly Christian book it had originally been intended to be. For them the Old Testament was, as Ellen Flesseman-van Leer puts it, 'a complete and true revelation of Jesus Christ',[22] not some kind of merely preliminary revelation.

It is true in a certain sense to say that for writers like Barnabas only the Old Testament is Scripture, that there is not yet a 'New Testament' placed alongside it; but this can be very misleading. For what is canonical is an Old Testament read in a highly Christianizing way, and corrected ('restored') as necessary to bring out the Christian reference more clearly. Such an attitude is in fact common to the Apostolic Fathers; as Frank puts it, 'Clement is very obviously of the opinion that it is permissible to correct and so clarify an obscure text in the *graphē* in order to demonstrate its fulfilment'[23] – see, for example, the doctored version of Isaiah 60.17 in 1 Clement 42.5, 'I will confirm their bishops in righteousness, and their deacons in faith'.

In Ptolemy's *To Flora*, the words of Jesus (probably from Matthew) are compared with the teaching of Moses, and found to conflict. A resolution lies through introducing the idea that there are three levels in the Old Testament Law. One Jesus ratified wholly; one he abrogated; and one he deepened and spiritualized. In some places, moreover, it is suggested that there have been interpolations into Moses' words, introducing discrepancies that were not intended by him. A similar theory of 'false pericopes' occurs in the Pseudo-Clementines.[24] Moses and Christ agreed in their teaching, so the discrepancies must have been introduced by a third hand. Christians have a duty to remove them.[25]

How difficult these discrepancies were felt to be can be seen from Theophilus' reworking of the ten commandments to make them 'fit' Jesus' teaching, and so 'save' the Old Testament from Marcion's attack. He could not simply deny the alleged inconsistencies.[26]

We can surely speak of a shift in interpretation when we meet writers who no longer see the Old Testament in these terms, but present it as the document of the pre-Christian dispensation, containing some things that continue in force and others that are abrogated or fulfilled in the Christian revelation. No early Christian thought that anything in the old scriptures was simply *irrelevant* to Christians, merely outmoded or unimportant. But there is a great difference between thinking that the relevance of the Old Testament consists in its having all been spoken by Christ (even though not the incarnate Christ), with a primary meaning which is the Christian one – blindly misunderstood by the Jews; and thinking, on the other hand, that it represents an earlier revelation of God, preparing the ground for his revelation in Christ, but now completed and superseded by it.

The first attitude has the effect of appropriating the Old Testament for Christians and denying it to the Jews. Thus in '2 Clement' it is Christ who speaks all through the Old Testament (see for example 3.5, 13.2), and, as Frank says, 'through this theologoumenon it is possible for the author of the Second Epistle of Clement to wrest the Old Testament out of the hands of the Jews and to open it up in principle to Christian-ecclesiastical interpretation'.[27] Such writers, like Matthew, feel that they as Christians understand the Jewish Scriptures better than the Jews – indeed, that the only real Jew is a Christian.[28] 'Israel' so-called is a nation of imposters for, as Paul had said, 'he is not a real Jew who is one outwardly, nor is true circumcision something external and physical. He is a Jew who is one inwardly' (Rom. 2.28–9).

But such a line of thought will not work once there is a body of distinctively Christian writing which is beginning to function for Christians as the Old Testament did for Jews. Then it will become apparent that the teachings in the Gospels represent a fresh stage in divine revelation, and some kind of 'dispensationalism' will become the order of the day, with the Old Testament as that which Jesus took for granted but moved beyond, or as predictions or types which he fulfilled.

Part of the quarrel between Marcion and Tertullian is conducted on exactly this ground, and yet again we see how Marcion represented an older, indeed by then outmoded, approach. Marcion's premiss is that if the God of the Old Testament is also the God of Jesus, they will speak with the same voice. Since they manifestly do not, it must be concluded that they are two different gods. Tertullian replies that the premiss is wrong. One should not assume that the one God will have spoken identically in his two successive dispensations of law and gospel, only that there is a linear and organic connection between the two stages: *sicut fructus separatur a semine, cum sit fructus ex semine, sic et evangelium separatur a lege, dum provenitur ex lege, aliud ab illa, sed non alienum, diversum, sed non contrarium* ('As the fruit is separated from the seed, although the fruit is from the seed, so too the gospel is separated from the law, while it proceeds from the law – different from it, yet not alien to it, diverse, yet not contradictory') (4:11:11). '*Aliud, sed non alienum*' makes a subtle point, and one that finds little echo in Barnabas or 1 Clement. Between them and Tertullian lies, surely, the growth of a body of material about Jesus which is being read in very much the same way as the Old Testament and whose conflict with the Old Testament has therefore come to be evident. The rise of a 'New Testament' is thus implicit in this subtle shift in the way the Old is treated.

'The Words of the Word'

Christian writers in the first two centuries often retain a sense that the Gospels are not holy texts but the records of living memory. They are corrigible in the light of fresh information, and especially of eyewitness testimony or reliable reporting of it. The vehicle for this testimony is seen as primarily oral in character.

We saw in the last chapter that this was essentially Marcion's perception of the matter. Nothing in his 'canonization' of the Gospel of Luke was meant to change it: for him, the written record could and should be corrected in the light of reliable tradition. It was important to have an accurate record, as memories faded; but the record was not in any sense a 'scripture'.

So far from accelerating the development of the Gospels into 'Scripture', Marcion would have retarded it if he could. He denied that the Gospels were written by apostles, and hence holy books. They were collections of traditions about Jesus which could be checked and tested. Tertullian's attempted demolition of Marcion's own revised Gospel, pointing out that Luke was not an apostle but only an *apostolicus*, was thus not just an unwise hostage to fortune but actually missed the entire point. Marcion was not interested in 'apostolic authority' as the warrant for sacred books. He was interested in the contents of the gospel, whose authority was the inherent authority of the authentic witnesses to the new revelation in Christ. For Marcion and the tradition in which he stands, which is by no means a minority or a heterodox tradition, the Gospels are not authoritative because they are apostolic writings. Indeed, apostolic authorship, when it is imputed, is often a conclusion based on the assumption that such accurate records 'must have had' apostles as authors. As von Campenhausen observes, 'The apostolic title is not the presupposition, but the result of an examination which was conducted, in the first instance not from a formal standpoint, but from the point of view of content, history and theology.' Of course this examination could only be conducted 'with the tools made available by the learning of the time'; but still it was the result of an examination, not something taken for granted.[29]

This older Christian perception of the Gospels survives in other Christian writers, not only in 'heretics' like Marcion. It has two aspects, both a matter of thinking of the traditions about Jesus as somehow inherently oral.

(i) Although in practice second-century writers treat the Gospels as entirely reliable, not to say infallible, sources of information, in principle they ascribe authority to the contents of the Gospels, considered as independent of the books in which they appear. One sign of this is the tendency to distinguish between the words of Jesus and the story of his life, passion, and resurrection.[30] There is little sense that these are two parts of a single whole. The early Church paid extremely great reverence to the *words* of Jesus. The authority of these words is certainly not that of the books in which they are recorded, but inheres in the words themselves because of who it was that uttered them. Thus for 1 Clement, writes Frank, 'Of equal value with the Scriptures, indeed, ranking higher than they, are the *logoi tou kuriou Iēsou*. And it should be noted that such authority is ascribed only to the *logoi*, not to the documents which record them.'[31] John Knox similarly argues that the occasional use even before Justin of *gegraptai* with a New Testament text is not to be explained as showing that there was already a canonical New Testament, since it is the words of Jesus which are always quoted: 'Is not reverence for these words – a reverence which placed them on a par with or even beyond the Scriptures in importance – a more likely explanation?'[32]

In the same way, the story of Jesus was felt to have a life of its own. The notion that what is authoritative is the story as recorded in one or other Gospel *rather than* what 'actually happened' is a sophisticated theological notion – in its full-blown form perhaps hardly to be found before the twentieth century, but certainly anticipated in the ancient Church once a four-Gospel canon was firmly established. But in the second century most writers still saw the story as essentially independent of any particular literary instantiation of it. It is 'the authoritative history of the Lord wondrously born, crucified, and risen again' that Tertullian calls the *originalia instrumenta Christi.*[33]

This is surely the position in Justin, whereas in many early Fathers there is a reluctance to speak of 'Gospels' in the plural (though the expression does occur), and the Gospels are referred to instead as the *apomnēmoneumata tōn apostolōn.*[34] It is not necessary, with Cosgrove, to maintain that this is deliberately minimizing, in the sense that it reflects a reluctance to accord authority to these books: 'the widespread use of the term "Gospel(s)" in the church during Justin's time by contrast with his own appellative, "memoirs", suggests that he conceives of them as purely historical documents and not as authorities'.[35] It is not that Justin is against the 'canonization' of the Gospels. It is simply that he does not yet have a sense of them as 'texts', scriptural books with their own independent authority. The important distinction is between the words of Jesus, which are quoted as if they do not come from any particular book and are never said to be in the 'memoirs', and the events of his life, where the apostles' memoirs are cited. There is no sense that different 'memoirs' tell a different story. The Gospels are simply not in focus as discrete documents enshrining both a story and a collection of sayings. This does not in the least mean that they did not exist, or that Justin did not use them. It means that his conception of what they were is quite different from his conception of the ancient holy books that made up the Old Testament. Nevertheless, Cosgrove sums up the general position well in a paragraph which is worth quoting:

> The second-century church tended not to conceive of the Gospels as discrete, theologically-shaped literary entities; this is a more modern notion of them. Narratives and sayings material even in Justin's day represented separate streams of oral tradition, and these strands of Gospel material continued to have a life of their own separate from their joint literary incorporation into written Gospels. Consequently, it is possible, even natural, for the second-century church of Justin's time to think of the logia of Jesus or the events of his life quite apart from the evangelical literature and to conceive of the Gospels as mere

guardians of such tradition. The 'orthodox' Gospel literature
represents not so much right interpretation, though this is not
entirely absent, as correct circumscription and preservation. It
is Marcion who most accentuates the redactional issue, and to
this extent he is the first *Tendenzkritiker*. . . . This forces the issue
of authority. . . . This meant that the authority of the Jesus
tradition no longer stood on its own as dynamic and self-attest-
ing. . . . The Gospels are now viewed not only as living guardians of the sacred tradition but as literary *guarantors* of the
tradition. This is the decisive move, and one which Justin
apparently resists. The words of Jesus (for him) need no
secondary props, for they possess intrinsic authority.[36]

One of the most striking witnesses to this way of thinking is
Irenaeus – striking because he is also a defender of the canon of
four Gospels and epistles in something like its present form. Irenaeus essentially follows Justin in separating the Lord's sayings –
which he handles as though they formed almost an independent
collection – from the testimony of the apostles. The Gospels are in
practice the source for both, but although Irenaeus believes in the
sanctity of these Gospels he continues to cite them as though the
sayings and the narratives were quite separate. If one did not know
the texts Irenaeus is quoting, one would probably guess that he
had two collections, a 'sayings-source' without narrative and a
narrative without sayings. The older perception of the internal
logic of appeals to the true source of authority – 'the Lord' and
'the Apostle' (or 'Apostles') – continues to dominate, even
though in practice the source for both is the same – the four canonical Gospels (plus Acts). As von Campenhausen puts it,

> that the words of the Lord are treated on their own without
> reference to the Gospels is . . . to be regarded as an archaic sur-
> vival, a practice which derives from the time when the tradition
> of the faith formed an unbroken unity. . . . The Gospels are not
> thought of as sources for the words of Jesus; their purpose is
> simply to provide documentary evidence of the teaching of
> 'that apostle' who wrote down the gospel.[37]

The attempt to combine this traditional idea with the Gospels
and Acts as scriptural books produces, as von Campenhausen has
argued in detail, a muddled impression. At the end of *adversus*

haereses 2 (in 35:4) Irenaeus sets out quite clearly how he intends to proceed. He will vindicate the true faith from four authorities: the preaching of the apostles, the authoritative teaching (*magisterium*) of the Lord, the predictions of the prophets, and the pronouncements of the Law – thus, the apostles and the Lord, the prophets and the Law, proceeding in each pair in ascending order of authority. To deal with the first pair, all that is logically needed is a tradition of what the apostles taught, and a tradition of the words of Jesus. But what, in this scheme, is one to do with the Gospels and Acts? Book 3 attempts to assimilate the Gospels to the model of 'the preaching of the apostles', by talking simply about the *beginnings* of each Gospel as evidence for the teachings of Matthew, Mark, Luke, and John. (This is a kind of redaction criticism affected by arrested development.) Irenaeus then proceeds to outline the teaching of the apostles who are mentioned in Acts, and from there moves to Paul's epistles. The generic difference between Gospels, Acts and epistles is thus ignored in order to accommodate the traditional norm 'the apostles'.

In book 4 Irenaeus turns to the words of Jesus, paying no attention to the fact that they actually occur in the Gospels discussed already, but treating them as an independent source of authority: 'the Lord' of earlier tradition. But (because it *is* actually the Gospels he is using) a lot of narrative material gets drawn in too. By the beginning of book 4 his retrospective summary of what has gone before correctly notes that he has now explained not only the teaching of the apostles but also much of what the Saviour both taught and *did* – even though he had not originally intended to include this last element, the deeds. This last book, he promises, will contain the rest of the Lord's sayings (those in which he taught openly about the Father, as opposed to the teaching in parables already summarized) and the epistles of Paul – now detached from his proper place with the other apostles. In all this we see, as von Campenhausen says, two systems cutting across each other. 'The explanation is simple, as soon as one realizes that the Gospels and Acts as "canonical books" constitute a new entity, which now has to be combined with those ancient authorities of long standing, "the Lord" and "the Apostle".'[38]

In all this nothing has changed so far as the actual source of information for Christians is concerned, but there has been a conceptual shift towards the idea of a Christian 'Scripture'. The shift is not yet complete in Irenaeus – hence the oddly disorganized air of his discussion. Indeed, this separation of the dominical *sayings* from the apostolic *narratives* was by no means a thing of the past even long after Irenaeus. The literary shape of the New Testament is not the same as its logical or, we might say, theological shape. In the Middle Ages Abelard drew a parallel between the threefold canon of the Old Testament (taken to be law, prophets, and histories) and that of the New, as follows:

> The teaching of the New Testament is also threefold. There the Gospel takes the place of the Law and teaches us the pattern (*forma*) of true and perfect justice. Then the Epistle and Apocalypse take the place of the prophets. They exhort us to obey the Gospel. The Acts of the Apostles and the various narrative accounts in the Gospel contain episodes of sacred history.[39]

The 'Gospel' which is the Christian equivalent of the Jewish Law cannot here mean the Gospels taken as a whole, for the narrative portions of the Gospels, like Acts, are supposed to be equivalent to the histories (understood primarily as collections of *exempla*). What is equivalent to the Law must be the dominical teachings in the Gospels. This is essentially Irenaeus' distinction, re-emerging eight hundred years later. Indeed, it is still not dead: there are still 'red-letter Bibles', in which the sayings of Jesus are marked out as a kind of 'canon within the canon' by typographical devices, typically rubrication.

There is evidence to suggest that some early Christians saw the Lord's words as salvific, rather than his deeds, or his passion and resurrection. Helmut Koester writes:

> One of the most striking features of the *Gospel of Thomas* is its silence on the matter of Jesus' death and resurrection – the keystone of Paul's missionary proclamation. But Thomas is not alone in this silence. The Synoptic Sayings Source (Q), used by Matthew and Luke, also does not consider Jesus' death a part of the Christian message.... The *Gospel of Thomas* and Q challenge the assumption that the early church was unanimous in making Jesus' death and resurrection the fulcrum of Christian faith. Both documents presuppose that Jesus' significance lay in his words, and in his words alone.[40]

For the followers of Jesus whose tradition is represented in the original composition of Q, the turning point of the ages is the proclamation of Jesus . . . Jesus may indeed have been viewed as the heavenly Wisdom.[41]

(ii) A feeling persists among writers of the second century that not only the sayings of the Lord but even the stories of his life do not properly belong in *books* in the formal sense, and hence that any documents in which they are recorded must be interpreted as 'non-books'. This is probably the position in Justin, where, as we have seen, there is a reluctance to speak of 'Gospels' in the plural, and the Gospels are rather referred to as the *apomnēmoneumata tōn apostolōn*. In using the term *apomnēmoneumata* Justin was using a term familiar from secular literature, as David Aune has stressed in his *The New Testament in its Literary Environment*;[42] *apomnēmoneumata*, he argues, is roughly synonymous with *hupomnēmata*, 'notes', though it may also refer more specifically to informal records of the teachings, for example, of a philosopher. The essence of such notes is that they are an *aide-mémoire*: the substance of them is meant to be transmitted by word of mouth and memorized. This is largely consistent with other early Christian perceptions of the Gospels, as recorded by Eusebius, and in particular the strong tradition that the writing down of gospel materials was an emergency measure when it was thought that oral tradition might not suffice.

> [Of all the apostles] Matthew and John alone have left us memoirs of the Lord's doings, and there is a firm tradition that they took to writing of necessity. Matthew had begun by preaching to Hebrews; and when he made up his mind to go to others too, he committed his own gospel to writing in his native tongue, so that for those with whom he was no longer present the gap left by his departure was filled by what he wrote. [As to John,] the three gospels already written were in general circulation and copies had come into John's hands. He welcomed them, we are told, and confirmed their accuracy, but remarked that the narrative only lacked the story of what Christ had done first of all at the beginning of his mission.[43]

(This is one of the oldest attempts to reconcile John and the Synoptics: the suggestion is that John recorded the things that happened between the Lord's temptations and the arrest of John the Baptist, a period passed over in silence in the Synoptics.) Mark, similarly, according to Clement of Alexandria, represented a piece of private enterprise on the part of an enthusiastic pupil of Peter: 'When Peter heard about it, he made no objection and gave no special encouragement.'[44] This Peter is not quite the impetuous figure we meet in the Gospels; he is a gentleman-philosopher, not easily swayed by his enthusiastic students.

When redaction critics, or modern literary enthusiasts for the Bible, tell us that the Gospels are works of literary art, we should by all means believe them;[45] but we should be aware that this was not a common perception in the ancient Church. There the Gospels were not seen as great 'texts', but as the raw materials for an essentially *oral* presentation of the 'things concerning Jesus'. 'Gospel', incidentally, though it became a literary term quite quickly (presumably before Justin), always retains an element of ambiguity. This survives at least residually in the designation of the canonical Gospels as 'the gospel, according to X' not 'the gospel of X'.

Origen is an interesting witness to this. Although he acknowledges that people generally use the term *euangelion* to mean one of the four Gospels, he argues (in the opposite way to Justin) that the term ought really to be applied to *more* texts than only these Gospels. *All* the New Testament is 'gospel'

> because it contains the praises and the teaching of him through whom the gospel is the gospel . . . the mark of an evangelist is his word of exhortation, intended to stir up faith in what has been handed down to us concerning Jesus; hence in a way everything written by apostles may be called 'gospel'.[46]

The shift from seeing the New Testament books as authoritative collections of sayings or memories to seeing them as 'Scripture' in the same sense as the Old Testament is thus a slow and spasmodic one, which in a sense is even yet not complete. It has hardly anything to do with 'canonization' as that is usually understood, since it has to do with the understanding of books whose authority in some sense is *already* granted. Even before the New Testament was complete, the author of 2 Peter was thinking of 'Paul' more as a text than as a person; and conversely, centuries after it was complete, writers like Abelard could still make a distinction between the first-order 'canonicity' of the Lord's sayings and the second- or third-order status of the narrative framework in which they were set. It is thus problematic how far the New

Testament ever became (before, perhaps, the Reformation) a uniformly 'canonical text' in quite the sense that the Old Testament had been and remained for Jews, and was for the first Christians – though in fact, the kinds of discrimination within New Testament material practised by writers like Justin and Irenaeus had a consequential effect on Christian reading of the Old Testament. Veneration of Christian writings as *old*, and therefore sacred, very soon replaced the original excitement with them as expressions of a revelation and an experience that were, above all, *new*. But the Church never entirely lost the awareness that they had not originally functioned as scriptural texts in quite this sense. In the second century such an awareness was still very much alive.

At this point an important distinction needs to be drawn. In examples such as we have mentioned, the contents of the Gospels are being treated and regarded as essentially oral tradition: reliable testimony passed on by the Church, for which written texts are mere receptacles. But this does not mean that the mode of transmission was *really* oral. Theories of actual oral tradition can introduce a giant red herring into the discussion. Thus, it is well known that many early Christian writers quote sayings of Jesus in a 'mixed' form, apparently dependent on all three Synoptics. Proponents of a 'late' canon, such as Sundberg, fall on such cases as evidence that the Gospels were not yet 'canonical', or even widely known in written form:

> Neither do the more frequent citations of Jesus in the Apostolic Fathers, largely synoptic in character, show much dependence on our written Gospels. Here, again, oral Jesus tradition is suggested. . . . The curious mixture of Matthaen and Lukan characteristics in the gospel-like material in the Apostolic Fathers is explicable within the context of such oral transmission.[47]

But it is entirely possible that the Gospels were in effect *deemed* to constitute oral tradition, or its convenient written summary; this does not necessarily mean that the material in them was *actually* transmitted orally. That is a false inference. The point is that Jesus' sayings, however transmitted, had their own authority, and the Gospels in which they were recorded were not seen as books with their own literary integrity and independence; they were mere receptacles for the words of life.[48]

This perception of the Gospels not only survived into the third

century, as we have already seen, well after the New Testament
had become a written text for everyone. At the other end of the
time-scale, if C. H. Roberts is correct, it was already current very
soon after the Gospels were written – which is just as odd, to a
modern way of thinking. We have already drawn on Roberts'
theories about the use of the codex for early Christian writings.[49]
Roberts' starting-point is that some explanation is needed for the
generally acknowledged fact that the adoption of the codex first
for biblical and then for other books occurred in Christian circles,
and especially that it had evidently established itself across a wide
area (Roberts' evidence is mostly from Egypt, and he may exaggerate the ubiquity of codices) by the very early second century.[50]
One could hold that Christians decided that they needed a distinctive form for their Scriptures. But it seems easier, in view of the
extremely early date and the fact that elsewhere codices were used
only for books of very *low* status, such as notebooks, to think that
the original use for the Gospels was linked not to a perception of
these works as holy books, 'Scripture', but to a sense that they
were not exactly *books*, but memoranda or notes. This would be
consistent with the classic designation of the Gospels as *Klein-
literatur* – casual or occasional writings – by K. L. Schmidt in the
1920s,[51] and with Justin's term *apomnēmoneumata*, already discussed.

   The swiftly enhanced status of the codex resulted from the success of the works it was being used to transmit, rather than because
Christians consciously decided to confer a special status on it.
Before long, Christians were copying the Old Testament also on
codices, as if to give the older scriptures the same status as the
Gospels – another example of how in Christianity authority
passed from the New Testament back to the Old, rather than
vice versa. But the first Christian codices, if Roberts is right,
were used because the works they carried were not really
'books'. However the evangelists may have perceived their own
work, their early readers saw it as merely a convenient repository
of the kind of oral Jesus-traditions that they already knew, and
were accustomed to pass on in teaching and preaching; and so
they wrote them on sheets sewn loosely together, rather than on
formal scrolls.

   To judge from their hands, the earliest Christian books were
essentially books for use, not, as Jewish Rolls of the Law some-

times were, almost cult objects; that was only possible for a publicly recognized and protected cult so that the Christian equivalent is not found before the great codices of the fourth century.[52]

Interestingly, even very early codices (including at least one containing the *Shepherd*) often bear marks for liturgical division or guides to public reading.

Roberts' first proposal about the original Christian reason for adopting the codex, while interesting, did not commend itself widely. This was that Mark's Gospel was originally so written because it really was Mark's 'lecture notes' taken down when listening to the reminiscences of Peter.[53] (This, incidentally, explains the lost ending neatly, more neatly than on the hypothesis that the autograph was on a scroll, where the closing words of the Gospel would have been safely at the centre.) Roberts himself later abandoned this suggestion, which was very fragile in depending on a shaky theory about a single hypothetical manscript, the original Mark. His second proposal followed a suggestion made in 1950 by S. Lieberman,[54] who thought there might be an analogy with the Oral Law in Judaism. According to rabbinic texts, if the Oral Law (*tôrāh she-be'al peh*) was recorded in writing, it was not supposed to be on a scroll, which could lead to confusion with a scroll of the (written) Torah, but on some less formal tablet or notebook.

If the Gospels had been written on scrolls, this would have implied to any Christian with a Jewish background that the contents were a holy *text*, whereas they were understood by Christians to be something more like an *aide-mémoire* to assist in oral proclamation. It will be clear that this theory is highly compatible with what we have just seen, from other evidence, to have been the typical early Christian attitude to gospel books. Roberts speculates that the use of the codex by Christian scribes writing out the Gospels arose from this early perception of them as non-books. Other Christian books came to be copied in the same way by a kind of attraction; then the codex began to be seen as sharing in the prestige which in due course gospel texts began to enjoy; and finally the codex came to be seen as a specially formal and holy vehicle, neatly reversing the original reason for its use. There have been less plausible hypotheses. The way in which what began as a deliberately non-sacred form in due time became the ultimately sacred one can be paralleled from many other phenomena in the history of the Church, in music, liturgy, and church order.

Roberts thought it might have been in Antioch (or perhaps in Jerusalem) that the Christians first adapted the Jewish use of joined payrus 'tablets' (*pinakes*) or leaves to record Jesus' sayings:

> It is possible . . . that papyrus tablets were used to record the Oral Law as pronounced by Jesus, and that these tablets might have developed into a primitive form of codex. To the records of these *logia* might have been added an account of the Passion, and the way would be clear for the production of a Proto-Gospel. Once the Jewish War began, the dominating position of Antioch as the metropolis of Christianity in the Greek-speaking world would have been unchallenged, and any development of the tablet into the codex is most likely to have taken place here, thus laying the foundation of the city as a centre of Biblical scholarship. If the first work on a papyrus codex was a Gospel, it is easy to understand that the codex rapidly became the sole format for the Christian scriptures, given the authority that a Gospel would carry.[55]

There is no doubt that this suggestion is extremely speculative. On the other hand, the astonishingly early success of the codex for Christian, and *thence* for other biblical literature, needs explanation, and no better one is currently on the table. If Roberts is correct, then we would have striking confirmation of the early Christian perception of the Gospels as essentially enshrining an oral teaching. This was succeeded first by an assimilation of the Old Testament to the same model but then, quite rapidly, the loss of this sense and its replacement by a belief that the codex was a particularly *sacred* form and hence suitable for the writing of all kinds of Scripture – simply the Christian equivalent of the holy scrolls of the Jews. This becomes part of a tendency summed up well by John Muddiman: 'Christianity reinvented equivalents for the religious institutions of Israel.'[56] But the original perception of the Gospels would have been quite different. Interestingly, if Roberts is right in thinking of a Jewish-Christian interest in preserving the *logia* of Jesus as a Christian form of Oral Law, that would help to explain the special status which *words* of Jesus

retained even long after it was in theory the Gospels as a whole
that formed the core of the 'New Testament'. We shall return to
the Oral Law later in this chapter.

Orality in Theory and Practice

Luther told his readers that their meditation on the word of God
in Scripture should not be merely, as we should say, intellectual or
mental, but should have a certain physical quality: 'Not only in the
heart, but outwardly as well continually hammer and grind the
oral speech and the word written in the book, read and re-read,
seeking with diligent attention and reflection what the Holy
Spirit means by it.'[57] The word of God for Luther has what is
now sometimes called 'orality'. Scripture may find a response
more readily in those who hear it than in those who read it silently.
We have already begun to see how important to some early Christian writers was the preservation of a picture of 'the gospel' in
which it was in essence transmitted orally, with books as a sometimes necessary expedient rather than something inherently desirable. This strikes a chord with some modern ideas about 'orality'
in Christian life. Walter Ong[58] and Werner Kelber[59] have elevated
orality to a dominant position, stressing how different are pre-literate cultures in the way they transmit and preserve information,
and arguing that the modern world has much to learn from them.

The gospel was 'oral' for early Christianity, however, in a rather
special sense that did not in practice rule out the use of books. A
more sophisticated account of 'orality', more fruitful for the kind
of study we are engaged in, can be found in W. A. Graham, *Beyond
the Written Word.*[60] This is particularly interesting for us because it
restricts itself specifically to those religious and cultural traditions
in which the texts that are encountered orally/aurally are texts
which have long existed in written form. Graham, that is to say,
is not concerned with non-literate societies, and his interest does
not lie with 'oral tradition' in the sense that term usually has in
biblical studies, where it refers to the transmission of tradition
before it becomes fixed in writing. He is concerned instead with
societies such as those where Islam is dominant, and where a written text is all-pervasive, yet that text is encountered by most people
in an oral form: learned by rote in the classroom (perhaps without
comprehension), chanted from minarets, broadcast on the radio,
murmured as the accompaniment to work and leisure.[61] And he

contends that the religous consciousness of many Western Christians has been impoverished because they have failed to understand that some texts, especially religious ones, are in fact best appropriated in this way, rather than read silently in the privacy of a living-room or study. At the same time, he reminds us that the 'orality' of the Bible is far from dead for modern Christians or Jews even in societies where there is widespread literacy, and he invites theologians to give an account of the oral dimensions of Bible reading that persist to this day, especially in liturgy.

I shall return later to Graham's work; but already it should be possible to see some lines of connection with our argument so far in this chapter. As we saw, some scholars have been attracted by the idea that much of the material in the Gospels was still being transmitted orally – that is, in a pre-literate form (or at any rate in a non-literate form as well as in a literary one) – even in the second century. The often inaccurate quotations in the Fathers, it is argued, show that they were drawing on 'synoptic traditions' but not actually on the Synoptic Gospels. Such a theory cannot be ruled out absolutely, but it is not the only or, probably, the best explanation for loose quotation. We should remember instead how loose are quotations from the *Old* Testament in many patristic texts, even though the Old Testament was unquestionably already fixed in writing. The explantion is to be found not in oral transmission in the strict sense, but in the oral *use* of texts which were already available in written form. Quotation of written texts from memory is not the same as quotation from an oral tradition. Most scholars would probably agree that even where early patristic citation of synoptic material is loose and appears to conflate material from several Gospels, that should not be taken as a sign that the material was still a collection of *agrapha*. Normally it simply means that it is being quoted from memory – much as when a modern Christian refers to the story of the 'rich young ruler', forgetting that though the man is rich in all the Synoptics, he is young only in Matthew and a ruler only in Luke.[62]

Form criticism of the Gospels usually supposes that the Jesus-tradition was originally transmitted orally, in preaching and teaching, and if we go back far enough behind the Gospels, this can hardly fail to be true. No one thinks that the very first proclamation of faith in Jesus was achieved by publishing books. It is usual, however, to see the writing of Gospels as putting an end to the oral transmission. The Gospels, it is thought, represent a fixing in

writing of Jesus-tradition, which henceforth is transmitted textually rather than orally. What continues to be orally transmitted
is the Church's *regula fidei*, the kind of summary of the gospel which
provides the basis for the creeds and in due course of short treatises
on the faith such as Irenaeus' *Demonstration of the Gospel* and the
catechetical instructions of such writers as Cyril of Jerusalem. In
many ways, however, this is misleadingly simple. As we have
argued, the written Gospels were not necessarily intended to put
an end to the oral communication of the traditions about Jesus;
they may have been meant to facilitate and improve that communication. So at least they were understood by many early Christians.

This is the underlying truth, it seems to me, in the various lectionary theories of the origin of the Gospels that have been proposed from time to time. The detail of many of these theories has
failed to convince most scholars. This is especially so when such
theories are linked with a matching theory about the liturgical
reading of the Old Testament, for there is much dispute about
what (if any) system for reading the Torah was in force in synago-
gues in Palestine or the Diaspora in New Testament times, let
alone whether any systematic reading of prophetic lessons as *haf-
taroth* had yet been devised. One of the great problems with M. D.
Goulder's schemes[63] has been the difficulty of establishing a firm
base in Jewish practice on which to build. But suppose the
Gospels not to have been a Christian equivalent of Jewish Scripture (and hence as requiring Jewish precedent if they are to be seen
as intended for lectionary use), but instead precisely as *unlike*
Jewish Scripture; as the fixing in writing of Christian *oral* tradition. In that case some of these difficulties may be avoided. The
possibility that the Gospels are texts for liturgical reading can
stand on its own merits, without needing to be corrleated strongly
with precedents from the practice of the synagogue.

Christians may have taken more of an initiative here than is
commonly supposed. The internal reasons for seeing the Gospels
as designed for reading in individual pericopes are quite strong
(even if we ignore early lectionary divisions). It is perhaps harder
to argue for Mark, which has a number of 'embedded' narratives
(e.g. the story of Jairus' daughter and the woman with the haem-
orrhage, in turn embedded in the story of John the Baptist[64]) and
Luke, the first part of an apparently literary history, than it is for
Matthew and John.[65] These latter Gospels are well adapted for
division into regular-sized sections. This does not mean that they

were written to be 'Scripture'; it may equally well mean that they were written to pass on the 'memoirs' of the apostles, just as Justin suggested. Reading the gospel accounts in worship is not necessarily the publication of a sacred text; it could be seen as a form of preaching or teaching, fulfilling exactly the same function that had been achieved by oral transmission of earlier versions of the same stories, but fulfilling it in a more orderly way. The transition from the units studied by the form critics to written Gospels may thus be much smoother and in a way less significant than we tend to think. We may be right to find all kinds of subtle nuances in the different evangelists' presentations of the central events, but we should not therefore conclude that even their earliest readers were aware of them. For the average Christian, probably, this was simply the local way of telling stories which, in one form or another, all Christians were (assumed to be) more or less aware of.

'Orality' in the case of the epistles is plainly intended from the first: the authentic letters of Paul are meant to be read aloud to the assembled congregation, and passed on to other congregations for their edification, too.[66] One of the difficulties in deciding where the outer edges of the canon lay, once this became a concern, was perhaps the fact that the epistles of distinguished church leaders tended in any case to be accorded this sort of treatment. Eusebius reports that 1 Clement, a 'long and wonderful' epistle, 'was read aloud to the assembled worshippers in early days, as it is in our own '.[67] The textual uncertainty at the beginning of Ephesians may be evidence that it was used, or even designed, as an 'encyclical' letter for several churches; and while few now follow John Knox's conjecture (following Goodspeed) that the whole Pauline corpus was put together to serve as a kind of composite encyclical, and indeed would otherwise have perished, surely we must think that it was continued public reading in at least the church addressed in each letter that saved Pauline letters for posterity.[68] The repeated reading of such a letter does not really constitute it 'Scripture'; yet it does imply a very authoritative status for the work.

The result of the public reading of both Gospels and epistles is the traditional dual authority of 'the Lord' and 'the Apostle' yet, as we saw above, the correlation never becomes complete, since the *stories* (as opposed to the sayings) of Jesus in the Gospels remain in a kind of twilight category, with a status that lags strangely behind that of the *words* of either Jesus or Paul. This bears witness to a primitive model of the public reading of Christian documents in which the telling of the story is a form of preaching or teaching, but the reading of dominical or apostolic words is a vehicle for mediating the *viva vox* of the Lord or the apostle. Neither is much like the public reading of Scripture, the precise words of the Law or the Prophets enshrined in a sacred book. ⟶ *Voice of Life*

But even this is not the whole story. The perception of traditional material as 'oral' may persist even when it not only exists in writing but has actually been encountered primarily in written form. (Conversely, a text may be considered to be a 'written' text, even when one has only in fact encountered it in oral renderings, as is the case of the Qur'an for illiterate Muslims.) During the short but formative period when Christian accounts of Jesus and his teachings were valued for their novelty rather than for their antiquity, they were also perceived as essentially oral tradition – memories – rather than as written texts. And looseness in citation may therefore not result only from poor recollection (though it may no doubt *also* result from that), but from an attitude towards Christian tradition which is significantly different from that felt towards the fixed texts which were the bedrock of Judaism, the Law and the Prophets. We might almost say that citation is loose *in principle*. Wellhausen, in his short book on the first Gospels, comments on the naïvety with which early Christian writers retouch the gospel stories and combine features from several Gospels, saying, 'There was no intention of doing violence to the original sense; people felt they were enhancing the truth, not distorting it.'[69]

No doubt the existence of more than one Gospel, and hence of variant versions of the same material, is an important factor here. But here we may distinguish an earlier from a later phase. To take the later phase first: once it became established in the Church that the four Gospels were sacred texts of equal status, Christian writers had a choice of two devices to make sense of this (on the face of it rather strange) situation. One was to practice careful and conscious harmonization, as in Augustine's *de consensu evangelistarum*. As we have seen, there is already some of this in Eusebius, where we find the explanation that most of the events recorded in John fit into the period between the temptations and the arrest of John the Baptist – a period which the Synoptics had left blank.

The other technique was to interpret the Gospels in the manner of a redaction critic, treating the discrepancies as pointers to the intentions of the evangelist rather than to historical uncertainties. Clement's suggestion that John is a 'spiritual Gospel' marks a beginning; but Origen is the primary source for this approach. Origen indeed began by trying to harmonize, but his acute intelligence soon showed him how limited the possibilities were, and he took a different path, as Helmut Merkel argues:

> Canonization itself led to a demand for exact exegesis, and thus to a recognition of difficulties which it had previously been possible to gloss over. Origen still tries to take seriously the character of the apostolic writings as historical accounts, and therefore has to concern himself with harmonizing the contradictions. But at the same time he recognizes the limits of harmonizability, and consequently moves to a strong emphasis on the kerygmatic character of the Gospels.[70]

The discords thus acquire a positive value, as different notes in the divine symphony, and the purely historical inconsistency of the Gospels is played down in the interests of the religious truths to be gained from their differing presentations. Thus Origen anticipates modern suggestions that the existence of four incompatible accounts is really a good thing because it points us away from an attachment to mere historical proof and calls forth religious faith instead.[71]

But, to return to the earlier understanding of the matter, in the early second century, gospel stories and sayings seldom seem to be treated in either of these ways. Writers in this period tend rather to assume that there is a pool of stories about, and sayings by, Jesus, which they quote in whatever form they have received them, and recast in slightly different words if that will bring out better the message they wish to illustrate from them. The use made of gospel materials is harmonistic in practice, but there is apparently no theoretical attention to the problems of harmonization. Otto Piper well characterizes the attitude to the text of the gospels in Justin, for example, as follows:

> Rather than regarding the apostolic memoirs as a circumscribed and limited group of books, Justin treats them as a literary type, with no clearly defined limits and from which one has a right to select as much or as little as one pleases as long as such material is compatible with the *euangelion*. . . .

> While some of the mutual assimilations of the text of the Synoptic Gospels may be credited to later scribes, the tendency to treat their text in that way must have originated in the age of Justin.... The manner in which Justin makes use of the Gospels known to him indicates a midrashic presentation of the *euangelion* rather than literal adherence to a given text.[72]

'Midrashic' here must be taken in the loose sense often adopted by biblical scholars: not 'verse-by-verse commentary on a sacred text', but 'imaginative expansion and use of a body of traditional material, of the kind often found in a midrash'. Whether or not that is a defensible use of the term, the point Piper was making is surely correct. The Gospels are not, for Justin, a sacred text, but a repository of tradition which can be cited and rearranged at will, provided the essential outlines are respected.

One attractive aspect of seeing the early reception of the Gospels in this way is that it blends smoothly into the process by which the Gospels were originally written. What did 'Matthew' think he was doing in expanding and altering 'Mark'? There are many theories about that, but all of them have to accommodate what may be seen as two equal and opposite data. First, the production of a second Gospel implies that the gospel form was regarded as a desirable thing, one to be imitated. What is more, the reproduction of so much of Mark's material in detail, and often with verbal identity, says something about the degree of authority which that book had already attained for Matthew's community, whatever that may have been. On the other hand, Mark clearly cannot yet have been regarded as a sacrosanct text, or even a completely accurate account of what Jesus did and taught; otherwise how could it have been changed so extensively? These simple and obvious points force us to the conclusion that for Matthew the material in Mark was highly important and authoritative, but the exact verbal form of Mark did not have the kind of fixity that a scriptural book would have. The present suggestion is simply that some such perception of the nature of the Gospels persisted into the second century, and faded only slowly. It survives today in popular knowledge of the story of Jesus in a version which is in practice a harmony – but an unconscious harmony – of all the Gospels, transmitted chiefly through oral tradition.

A crucially important point, already discussed above, is that 'orality' and its converse, 'textuality' or 'literarity', may be matters

of perception rather than of objective, observable distinction. Inherently oral genres, such as plays, exist as written texts, just as
music is encoded on paper through various systems of notation;
while on the other hand works which never had anything but a
written existence may be perceived by those who value and use
them as inherently oral. A classic case, already mentioned, is the
so-called Oral Law in Judaism, which fills many shelves in
libraries. There are extreme cases of oral versus written material:
the traditions of a non-literate culture are, inevitably, purely oral, a
computer print-out is purely 'written'. But in literate societies
many cases are mixed, and subjective perception may be more important than what appears to be the case to the detached observer.
Thus we may continue to allow for the possibility that the earliest
Christians perceived the traditions about Jesus as 'oral', even
though they were already being recorded in Gospels; while they,
like their Jewish contemporaries, thought of the Old Testament
Scripture as a written text, even though many of them encountered it only when they heard it read aloud, and had generally to
quote it from memory.

To take this a little further: it is well known that many of the
Fathers cite sayings of Jesus not recorded in any existing Gospel,
the so-called *agrapha*. Certainly it is still true for Irenaeus that
words of Jesus have an authority which has little to do with
whether or not they stand in a written Gospel, and that although
Irenaeus himself is keen to defend exactly the four canonical Gospels as all-sufficient. And besides unwritten *sayings*, there are also
many traditions which the Fathers use that cannot come from our
Gospels: the idea, for example, that Jesus was born in a cave, that a
light shone at his baptism, or that when working as a carpenter he
made ploughs and yokes. (All these examples can be found in
Justin.[73]) These traditions are cited as 'what all Christians know',
not as facts attested by specific documents. Rather than saying that
such 'unwritten' traditions had a status equal to that of the written
Gospels – as though thereby the 'canonicity' of the Gospels were
impugned – perhaps we should argue in the opposite direction:
the Gospels were felt to have much the same kind of authority
as *agrapha*.[74] They were convenient summaries of the core of the
tradition about Jesus, and what was known of him coincided
more or less with the contents of the Gospels, but not exactly. In
principle the traditions about Jesus' life and teaching are passed on
by word of mouth, though as a matter of fact the Gospels contain

most of them. Christians who saw things in this way agreed in principle with Papias that 'I did not think that what was taken from books would profit me so much as what came from the living and abiding voice.'[75]

The difference can be seen more clearly if we contrast it with what we find once we read the works of Clement and Origen, for whom the two Testaments are much more two examples of the same kind of thing, scriptural books. Oral tradition here is far more clearly something other than the text of these 'Scriptures' themselves. Clement regards his own teaching as teaching he had received himself from those who had known the apostles, teaching which had been handed down by a line of oral transmission going back ultimately to the teachings given by the risen Lord and thus additional to what is recorded in the Gospels. Clement describes this in terms uncannily similar to the way the Oral Law is described at the beginning of Pirqe Aboth: 'After his resurrection the Lord imparted knowledge to James the Just and John and Peter, they imparted it to the remaining apostles, and the remaining apostles gave it to the seventy, of whom Barnabas was one.'[76] Clement comments in *Stromateis* 6:61:2–3 that 'knowledge' (*gnōsis*) of the interrelation of past, present, and future, 'has descended from the apostles in unbroken sequence to a few through oral tradition'. The 'knowledge' is thus in the nature of the case arcane, and if it is to be found in the New Testament it can only be because it is there in an encoded form, which the enlightened can discover by reading between the lines. The letter of the New Testament, just as much as that of the Old, is to be distinguished from this oral tradition.

This is a different perception of the matter from what we find in Justin or Irenaeus, and tends to confirm that there was an important shift during the second century, in which the New Testament came like the Old to be seen as a holy, ancient text, capable of containing hints of hidden meaning but clearly distinguished from a secret, and in many ways superior, oral tradition going back through the apostolic line to the risen Lord himself. The citation of *agrapha* as of equal authority with gospel sayings belongs in a period before this shift has occurred, in a time when the Lord's sayings, and traditions about his life, formed an indivisible whole, and whether or not they had as a matter of fact been recorded in writing made little or no difference to how they were treated. It would certainly make sense to say that they were 'canonical', yet their canonicity neither derived from, nor rubbed off on, the documents which might be a convenient receptacle for them.

I discussed above the theory of C. H. Roberts that the Gospels were seen by Christians as analogous to the Oral Law in Judaism, and that that is why they were written on codices, as a kind of *aide-mémoire* for an essentially oral transmission of the gospel. It may be worth spending a few moments on this parallel. There are two particularly instructive points for our purposes.

1. The 'Oral Law' (*tôrāh she-b^e'al-peh*) is supposed to have been handed down by a secret tradition from Moses alongside the written Torah codified in the Pentateuch. The Oral Law is a tradition about how the Written Law is to be interpreted. But it can be argued that its 'orality' must be understood in a somewhat special sense, to be distinguished from the 'orality' of traditions in pre-literate societies, and even from the informal orality of anecdotal material in our own culture. What is meant in Judaism by saying that *mishnayoth* are oral is that they do not form part of the written code of the Scriptures, and that oral transmission is somehow their natural habitat. It may not necessarily be meant to rule out the possibility of writing them down in some form. The Written Law has 'inscripturation' as part of its definition, but of course is frequently read aloud and indeed committed to memory; correspondingly, the Oral Law has 'orality' as part of its definition, but it can be jotted down as an aid to memory, read and worked upon in private.

Thus in the Talmudic prohibitions of writing down the Oral Law,[77] what is objected to is anything that could lead to confusion between the Oral and the Written Law. Accordingly it is held that the Oral Law must not be written in a *sepher* or formal scroll. But it could apparently be jotted down on a *pinax* – as we have seen, this can be interpreted as meaning a notebook, a kind of mini-codex, which could not possibly be confused with a Torah-scroll. Indeed, the prescriptions about the Oral and Written Law are symmetrical: the Oral Law may not be written and the Written Law may not be recited from memory.

The second part of this ruling does not mean that in no circumstances may anyone 'recite' a piece of the Torah; it means that when the Torah is being read aloud formally, in liturgy or teaching, it must be read from a scroll and not recited from memory. (Similar rulings are found about the reading of the scroll of Esther at Purim: even someone who knows the book by heart has not fulfilled the obligation to read it unless he has read it from a text.[78]) Conversely, the Oral Law must not be taught by reading it aloud from a scroll, as if its text were fixed in the way that the text of Scripture is fixed; its essential orality must be safeguarded. Jottings are allowed, but exact recitation from them is discouraged – much as speeches in the House of Commons may be delivered from notes, but are not supposed to be 'read'.[79] The element of 'orality' we have found in early Christian perceptions of the Gospels is quite close in spirit to this way of understanding the Oral Law.

2. Secondly, the relative status of Oral and Written Law in Judaism exhibits many of the same paradoxes as the relation in the early Church between the Christian gospel (and the texts by which it is communicated) and the older Scriptures. In one sense, the ultimate authority in rabbinic Judaism is of course the Written Torah, enshrined in the holy scrolls in the Ark. But in another sense, it is the Oral Law, which makes it possible actually to keep the Torah in practice, that is Israel's supreme possession. A passage quoted by Lieberman puts this nicely:

> R. Judah b. Shalom said, When the Holy One told Moses 'write down' (Exod. 34.22), the latter wanted the Mishnah also to be in writing. However, the Holy One foresaw that a time would come when the nations of the world would translate the Torah and read it in Greek and then say, 'We are Israel, and now the scales are balanced!' The Holy One will then say to the nations: you contend that you are my children. That may be, but only those who possess my mysteries are my children, i.e. [those who have] the Mishnah which is given orally.[80]

The Oral Law is not 'Scripture', yet in a way its status is higher than that of Scripture, since without it the Torah is mute and ineffective.

In the medieval Jewish mystical tradition the Written Torah exists in such a rarefied atmosphere that, without the Oral Torah, it would have scarcely any authority in practice.

> The Torah was likened to the Tree of Life in Paradise. But the Bible speaks of two trees in Paradise, each of which was related

to a different sphere of the divine realm. The Tree of Life was identified (even before the *Zohar*) with the written Torah, while the Tree of Knowledge of good and evil was identified with the oral Torah. In this connection the written Torah, it goes without saying, is considered as an absolute, while the oral Torah deals with the modalities of the Torah's application in the earthly world.... It is the tradition which first makes the Torah accessible to the human understanding, by showing the ways and means by which it can be applied to Jewish life. For an orthodox Jew ... the written Torah alone, without the tradition, which is the oral Torah, would be open to all sorts of heretical misinterpretation. It is the oral Torah that determines a Jews's actual conduct. It is easy to see how the oral Torah came to be identified – as it was by all the early Kabbalists – with the new mystical conception of the *Shekhinah*, which was regarded as the divine potency that governs the Congregation of Israel and is manifested in it.[81]

Of course these developments lie far in the future for the writers we are considering. But it is universally true that traditions giving an authoritative interpretration of a written text are in effect – though not in intention – more authoritative than the text they interpret. In that sense the Oral Law was always more important than the Written. Likewise the Christian Scriptures were more authoritative for Christians than the Old Testament long before they became *graphē*, 'Scripture', themselves. Indeed, once they did become Scripture, they at once attracted a kind of Oral Law themselves – a 'secret' tradition held to be as venerable as they were. Their 'promotion' to the rank of written Scripture put them at the mercy of 'authoritative' interpreters. In origin, however, the formal relation of Gospels and Old Testament does have some significant analogies with the relation of Oral and Written Torah in Judaism.

There are important respects in which the Gospels are not at all like the Oral Law:

(i) They are narratives, not merely sayings: a better Christian parallel to the Oral Law would be the 'Sayings Source' (Q) if it ever existed, but this was displaced by our present Gospels with their combination of sayings and narrative. All the same, the preception of sayings of Jesus as existing in their own right, apart from the gospel texts in which they now stand, would suggest that some such model as the Oral Law may well have been in the minds of some early Christians, and one could even guess that it was the transition from a Jewish to a Gentile context that resulted in a loss of the independent integrity of a sayings tradition and its subsumption into something more like a Hellenistic 'biography'. (On the other hand, in rabbinic Judaism too the deeds (*ma'ªsîm*) of great teachers are cited as authoritative for halakah alongside their sayings (*d*ᵉ*bārîm*).)

(ii) The teachings of Jesus in the Gospels are for the most part not an interpretation of Old Testament texts at all, not even ostensibly so. Some of the Sermon on the Mount, for example the Antitheses (Matt. 5.21–48), can be read as a Christian Torah, and there have been theories to the effect that the Gospel according to Matthew was meant as a Christian 'Pentateuch'.[82] But most of the sayings-material in the Gospels is not of this type. This does not rule out the possibility, however, that Christians, especially Jewish Christians, may have *thought of* the sayings of Jesus as analogous to the Oral Law: Matthew's community may have read Matthew in this sense, whatever the evangelist's own intentions may have been. Here again, the question how the Gospels were *perceived* may matter more, for the second century, than how they would be classified either by us or by their writers and compilers.

(iii) A feature not really paralleled in the Oral Law but perhaps crucial to the Christian tradition takes us back to our starting-point in this chapter: the sense that the Gospels need not be remembered and reproduced verbatim, that the general gist is enough. Oral Law in Judaism is not loose, just because it is oral. Those who hand it on are supposed to memorize the precise words of their master and reproduce them exactly. A talmudic passage discussed by Birger Gerhardsson may show how this kind of accurate transmission was ensured:

In what way was mishnah published? Moses learned from the mouth of the Almighty. Then Aaron entered and Moses repeated to him his chapter. Then Aaron moved and sat on Moses' left. Thereupon Aaron's sons entered and Moses repeated to them their chapter. Thereupon his sons moved and Eleazar sat down on Moses' right and Ithamar on Aaron's left. Thereupon the elders entered and Moses repeated to them their chapter, and when the elders had moved to one side all the people entered and Moses repeated to them their chapter.

Aaron had thus heard what was transmitted four times, his sons three times, the elders twice and all the people once. Moses now left them and Aaron repeated his chapter to them. Then Aaron went out and his sons repeated their chapter to them. Then his sons went out and the elders repeated their chapter to them. Thus everyone had heard (every) chapter four times. From this R. Eliezer drew the conclusion that a man is bound to repeat (every tradition) four times for his pupil.[83]

In such a method exact repetition is all-important: as Gerhardsson says, 'The art of reproducing another person's statements in one's own words, and of abstracting points of view and ideas from someone's words, has been carried to considerable lengths in the Hellenized West. But the art was not practised in ancient Israel.'[84] And the transmission of gospel traditions surely stands more in the Western art of epitomizing than it does in the rabbinic tradition of exact repetition. Indeed, once Jesus' sayings came to be transmitted purely in Greek, that is, in translation, this was probably inevitable. But the contrast here reminds us again of an important point: orality is not simply synonymous with fluidity. There can be a loosely transmitted textual tradition or a tightly transmitted oral one, and there are many intermediate possibilities.[85]

The Gospel and the Gospels

To sum up. In retaining a sense that the gospel message was essentially something oral, early Christians were not in practice setting their faces against books, nor against a certain fixity in their traditions. Some modern accounts of the essential 'orality' of the primitive gospel, such as that by Werner Kelber, have gone too far in this direction, even arguing (as Gerhardsson puts it) that 'the written Gospel is a direct counter-move against the oral tradition . . . the evangelist who writes wants to dethrone the authorities of the existing gospel proclamation'.[86] But though this is an exaggeration, it remains true that Christians long retained a sense that the gospel and the Gospels were not simply identical. The flavour of the first Christians' thinking is captured well by Gerhardsson:

In the hermeneutical debate today, there are reasons for thinking once more about the early church Fathers' theme . . . that the gospel is a spoken word (*viva vox*). The double point of

departure is that books surely are permitted and important . . .
but that the gospel was from the beginning a markedly oral
word, which should be written 'in the heart' of the listeners. . . .
To achieve this aim, it was vital that the message was living,
flexible speech.[87]

The practical consequence of this, once there were written Gospels, was that authority was accorded not to these books directly,
but more obliquely to what they stood for or what was taken to be
at the heart of them. The 'New Testament canon' of the early
Church was thus organized rather differently in people's minds
from the way it was organized on paper. So far as we know,
there has never been a physical New Testament consisting of (a)
Jesus' sayings, (b) accounts of Jesus' actions, and (c) the teachings
of the apostles: one would have to reshuffle the material in the
Christian books to produce such a New Testament. But from
very early times the New Testament was *perceived* as consisting of
these elements, and that is the shape the Christian 'oral law', as we
might call it, had in people's minds. I do not think that traditional
studies of 'canonization' have seen how difficult this makes it to
answer 'yes or no' questions about the status of our written New
Testament texts in the first two centuries.

↩4↪
'Writings of Holiness'

> There is Kabbalistic speculation ... about a day on which
> words will shake off 'the burden of having to mean' and will
> be only themselves, blank and replete as stone.
>
> George Steiner, *After Babel*, London 1975, p. 297

'CANONIZATION' SOUNDS LIKE a simple concept: the attribution
of authority to a corpus of literature. We have begun to see that it
is far from simple. The preceding chapters have been an exercise in
map-work, as I have tried to explore a number of sets of alterna-
tives in the way the authority of a body of texts can be understood.
We have seen that a text can be authoritative as a written document, or as the repository of an oral tradition. Its exact wording
can be regarded as essential, or more may be felt to depend on its
general gist. What is more, this pair of contrasts does not always
correlate in the most obvious way. We tend to assume that writing
preserves the exact wording of a tradition, while oral transmission
correlates with interest in its 'gist'. But this is not always so, or at
least, it was not always thought to be so by the cultures we are
interested in. Many people in the ancient world thought that oral
transmission was more reliable than written; and conversely, as we
have seen, some Christians may have written down sayings of
Jesus in order to have a text from which to extemporize. On the
other hand, some early rabbinic authorities believed that essential
traditions *ought* to be transmitted orally rather than in writing, but
that the oral tradition should be scrupulously exact as to the wording adopted. Thus orality and 'inscripturation' may each be correlated with either flexibility or rigidity in the transmission of texts
and their content.

Worse still, if one is trying to draw up a tidy scheme, the
recipient of a text or a tradition may not experience it in the
mode deliberately adopted by the sender. To take an extreme

case, a theoretically very fluid oral tradition may come to exercise its authority and influence through a rigidly fixed written form – this was often the case for the Oral Law; while on the other hand a work such as the Qur'an, which is fixed in writing to the smallest detail, is know to many only through an oral realization.

With all this complexity in mind, I should perhaps apologize to the reader for the present chapter, whose purpose is to thicken the plot still further. I wrote above that orality and 'inscripturation' may each be correlated with either flexibility or rigidity in the transmission of texts *and their content*. The expression 'and their content' may have seemed redundant. Surely in passing on a text we are *ipso facto* transmitting a content, a 'message' which the text exists to convey? Any collection of words presents itself to us as the vehicle for conveying some information. Hence to say that a text is 'canonical' or 'authoritative' is to say (we normally assume) that the content of the text's message or meaning is being affirmed as important and definitive: to canonize the text is to declare that this content must be assented to. Different people may see the interrelation of verbal form and semantic content differently – some, as we have just recalled, may think that the exact verbal form matters deeply, others that the gist of the text might be conveyed equally well by several different sequences of words. But in either case, it is assumed, the words exist to convey a meaning, and, if the text is 'canonical', then a very important meaning. Because this is how we naturally think of texts, in discussing canonization we usually think of it as a process by which Jews or Christians came to agree on the texts whose meanings they affirmed as authoritative. These texts, we then suppose, were carefully copied (textually) or scrupulously recited (orally) precisely because their *contents* were important – because of what they *meant*.

The additional complication which I want to introduce in this chapter is the question whether this is necessarily the case. A concentration on the semantic contents of religious works is far from doing justice to the varied purposes and functions of holy books in religious practice. There are many uses a written (or indeed oral) text can have besides conveying information. As Rosalind Thomas puts it, 'It is ... assumed that writing simply conveys the message of its written content without any further meaning. ... But such modern perceptions may not always be appropriate for the ancient world. The symbolic or non-documentary use of writing is often recognized in other cultures.'[1]

So in this chapter I shall reflect on attitudes to Scripture (whether written or oral) in which the semantic content is not the primary concern, where the text is not thought of as essentially a repository of meaning. In the final chapter we shall turn to the polar opposite: ways of reading or hearing texts in which meaning is extracted from features other than the text's 'content'.

'All Holy Scriptures Defile the Hands'

To think one's way into a mentality for which texts are not primarily important because of their content is difficult for the modern reader. I propose to approach it by examining an old crux in the study of the biblical canon, a passage in the Mishnah which tells of disputes about whether certain books 'defile the hands' (*m^etam'îm et-ha-yādaim*). It is fair to warn the reader that it will be some time before the relevance of this issue to the theme of the chapter becomes clear, but patience will be rewarded.

A received opinion about the canon of the Hebrew Scriptures is that there are certain books in our present Old Testament whose status as inspired Scripture was still doubtful in the New Testament period, and which were accepted by Judaism as 'canonical' only as the result of the so-called 'council of Jamnia' – supposedly a special meeting of the Jewish academy at Jamnia (otherwise Yabneh) at the end of the first century AD. Scholarship in recent years has begun to abandon the idea that there was ever a formal 'council'.[2] But the impression has persisted that, so far as the establishment of the Old Testament canon is concerned, this may be something of a quibble. Council or no council, it was among the rabbinic authorities gathered at Yabneh after the destruction of the Temple that disputes about the exact limits of Scripture began to be settled. The books which are said to have been in dispute are the Song of Songs and Ecclesiastes (and we shall see that elsewhere Esther is sometimes also mentioned), and the primary text which refers to the rabbinic disputes is in the Mishnah, in the tractate Yadaim 3:5:

> All holy scriptures (*kitbē-ha-qôdesh*, 'writing of holiness') make the hands unclean (*m^etam'îm 'et-ha-yādaim*). The Song of Songs and Ecclesiastes make the hands unclean. R. Judah said: The Song of Songs makes the hands unclean but there is a dispute concerning Ecclesiastes. R. Jose said: Ecclesiastes does not

make the hands unclean but there is a dispute concerning the Song of Songs. R. Simeon said: Ecclesiastes is among the lenient decisions of the School of Shammai and among the stringent decisions of the School of Hillel. R. Simeon b. Azzai said: I have heard a tradition from the seventy-two elders on the day that R. Eleazar b. Azariah was appointed head of the Academy, that the Song of Songs and Ecclesiastes make the hands unclean. R. Akiba said: God forbid that any man in Israel ever disputed concerning the Song of Songs, saying that it does not make the hands unclean, for the whole world is not worth the day on which the Song of Songs was given to Israel, for all the scriptures [or, all the Writings] are holy, but the Song of Songs is the holiest of the holy. If there was a dispute, it concerned Ecclesiastes. R. Johanan b. Joshua, the son of R. Akiba's father-in-law, said: According to what was said by Ben Azzai, thus they disputed and thus they decided.

It can easily be seen that the idea of a 'council' which ruled on the status of these books rests on the narrowest of bases: a tradition about the day on which R. Eleazar was elected president of the Academy. But it can also be seen that the Mishnah was aware of some kind of dispute about the two books, and most scholars who have studied the passage continue to think that it has something to do with 'canonicity'.[3]

The two questions that naturally arise in reading M. Yadaim are these: what is it about 'holy scriptures' that make them 'defile the hands' of those who handle them; and why are the Song of Songs and Ecclesiastes at least thinkable exceptions?

1. To Christian eyes the idea that the holiness of a book consists in its ability to make the hands that hold it *un*clean seems highly paradoxical. But it is quite plain from the passage that this ability is indeed a mark of higher rather than lower status; for we know from many other rabbinic texts that scrolls of the Torah were thought to possess this property. The paradox was apparent not only to Christian but also to Jewish eyes – it is not simply a Christian misunderstanding of Jewish institutions – for several rabbinic texts concern themselves with the question how something as holy as the Torah can be said to defile. The Sadducees in particular are supposed to have regarded such a notion as nonsensical. Even our present passage may contain an awareness of paradox, in that

the notoriously strict school of Shammai is said to have been lenient about Ecclesiastes (that is, to have said that it did *not* defile the
hands, so that no elaborate ritual purifications were needed after
handling it), while the normally lenient school of Hillel ruled the
other way.

There is a sense here that the whole thing is decidedly odd, and
most of the explanations the rabbis themselves give are far-
fetched, and fairly obviously contrived – explaining customs
they observed as traditional but did not understand. The most
plausible account I have yet seen is in an article by Martin Goodman.[4] Goodman suggests that the Pharisees quite deliberately attributed this somewhat unnatural and counter-intuitive stigma of
uncleanness to scriptural books because they wanted to give an
explanation of ritual practices in which Jews treated scriptural
scrolls much as pagans treated idols, handling them with reverence and carrying them around in procession – customs, of
course, which persist to this day. Some account was needed of
this custom that would rebut the implication of idolatry towards
the scrolls of the Law, for 'after all', says Goodman, 'the Bible
itself is clear enough in its prohibition on the worship of objects
made by men. [Accordingly] rabbinic texts systematically avoid
describing the scrolls themselves as sacred: they are termed *kitbē
ha-qôdesh* ("writings of the holy"), rather than *kethûbîm ha-
qedôshim*.' 'I suggest', he goes on,

> that the origins of the notion that sacred books defile the hands
> lie in this embarrassment.... Faced by the fact that ordinary
> Jews treated scrolls of scripture as too special to be used as or-
> dinary objects, and unwilling to accept that such behaviour
> could be put down to the semi-idolatrous notion that pieces
> of parchment could be sacred, the Pharisees explained custom-
> ary behaviour by asserting that the scrolls of the Torah must be
> handled with care because when touched they would defile the
> hands.[5]

Thus attributing uncleanness had the same practical effect as
attributing holiness. It made people handle the texts very carefully, much as people in many religions handle sacred objects.
But it gave an opposite explanation of the reason for the custom,
which protected Judaism (in theory at least) from the charge of
idolatry. I find this theory attractive, but I shall go on to suggest

that it is part of a more general tendency in Judaism, a tendency which has an even more powerful explanatory value in handling questions about this text from the Mishnah than Goodman has proposed.

2. If Goodman is right, the idea of texts 'defiling the hands' began with an attempt to give a theologically acceptable account of popular reverence for the scrolls of the Torah, and was then extended by analogy to cover other books and objects that were associated with, or looked like, Torah scrolls – a normal rabbinic procedure. Hence the wrappings of Torah scolls and the thongs used to tie them up were also thought to confer uncleanness.[6] So were other sacred writings which had the same form as the Torah: thus a scroll of Isaiah would also confer uncleanness. But why does the Mishnah single out the two books, Song of Songs and Ecclesiastes, and say that there were disputes about their ability to defile?

James Barr has argued[7] that the question is not about the scriptural status of such texts in general, but only about the constraints on their use in a liturgical context. In other words, Christian concern about 'canonicity' should not be read back into rabbinic disputes about the physical properties of certain scrolls. This is true, I am sure, as far as it goes: the whole concern of these rulings on what does and does not defile the hands is indeed concerned with the handling of physical objects, not with the status of books considered as having a metaphysical existence. Nothing makes this clearer than the ruling in m. Yadaim 4:5, very close to the passage we are considering, that books of the Torah do not defile the hands if they are in the wrong script, e.g. in proto-Hebraic rather than square script (what the Mishnah calls Assyrian characters). Furthermore, if it is to defile, a book must be written in ink on parchment. An additional reason for thinking that 'defiling the hands' is not the same as 'being canonical' is the ruling, also in m. Yadaim 4:5, that the Hebrew text does not defile the hands when translated into Aramaic and (perhaps more surprisingly) vice versa:

The [Aramaic] version that is in Ezra and Daniel renders the hands unclean. If an [Aramaic] version [contained in the Scriptures] was written in Hebrew, or if [Scripture that is in] Hebrew was written in an Aramaic version, or in Hebrew script, it does not render the hands unclean. [The Holy Scriptures] render the hands unclean only if they are written in the Assyrian character, on leather, and in ink.

But Goodman rightly observes that 'this negative conclusion can hardly be the end of the matter. If the authority of their contents did not distinguish texts which defile the hands from other texts, on what other grounds did the rabbis make the distinction?'[8] Granted that the debates were not directly about the 'canonicity' of Ecclesiastes or the Song of Songs, but about their use, why should it be only with these books that such debates arose, if not that people were unclear whether they counted as 'holy scriptures' or 'writings of holiness'?

We may recall that these two books are generally regarded as among the latest in the Old Testament; that they appear in the third section of the Hebrew canon, the Writings, often thought to be the last part to be canonized anyway; and that both Christians and Jews have sometimes been doubtful of their religious value, for reasons obvious to any reader. Can it be a coincidence, then, that they are also the two books that some thought incapable of defiling the hands? Was not this practice a way of indicating that they were not part of the Scriptures, but because of their doubtful *content* had the same status as secular books? And is not the traditional interpretation of the mishnaic passage therefore essentially correct in thinking that the Old Testament canon was still not completely settled in the first century, and that these two books were still in an ambiguous position?

The problem I have with this is that (for reasons I have discussed elsewhere[9]) I find it hard to believe that these or any other parts of the present Hebrew Bible were of doubtful status as late as the end of the first century AD.[10] The canon was indeed not *closed* by then – indeed, I am inclined to think it remained fluid long after the date when the non-existent council of Jamnia failed to take place. But its fluidity means, precisely, that in the first century *more* books than the present list were serious contenders for canonical status, not that any of the existing ones were candidates for exclusion. Yet what alternative account can be given of our text?

3. The solution lies, I believe, in first going even further than Goodman in accounting for the strange idea that holy books in general defile the hands. The paradoxical character of this idea

has, in fact, parallels elsewhere in Jewish tradition, and perhaps in other cultures in which taboos of various sorts are culturally important. Within rabbinic Judaism, the law of blasphemy offers striking analogies, in its attitude towards another supremely holy thing: the name of God which we now conventionally render 'Yahweh'.

The name of the God of Israel must not be uttered under any normal circumstances. To utter it in blessing is no more acceptable than to use it for a curse. The Mishnah (m. Shebuoth 4:13) condemns those who swear even by individual letters of the name of God or even of the word 'God', *elohim*: 'swearing by aleph or daleth, by yodh or he', and there is a similar provision in the Qumran Damascus Document.[11] The name of God is so holy that to utter it places one under a curse, and this irrespective of whether one does so to show respect or disrespect for the deity. Accordingly, as is well known, the Mishnah defined blasphemy entirely in terms of the utterance of the Name. The one legitimate occasion for uttering the Name was the moment at which the High Priest pronounced it during his annual entry into the Holy of Holies on the day of Atonement. Within the holiest place of Judaism his utterance of the Name was not blasphemy, and did not render him subject to divine punishment. But in any other circumstances to utter the Name was to blaspheme, and blasphemy could not in fact be committed in any other way. This is perhaps part of the Mishnah's proverbial kindliness, for – since it may be that no one knew how the Name was meant to be pronounced anyway – it may well have made blasphemy into an uncommittable sin.

It is interesting to see how a trial for blasphemy was supposed to be conducted. At some point, of course, in accordance with the law specifying the need for witnesses, someone had to testify that he had heard the Name uttered. But how was he to do so without committing blasphemy himself? In fact the witnesses were supposed until the last moment to use a pseudonym, saying, 'I heard him say, May Jose smite Jose', as we might say 'Bloggs'. But before sentence could be passed one of them had to pronounce the very word they had heard:

> When sentence was to be given they did not declare him guilty of death with the substituted name, but they sent out all the people and asked the chief among the witnesses and said to

him, 'Say expressly what thou heardest,' and he says it; and the judges stand up on their feet and rend their garments, and they may not mend them again. And the second witness says, 'I also heard the like,' and the third says, 'I also heard the like.'[12]

The *intention* with which even the witness pronounced the Name did not make the act of doing so a holy act. It was clearly felt to be gravely dangerous. Outside the Holy of Holies, the Name could not be pronounced without the risk of blasphemy.[13]

Now I think we have here at least a partial analogy to the theory that Scriptures, because of their intense holiness, bring those who handle them defilement rather than blessing. Of course, to destroy a scriptural text is a sin; but that does not mean that to handle one with reverence is simply and unproblematically praiseworthy. The text is too charged with sanctity for such a simple contrast to be applicable.[14] Any human being handling the Torah, like anyone uttering the holy name of God, is running a high risk. Rituals of cleansing are needed to neutralize this risk. Handling Scripture for a good cause, such as reading it liturgically, is of course not *sinful*, any more than bearing witness to blasphemy and so getting the blasphemer convicted is sinful: both are acts of piety. But they bring the person concerned into dangerous contact with the divine, and, like Uzzah steadying the ark when the oxen stumbled (2 Sam. 6:6–7), he may be harmed by the contact. The religious system has to provide a means whereby, as it were, the electric charge can run to earth without harming the innocent victim. The way to do this is to treat him as unclean, and put him through the normal rituals which remove such uncleanness and restore normality.

One small point which may help to confirm that the analogy I am developing here is in fact quite a close one is to be found in rabbinic statements about what is called the 'scroll of the Temple Court'. This is supposed to have been the standard copy of the Torah,[15] against which other copies were periodically checked, and it was kept within the precincts of the Temple. Whether or not such a scroll ever in fact existed is an interesting question, but does not matter for our purposes. What is notable is that the rabbis maintained that this scroll, alone of all copies of the Torah, did not make the hands unclean so long as it remained within the Temple;[16] though if taken outside it would, at least according to the Tosephta,[17] start to confer uncleanness like any normal Torah scroll. There is no doubt that a book which could not be handled without causing ritual impurity would have been an extremely inconvenient object in a place where *par excellence* people must at all times be ritually pure; so we might argue (as Goodman does) that the inconsistent exception in favour of this one scroll was simply forced on the rabbis though they could give no coherent reason of principle for it.

But the analogy with the High Priest's privileged utterance of the divine Name might suggest a better explanation. Within the Temple, in its proper and natural place, the definitive Torah scroll had no power to convey uncleanness. It was only outside the precinct that the holiness of the Torah was a dangerous force. The holy book handled by ritually pure people in the holiest place on earth is not part of a structure of unbalanced forces pulling against each other, but is in perfect equilibrium. Uncleanness occurs when the balance is disturbed.[18] Just as blasphemy occurs when there is an inappropriate utterance of the great Name of God in profane surroundings, so the power in the Torah becomes a dangerous force bringing ritual impurity when the scrolls are handled at ordinary times by people who lack the complete ritual purity of priests in the Temple. This whole way of thinking seems strange in many ways to many modern people – though not to all: there are plenty of Christian parallels attaching to the Blessed Sacrament, or to liturgical books of the Gospels, which are still second nature to some. But once we are inside this world of thought, the idea that holy Scriptures defile the hands, and the idea that speaking God's name is blasphemy, seem to have the same kind of logic.

4. All of this helps considerably, I believe, in explaining why the status of certain books is defined as their ability to make the hands unclean. But it does not get us much further towards identifying the criterion by which it could be decided whether or not a book is of this kind, and on what basis therefore anyone might have held that two books which were undoubtedly of very high prestige, Ecclesiastes and the Song of Songs, were nevertheless incapable of causing defilement. The analogy I have just developed, however, suggests to me that the answer could be extremely simple.

There are in fact, as noted above, *three* books whose ability to defile the hands, rabbinic authorities claim, was at some time or other in dispute. Alongside the two mentioned in m. Yadaim

3:5, there is a passage from a later source, the tractate Megillah of
the Babylonian Talmud (7a), which says that there was also doubt
about Esther. Various rabbis gave assorted reasons for saying that
it too did not make the hands unclean. Now even if there were any
plausibility in saying that Ecclesiastes and the Song of Songs were
not yet regarded as Scripture in the first century, it would be very
odd to say the same of Esther, which has a whole tractate of the
Mishnah (m. Megillah) devoted to the rules for reading it at the
feast of Purim.

Much later *Christian* doubts about the canonical status of
Esther, however, may point us towards the solution of our problem. Esther, it is sometimes said by Christians, should not really
be in the Bible because God is not mentioned in it. From a modern
exegetical perspective this is misleading, for Esther clearly works
with a high doctrine of divine providence, and is in fact a very
religious book, even if the religion is (for good reasons) of a
rather aggressive kind. But at a much more obvious level it is perfectly true that God is not mentioned in Esther: that is, the *word*
'God' nowhere occurs in the book. If we take our cue from this
and try to approach the matter from a Jewish rather than a Christian perspective, we can easily establish that Esther, Ecclesiastes,
and the Song of Songs have one simple characteristic in common.
Though Esther is alone in not mentioning God at all, all three
books share a much more important feature, seen through
Jewish eyes: none of them contains the divine Name, that is, the
sacred Tetragrammaton. Furthermore, they are the only books in
the Hebrew Bible of which this is true. It is the one thing that
marks them off from the rest of the canon. This has nothing to
do with the books' *content*, in the sense of their message or meaning
or theme; nothing to do with their date of writing; nothing to do
with which section of the canon they belong to, or with how they
were interpreted. It is an entirely external, physical fact about
them. But for rabbinic Judaism it may well have been an all-
important fact. That at any rate is the hypothesis I should like to
develop. It will help to confirm that the sacredness of the physical
scrolls containing holy texts may be quite independent of questions of meaning and interpretation.

The effect of this proposal is to move from an *analogy* between
the law of blasphemy and the ritual uncleanness of Scripture to a
virtual *equivalence* between the two. The divine Name is central to
both. Just as an utterance containing the spoken Name is the

ultimately holy utterance in Judaism, but for that very reason normally a blasphemy, so a book containing the written form of the Name is a truly holy book, but therefore contaminates any ordinary human hands that hold it.

If this is correct, we could go further and suggest a reinterpretation of the phrase 'writings of holiness' (*kitbē ha-qôdesh*). Perhaps this is not synonymous with 'sacred scriptures'. The expression *kitbē ha-qôdesh* occurs (according to Blau[19]) only seven or eight times in the Mishnah and four times in the Tosephta – it is not simply an everyday term for scriptural books. Perhaps it means not 'holy scriptures' but 'writings containing holiness' – that is, containing the Name. Of course this is quite compatible with the idea that the *reference* (or denotation) of the phrase is in practice almost exactly the present Hebrew Scriptures, minus only the three books that are in dispute. But its *sense* (or connotation) is 'writings containing the Name'.

In that case the next sentence in the passage from m. Yadaim is not discussing whether the Song and Ecclesiastes are 'writings of holiness' – which, obviously, they are not – but whether *in spite of this* they defile the hands. The question only arises because these books are 'Scripture' anyway; if they were not, the answer would be obviously negative. The question is this: given that these scriptural books are read in the same way as the other Scriptures, need they be handled, as it were, with gloves on;[20] or does the fact that they lack the feature from which divine power emanates – the ineffable Name – mean that they need fewer safeguards? This would agree with what I take on other grounds to be the case, that these books were already 'scriptural' or 'canonical' well before AD 90. It would also confirm Barr's point that the question really is what it purports to be, a question about ritual. But it would give a reason why the question needed to be asked. It might also. incidentally, help to explain the uncharacteristic judgements of the schools of Shammai and Hillel. The school of Shammai may well have taken the rigorist line that books lacking the Name should not be treated as though they had it, even though this would have *appeared* lax to a superficial observer.

Even if this interpretation of the phrase 'writings of holiness' is rejected, however, the hypothesis that it was the absence of the Name that made these books arguably unable to defile the hands remains on the table. The main objection to it, I believe, is that it is pure speculation. If this was the true reason for the debate, why did no one say so? This may not be fatal, however; for there is quite a lot of circumstantial evidence that may make it at least plausible.

Our starting-point might be the widely held supposition that it was the presence of the Tetragrammaton which made scriptural books candidates for storage in a genizah.[21] The fact that texts were inaccurate meant that they could not be used, but the fact that they contained the Name meant they could not be destroyed. This is why there have to be special rabbinic rulings on the legitimacy of destroying heretical (especially Christian) books 'with their names'.[22] The reason why this was seldom a problem in the case of orthodox but non-biblical Jewish works seems to be that it was in practice only in scriptural texts that the Tetragrammaton was actually written out. This is why I remarked that the logical distinction between the sense and reference of the phrase 'writings of holiness' does not in practice make much difference, even though it does affect the interpretation of the mishnaic passage we have been considering. A 'writing of holiness' does not *mean* 'a scriptural book'; but in fact only scriptural books ever are 'writings of holiness', since it is only in them that people dared to write out the divine Name. Christian books could apparently be a problem because they were not scriptural, yet did contain the Name. The problem addressed in m. Yadaim 3:5 is the equal and opposite one, of books that were scriptural yet lacked the Name. It is this that is anomalous about them, and that is the reason why they were debated. It has nothing to do with any attempts to expel them from the canon.

The Qumran evidence is interesting here. Outside the community's copies of those books which are now in the Hebrew canon, there are very few places where the Tetragrammaton occurs, and almost all of these are textually suspect.[23] Where Scripture is *quoted* in some other book, as in a famous place in the Community Rule where Isaiah 40.3 is cited, four dots are placed where the Name ought to stand. It is possible they are a reminder to another scribe entrusted with inserting the sacred word; but it is also possible that the dots are a substitute for a word that might not be written in a mere *quotation* from Isaiah, within a book which was not itself scriptural. Sometimes the word is written in palaeo-Hebrew chracters rather than in the 'square script' – proscribed in the Mishnah (see above). Perhaps a definition of a canonical text for Judaism in our period would be: a text in which it is legitimate to write the Tetragrammaton. Otto Betz argues along exactly these lines that the Qumran Temple Scroll was regarded by the community as 'canonical': it contains the Tetragrammaton (in square script).[24] This is an entirely *physical* idea of the nature of a sacred book, and one which students of the canon may not have been sufficiently sensitive to.

In the Middle Ages the idea that the divine Name or names were what gave the Bible its sanctity was more or less taken for granted within the Jewish mystical tradition.[25] In the Kabbalah it is assumed that the Torah has a hidden meaning which bears no connection with the surface sense. The present form of the Torah appears to be a series of histories and of commandments, but this is because as it now stands it has been divided into ordinary Hebrew words. The original Torah, the Torah that was written 'with black fire on white fire', was a continuous sequence of divine names; and the oral tradition, which the Kabbalists believed they had inherited, told the student how to reconstruct them, an esoteric task of great difficulty and danger but much promise. That is why the exact copying of the smallest details mattered:[26] the point was to preserve, not the *gist* of the Torah, but the definitive sequence of graphic signs – signs which could be recombined to make the many names of God which in the end form his one great Name. As Joseph Gikatila put it in the late thirteenth century, the Torah in its entirety is nothing but an exposition of the Tetragrammaton, indeed, it is 'woven' from the name of God:

> The whole Torah is a fabric of epithets describing God, and these epithets in turn are woven from the various names of God. But all these holy names are connected with the Tetragrammaton and dependent upon it. Thus the entire Torah is woven ultimately from the Tetragrammaton.[27]

Writing the Tetragrammaton was from quite early times hedged about with many restrictions which at least approach the rigour of the taboo against uttering it. According to the Minor Tractate of the Talmud called Soferim (in its present form, it is said, from the eighth century AD, but probably codifying older practices), anyone who wrote a divine Name on his body would soon wish he had not done so; for it would be impiety to wash, in case he destroyed it, and yet the presence of the Name would make it illicit for him to be in a condition of uncleanness – quite a tricky situation to get out of.[28] The same tractate prescribes in detail the precautions to be taken by scribes copying the Scriptures. One must 'sanctify' the Name, that is, write it only after saying a prayer and with the conscious intention of writing it as a divine word. This leads to complicated rules for correcting errors:

> If one writes *Yehudah* and omits the *daleth*, he inserts it above the line. If he intended to write the Tetragrammaton and wrote *Yehudah* instead, he alters the *daleth* into a *he* and wipes away the final letter *he*. If it was required to write *Yehudah* and he intended to write the Tetragrammaton, although he [inadvertently] inserted the *daleth*, he erases it and writes another *Yehudah*. If it was required to write the Tetragrammaton but he intended to write *Yehudah*, although he did not insert the *daleth* [so that the Tetragrammaton was written correctly but unintentionally so], he must wipe away [the entire word] and rewrite the Tetragrammaton.[29]

Soferim gives a certain indirect confirmation that the presence of the divine Name was at least in this later period felt to be critical to the sacredness of a scriptural book. It rules that almost all instances of the name 'Solomon' in the Song of Songs are to be treated as divine names.[30] By this time, it is true, several other names besides the Tetragrammaton have to be sanctified – El Shaddai, Elohim, and so on – though with a lower degree of intensity. But the very strange idea that 'Solomon' is a divine name seems to me very probably an attempt to provide such a name in a book that would otherwise lack any, and might therefore seem lacking in holiness.[31]

The power of the Name is widely attested in Jewish mystical and magical tradition.[32] Gershom Scholem drew attention to a Talmudic passage which records how Elisha cut one of the names of God into the muzzles of Jeroboam I's bull idols, whereupon the idols began to recite the ten commandments:

> Elisha . . . by magnetism made the golden calves at Bethel float in the air, and many were brought to believe in the divinity of these idols. Moreover, he engraved the great and awful Name of God in their mouth. Thus they were enabled to speak and

they gave forth the same words God had proclaimed from Sinai: 'I am the Lord thy God – Thou shalt have no other gods before me.'[33]

Thus the power of the Name leads the idols of the heathen to condemn themselves out of their own mouths. Song of Songs Rabbah records a similar legend about Nebuchadnezzar: he made his golden image (Dan. 3) come to life by placing on it the High Priest's crown, which bore the Tetragrammaton. Daniel removed the crown, and the image slumped lifeless to the ground.

Nomina sacra and Related Customs

Thus if we consider sacred books primarily as written texts, we find that many of the significant features of the text are not significant because of their contribution to the books' content or 'message', but matter for some physical quality deemed to inhere in them. (And on the other hand, meaning *is* conveyed by things other than the sequence of written words, a phenomenon we shall discuss in the next chapter.) In Judaism, the exact graphic form of the Torah is holy, but that is not necessarily because the meaning, in the sense of the informational content conveyed to a reader by the words, is sacred. A paraphrase or a translation, however accurate, would not have the holiness of the Hebrew text just because it 'said the same thing'. The graphic signs of the Hebrew Scriptures contain divine power within themselves. When R. Hanina b. Teradion was being martyred by burning, according to the Talmud,[34] a Torah scroll was burned with him; and the letters of the Torah flew up to God from the flames ahead of him. The sacred text itself was being martyred. The Torah here is a holy object, not a meaningful discourse.

Given the understanding of early Christian books that has emerged so far, it would seem unlikely that any of them, even the Gospels, were thought of in this way in the first two centuries or so of the Christian era. If the Gospels were 'mere' repositories of essentially oral tradition they cannot also have been holy objects in this sense. Nevertheless such a way of seeing the Christian holy books was not long in coming. C. H. Roberts points out two ways in which Christian Scriptures came to be important as physical objects, where the graphic form is important as well as (or even instead of) the semantic content.[35]

One such practice is the use of Christian texts as amulets, attested by John Chrysostom.[36] Upper-class Christian women in his day wore gospel-texts around their necks, in the same manner as others wore pagan epigrams or love-poems. Roberts speculates that some of the pocket-sized codices of the first few centuries – which he regards as a Christian invention – served a similar purpose. It is interesting that many of these include books now not canonical, as well as some of the very texts about whose status there was much debate in the Church; for example, there are miniature codices of Tobit, the Acts of John, Peter, and Paul and Thecla, the *Shepherd*, Revelation, and 4 Ezra. The use of such books may not have been magical – they may have been carried around as pocket handbooks to be read in spare moments. Among the papyri, P[50] and P[87] are thought to have been talismans.[37]

The other feature is the phenomenon of the *nomina sacra*, which have already been discussed. These standard contractions of certain sacred words are found in Christian manuscripts from a very early period.[38] The great majority of extant Christian biblical manuscripts contract *iēsous*, *christos*, *kurios*, and *theos*; many contract *pneuma*, *anthrōpos*, and *stauros*. A few contract other words, such as *patēr*, *huios*, *sōtēr*, *mētēr*, *ouranos*, *israēl*, *daueid*, and *hierousalēm*.[39] The system is sophisticated: whether or not the word in question is contracted will often depend on whether it has a sacred reference. Thus *iēsous* is not normally contracted when it means the Old Testament character Joshua, though in some Old Testament texts this is done, probably by mistake. There can even be a graded system: the Codex Purpureus Petropolitanus (N) writes *patēr*, *pneuma*, and *huios* in gold, the other *nomina sacra* in silver.

Clearly in a sense the *nomina sacra* are related to the meaning of the texts, in that they are words with a special significance for Christians: Roberts remarks that they almost form a little creed – Jesus, Christ, Lord, and God could be treated as a quick guide to the essence of Christian faith. Each of the five words that give the acronym *ICHTHUS* is a *nomen sacrum* – *iēsous christos theou huios sōtēr*. But the convention of writing them contracted is a purely graphic convention and does not affect the meaning of the texts so written. It does, however, mark them out as Christian manuscripts; and the fact that Christian scribes applied the same convention in writing Old Testament texts is one clear indication that they had begun to treat Old and New Testament books as sacred texts in much the same sense – transferring special features of the New Testament back on to the Old. This is a further example of how 'canonization' could work in the reverse direction from that usually expected. This graphic feature is thus important for the history of the canon. It is widely recognized that the most important *nomen sacrum* of all, the contraction of *iēsous*, is already attested in the Epistle of Barnabas;[40] Clement of Alexandria discusses it (and its numerological uses) in detail.[41]

Now it may be that the Christians who devised the system of *nomina sacra* were engaged in the task of 'reinvent[ing] the sacred institutions of Judaism'[42] – providing a Christian equivalent for the Name in Judaism. It would be characteristic that the equivalent is a kind of inversion, so that sanctity is marked by contracting a word, where for Jews it is registered by the care with which the whole word is copied. Whatever the explanation, the existence of the *nomina sacra* indicates that for Christians as for Jews there were features of the text as a physical object that were used to express its sacredness, and which were not connected with its semantic content in the sense of its 'message'.

Kethibh and *Qere*: Performing the Text

In Judaism, the ultimate monument to care for the graphic form of the Bible is the Masorah – a work in its finished form later by many centuries than the period we are directly concerned with at the moment, but the logical outcome of an understanding of sacred Scripture in which what stands written matters in itself, apart from and without relation to the meaning it conveys.

It might be thought that the Masoretes guarded and protected the graphic form of the text that had come down to them in order to safeguard its meaning; but I doubt if that is the right way to interpret their work. What was sacred was this particular collection of signs on parchment. One can see this most clearly if one considers the system of *kethibh* and *qere*. For this I depend heavily on the work of James Barr.[43]

The Masoretic text of the Hebrew Bible records two parallel versions of the sacred texts: the scribal version, and the version which was known through the tradition of oral recitation. The device of *qere* and *kethibh* is the method by which these two 'texts' can be recorded through a single written text. The marginal *qere* registers those places where the traditional recited version of the text would suggest a different set of graphic signs from those that actually appear in the text transmitted by scribal tradition, and registered in the body of the written Hebrew text. We often say, loosely, that the *qere* is a kind of instruction to the reader: do not read what is before you on the page, read this instead. But this is probably, as Barr has argued, to put it the wrong way round. The person reading aloud did not need instructions on what to read, since he recited the text from memory, with the signs on the page acting at most as a reminder. The danger which the KQ system is designed to eliminate is not that the reader might read the wrong words, but rather that the scribe, misled by the remembered recitation tradition, might write the wrong signs. The authority of the oral reading tradition was such that a scribe, unless warned, might well falsify the traditional graphic form of the text; after all, the oral reading tradition was the form of the sacred text that would come into his mind unbidden and usually made better sense. The Q is not a *correction* of the K, but a registration of the reading tradition which enables the scribe not to be misled by it.

qere is in fact close in meaning to *sebir*, the Masoretic equivalent of our *sic*, or rather its opposite. *sebir* marks words and spellings which some think should be read instead of the *kethibh*, but which the Masoretes considered were mistakes. *qere* marks alternative words or spellings which are a correct part of the reading tradition, but which ought equally not to be allowed to distort the written text. As is well known, many alternative readings appear in some manuscripts as *qere* and in others as *sebir*, and the simplest explanation is that the two terms are quite close in what they imply. In either case, an oral reading is being registered as a guard against its being unconsciously inserted into the *kethibh*. The *qere* marks such readings when they are judged an authentic part of the oral tradition, *sebir* marks those judged to be erroneous.

Here is a clear case, admittedly attested only much later than the New Testament period, where a text which unquestionably existed in written form and was perceived very much as a written document was none the less received and appropriated largely through an oral tradition – so much so, that there was always a danger that the oral tradition would contaminate the scribal transmission. The Hebrew Bible exists simultaneously as a written text and as an orally transmitted recitation, and there are small but significant differences between the two 'texts'. But neither is in a 'pure' form. The written tradition cannot be read at all without some knowledge of the oral tradition, or only with the greatest difficulty, since it is unvocalized; in many places one needs to know, from the oral tradition, how the text should be read before one can understand it. Conversely, the reading tradition, thanks to the Masoretes, exists in written form, through (a) the vowel points and (b) the marginal *qere*s. Rather as with the distinction between Oral and Written Torah, the difference between the graphic and oral traditions of the text of the Hebrew Bible is not *literally* a distinction of 'oral' and 'written' in the ordinary sense of those terms. Yet the two systems are kept scrupulously separate by the KQ system.

The system is designed to ensure that the traditional graphic form is faithfully preserved and transmitted *even when it is apparently meaningless*.[44] It is meant to prevent the text from being corrected into a more meaningful form from the oral reading tradition. God, it was believed, had given precisely these graphic signs, and it was not for humans to change them because they could not understand them.

In point of fact one can argue that neither the oral nor the written form of the Torah, neither K nor Q, was valued because of the meaning it was believed to convey. The thinking works rather in the opposite direction: here is a sacred text, whose sacredness inheres in the very sounds one hears when it is recited and in the very signs which appear on the paper when it is copied. Of course a lot of meaning will be present in such a holy text, and some of it at least can be extracted by suitable exegetical techniques. But, in a mysterious way, the text exists before its meaning. The graphic signs, or the uttered sounds, are not seen as registrations of a meaning; rather, the meaning is seen as a deduction from the sounds or signs.

The KQ system is part of the drive in Judaism to preserve the purity of the biblical text at any cost – even at the cost of its meaningfulness. The Masoretes' motto might have been Ecclesiastes 7.13: 'Consider the work of God; who can make straight what he has made crooked?' It is not for human beings to force meaningfulness upon texts; their task is to accept them as they came from the hand of God, meaningful or not.

It is above all in the written form of the text that reverence for the correct form at the expense of content is to be found.[45] The reading tradition more often reflects the need to read aloud a comprehensible, not a nonsensical text. And in general the examples presented in this chapter of the priority of texts over their meanings, in the religious cultures of Judaism and Christianity, have involved graphic aspects of biblical texts. None the less, it should not be assumed that orality is always correlated with a concern for 'the message' of a text: an oral culture can privilege sound over content just as much as scribal culture can defend the inherited wording of a text against emendations designed to make sense of it.[46]

If early Christians saw their books, and especially the Gospels, not so much as holy texts but more as the raw materials with which an oral proclamation and presentation of the gospel could be achieved, then we would not expect to find them showing such a concern for exact verbal form – indeed, just the opposite. Christian preachers could improvise by drawing on the materials in the Gospels, rather than insist on their exact verbal form. In any case, whether the gospel was proclaimed by such improvisation or by an exact recitation of the words of one particular Gospel, the original object was clearly to use the words to convey a message.

But parallels from other religious cultures, and from the later history of Christian and Jewish uses of Scripture, should make us aware that this may not be the whole story. William A. Graham reminds us that it is not just the written form, but also the 'orality' of texts that in many cultures has purposes going beyond the communication of meaningful content. He suggests that we should be aware also of what he calls the 'sensual' dimension of texts:

> I use this word . . . to suggest that seeing, hearing, and touching in particular are essential elements in religious life as we can observe it. . . . They deserve greater attention than our bias in favour of the mental and emotional aspects of religion (in the case of scripture, towards the 'original message' or 'theological meaning' of the text) typically allows. A sacred text can be read laboriously in silent study, chanted or sung in unthinking repetition, copied or illuminated in loving devotion, imaginatively depicted in art or drama, solemnly processed in religious pageantry, or devoutly touched in hope of luck or blessing.[47]

Compare also Wilfred Cantwell Smith:

> Thus in the accepted approach the overt meaning of the words of the text not only is transcended by far in the loftier, deeper,

more inner realms of what is inherently present in or through
the scriptures, but also is seen as derivative from them – and
even, perhaps, as superseded by them. This last sometimes
takes the form of neglecting or even rejecting those lower
levels of narrower or shallower ranges of more immediate significance, as a way of better holding on to the higher, wider,
deeper. Resistance in Turkey earlier this century to the public
reciting, proclaiming, of the Qur'an in Turkish translation ...
or the sense that the sounds, rather than the meaning, of the
Rig-Veda are its ultimate significance ... are indications of a
deep sense of the holy associated with scripture, where the
sense of holiness, transcendence, is more important than any
concrete detail that it may offer.[48]

Graham recalls that in many societies (within the modern
world, especially those dominated by Islam) oral realization of a
fixed written text is the main channel by which ordinary people
encounter it; and the conceptual content of the text may not be
what matters most.

The discursive understanding, at whatever level, of qur'anic
teaching is not the only access to meaning in the interaction of
the faithful with the text. There is also a nondiscursive understanding or [?of] meaning that is part of the experience of overt
encounter with the text itself – an encounter that is primarily
oral/aural in character, rooted as it is in the recitation, or listening to the recitation, of the text. . . . Because we as modern students of religion typically invest most of our time and effort
poring over precisely the linguistic meaning of the words of
religious texts, we are least prepared to tackle the question of
meaning when it seems to be divorced from, or at least independent of, the literal, word-by-word content of the text in a linguistic sense.[49]

Thus, though *one* of the functions of reading scriptural texts
aloud is to impress them on the memories of those who will transmit them to later generations, recitation may also have a 'higher'
function. People may believe that the solemn public recitation of
texts is valuable in itself, almost apart from any communication of
meaning or content to an audience. In both Judaism and Islam
recitation in teaching and learning stands alongside public liturgi-

cal reading, and the latter does not have as its only function the instruction of a congregation. As Graham points out, in Islam the recitation of the Qur'an is seen as having a value even for those who cannot understand it: it underlines the 'inherent sacrality of the original Arabic sounds',[50] spoken by God himself. Similarly, when a portion of the Pentateuch is read in the synagogue, the Jewish community's identity is affirmed; its religious faith is attested; God is worshipped. The precise content of the portion is often neither here nor there.

Whatever may have been the case in the earliest Christian generations, there are strong parallels in traditional Christian use of both Old and New Testaments. In Catholic and Orthodox liturgy, the reading of the Gospel is attended with special ceremonies that emphasize the holiness of the 'message' it communicates, and 'the gospel' is felt to be proclaimed through the chosen pericope whatever it may be, even if (to take the extreme case) it happens to be one of the genealogies in Matthew or Luke. I learned as a child (from oral tradition!) that in Anglican liturgy one begins the reading, 'The holy gospel is written in the Gospel according to Saint X, in the nth chapter' – emphasizing, that is, that the whole gospel is present in any given portion; and that one does not say, 'Here endeth the gospel', whereas one does (or did) say, 'Here endeth the epistle', because the gospel has no end. A gospel text read within this framework of assumptions communicates (in some sense) 'the gospel' even if one cannot hear it, even if it is read in a foreign language, even if (by mistake) it is the wrong passage. Liturgical reading is a form of kerygma or, perhaps, a form of doxology. In reading 'God's Word' in the presence of God, the community reaffirms its relationship with God. There is an analogy with what linguists call 'phatic communion', where we speak to someone else not in order to communicate information, ask questions, or give instructions, but simply to 'service' our relationship with them. 'Sharing between friends is not merely informational: friends add to the information they share, a joy in the act of recounting it and a vicarious sharing in each other's experience on terms special to the friendship.'[51]

Such an oral *use* may be imposed artificially on texts that were originally composed for some quite other purpose. For example, if one reads aloud some of the annalistic notices in the books of Kings, one is probably not using them for their original purpose. But we should be on our guard against assuming too readily that ancient texts were *not* meant for oral delivery. Ancient cultures, even when highly literate, were often far more attuned than ours to the oral *performance* of written texts, and saw writing as more akin to producing a script or a musical score than to making a written record to be consulted privately. J. A. Burrow sums up the position in medieval England:

> People in the Middle Ages treated books rather as musical scores are treated today. The normal thing to do with a written literary text, that is, was to *perform* it, by reading or chanting it aloud. Reading was a kind of performance. Even the solitary reader most often read aloud, or at least muttered, the words of his text – performing it to himself, as it were – and most reading was not solitary. The performance of a text was most often a social occasion.[52]

The Gospels in particular, but much other early Christian material too, may soon have begun to function in this way in many communities. Scripture as a text to be performed is seldom actively present in the minds of modern scholars studying Jewish or Christian texts; perhaps it should have a higher profile than it has.

For just because the oral performance of a text may be more important than minute attention to its linguistic meaning, there is always the possibility that texts may come to function almost as meaningless formulas, whose power is unrelated to their content. Leipoldt and Morenz cite a startling observation by Origen. How, asks Origen, should we deal with passages in the Bible whose meaning we do not understand? Certainly, we should do our best to comprehend them; but if understanding fails, we should read the words aloud: for 'even if we do not understand the words we utter, yet those powers which are present with us do understand, and they delight to be with us as though summoned by the words of a charm, and to lend us their aid'.[53]

Without perhaps going so far as to think that the Gospels were ever perceived as meaningless, we ought to be on our guard against too much confidence in thinking we know what their early hearers heard. Redaction criticism in particular has sensitized us to very subtle layers of meaning in the Gospels. A study like the present is not meant to challenge such interpretations in so far as they unpack the inherent possibilities for meaning within these texts, or even in so far as they impute an original audience which could receive them. But I think some of the parallels adduced from other religious cultures should at least encourage us to ask *also* what, say, an average worshipper two generations after one of the Gospels was written is likely to have made of it, when it was read in pericopes in Sunday worship. That he or she will have missed some of the nuances we notice seems clear; and it is possible that such a worshipper will sometimes have been aware predominantly of the presence of God, mysteriously mediated through obscure words, rather than of the conceptual content of the text.

ᴖ 5 ᴖ
Canon and Meaning

Art is limitation: the essence of every picture is the frame.

G. K. Chesterton, *Orthodoxy*, London 1908, ch. 3

PEOPLE WHO HAVE not read any literary theory usually assume that a text exists to convey meaning. The kind of meaning will vary according to the genre of the text. It may be a story, a line of argument, a body of information, an emotional state, or a set of instructions. But in every case the text will have a gist, or drift, or 'message', which its individual sentences and paragraphs are designed to convey, and which readers are meant to grasp and then assimilate, so that what the author was saying becomes part of their own understanding.

In the ancient world many texts were approached with much the same assumption. People read personal letters, commercial documents, and works of philosophy, with the same attention to the flow of the argument or the information contained in them as we do today. But religious texts were often read according to different principles. Indeed, the purpose of the preceding chapter was to try and enter a world in which sacred books were sometimes not exactly 'read' at all, in our sense of the word, but treated as holy objects or talismans. I suggested that the presence or absence of the Tetragrammaton was regarded by Jews as making a crucial difference to the sacredness of texts, so that its use was often avoided in secular writing and, conversely, in the case of scriptural texts its absence had to be explained and justified. The work of the Masoretes seems exotic to us because in it a concern (amounting to obsession) with the exact graphic form of the Scriptures exists alongside a comparative indifference to what the text means. If it was so important to copy the text precisely that it might not be emended even where it made no sense, then surely the Masoretes were not textual critics in our sense, striving to discover what the text originally said so that its true meaning might be discerned, but infinitely sophisticated copy-typists. Meaning does not lie at the heart of the Masoretic task: what matters is the precise set of graphic signs given to Israel by God. The text is not so much a vehicle of meaning as an object in its own right.

This is not to imply that ancient readers were indifferent to the meaning of the texts that they regarded also as sacred objects. It does imply that their concern for meaning, in the straightforward sense, must be seen within a wider context in which there were other, and different, expectations as well. The previous chapter tried to set out some of these expectations, and to note in particular how Jews and Christians developed contrasting ideas about the nature of holy books. Indeed, their respective attitudes often contrast so diametrically that it is hard not to think that each was at least partly formed by deliberate contrast with the other. Jews insisted on the exact writing of God's name, Christians contracted holy words; Jews used scrolls, Christians codices; Jews stressed the exact wording of the text, Christians saw it as a prompt for extemporization.

In both cases, Jewish and Christian, there is a wide gulf between ancient readers and ourselves, if we are 'critical', 'modern' students of the Bible – though I have noted ways in which popular religious culture preserves much from the old ways of thinking. The Bible mattered to many Jews and Christians in ancient times not for what it 'said' or 'meant', but for what it *was*; and for many today this is still the case. When a bride, for example, in England today carries a white leather-bound Bible instead of a bouquet, she is making a powerful statement about her commitments, priorities, and beliefs. She is not expressing a view about the meaning of this or that biblical text. But she has more in common with many religious people of two thousand years ago than does a critical reader, who analyses the Bible and asks what it is 'about'.

All of this being said, it is time now to turn the enquiry on its head, and remind ourselves that many people in ancient times were very interested indeed in the meaning of Scripture. To say this is not to unsay our conclusions so far, for what they understood to be the Bible's 'meaning', and the methods by which they extracted it, were often just as exotic (from our point of view) as the work of the Masoretes. What is clear is this: the fact that a book was sacred made a difference to how it was interpreted, to the kinds of meaning that would be looked for in it, and to the methods used to extract that meaning. The canon, as a number of recent scholars have emphasized, contains a 'hermeneutical imperative'. The canon dictates how the books that fall within it are to be read. And here ancient exegetical practice and recent literary and theological theory may join hands.

In their important book on the biblical (in fact principally the Old Testament) canon, Dohmen and Oeming[1] examine the classic formulation of canonicity which was discussed in chapter 1: 'neither to add nor to take away'. They point out that, though borrowed for use in discussing the biblical canon, this formulation was in fact a commonplace slogan in the Hellenistic world in the realm of *aesthetics*. A 'canonical' work in classical literature was defined, from Aristotle onwards, as one to which nothing could be added and from which nothing could be subtracted without harming its aesthetic unity.[2] When the phrase was applied to the biblical canon, it was, certainly, understood more as a prohibition than as an expression of aesthetic satisfaction; nevertheless, the implication may well have been that the Scriptures were perfect in form and content.

The formula does point, however, to a duality within the concept of 'canonicity' which I have commented on more than once, and which proved critical for understanding second-century developments in the formation of the Bible. Though the two parts of the formula look symmetrical, and are so once we know we are talking about a fixed Bible, the logic of them is rather different.

(i) To say that nothing may be subtracted from the canon is to say that certain books have a status which may not be denied. This attitude is the end-product of the *growth* of Scripture. It belongs to what Dohmen and Oeming dub 'the canonical process' (*der kanonische Prozeß*) – the gradual building up, first of traditions, and then of books, which are felt to be so sacred that no one would dare to remove anything from them. This kind of 'canonization' was, I believe, an early development in the literature of ancient Israel, and I would concur with their argument that it is already present in Deuteronomy (Deut. 17.18–20, for example), which is presented in the text itself as a document that no one must in any way downgrade from its status as divinely given law.

(ii) To say, on the other hand, that nothing may be added to the canonical collection is to speak of the *delimitation* of the sacred writings, and this – called by Dohmen and Oeming 'canonization' (*Kanonisierung*) – belongs in a world where official decrees may anathematize this or that book, declaring it unfit for inclusion in the canon. This is not necessarily a later development than the first: as we saw, Tertullian already witnesses to 'forbidden' books, and the Pauline corpus includes a warning against reading 'spurious' letters (2 Thess. 2.2). It is, rather, a different kind of concern, a concern for purity and reliability of teaching, the imposition of a limit on the possible growth of Scripture. This second half of the formula describes the process for which I tend to reserve the term 'canonization', preferring to call the other simply 'the growth of Scripture': as we saw in chapter 1, scholars' terminology has registered many real disagreements but has also, and perhaps more often, obscured substantial agreements. The question of dating the 'canonization' of the Bible, in particular, has fallen prey to serious misunderstandings arising from nothing more than divergent use of the terms 'canon' and 'canonization'.

All this should be clear in principle from the discussion in chapter 1 above, but I rehearse it here because it provides a convenient way of structuring the discussion of 'canonical meaning'. I shall distinguish aspects of meaning related to the growth of Scripture (Dohmen and Oeming's 'canonical process') from those related to 'canonization', the drawing up of a maximal list of scriptural books and their arrangement to produce the 'final form' the biblical canon now has.

Implications of Scriptural Status

To treat a book as 'Scripture', not only in Judaism and Christianity but in some other religions too, implies that it is seen as possessing certain distinctive characteristics.[3] Perceiving texts in this way does not in itself imply that they form part of a 'canon', only that they are 'scriptural' – or 'canonical' in the weaker sense: at most what Sundberg called 'scripture on the way to a canon', and perhaps not even that. The characteristics we shall consider (there are others, but these seem to be the main ones) are: the importance or non-triviality of the text; its relevance to every reader; its internal consistency; and its excess of meaning. These characteristics interlock closely, but can conveniently be separated out for our present purposes. All are apparent in the way Jewish scriptural books were treated by Jews and early Christians. How soon they came to apply to the New Testament writings is a difficult question to answer, but we shall look at some possibilities.

1. A scriptural text is an important text, a text that matters and that contains no trivialities, nothing ephemeral. A clear case of this would be Paul's treatment of Deuteronomy 25.4 in 1 Corinthians 9.9 – 'You shall not muzzle an ox when it treads out the grain.' To us this text probably does not look trivial: on the contrary it is an early recognition of the rights of animals, and forbids the cruelty of making an ox spend the day looking at food which it is forcibly prevented from eating. Paul, however, takes it for granted that God has no particular concern for dumb animals, so for him the text is prima facie trivial. But because it is in Scripture, it cannot be trivial: hence it must have a deeper (or in a loose sense 'allegorical') meaning. This meaning turns out to concern ministers of the gospel, and their right to be paid by their converts.

A literary theorist might say that perceiving texts as non-trivial is not a matter of their inherent content, but of the expectations we bring to them, and that this is true of all texts, not just of 'sacred' ones. It will be noted that my 'modern' interpretation of this text in terms of the rights of animals is also driven by a wish to see the content as non-trivial. 'Critical' and 'post-critical' commentators on the Bible tend in fact to be united by a commitment to its non-triviality. It would be interesting to find a commentator on Deuteronomy 25.4 who *agreed* with Paul that oxen do not matter, but still insisted that the verse was to be taken literally – who defended, that is, the essential triviality or pointlessness of the text.

Even without a religious commitment, we choose to read texts we think important, and we have a natural bias to reading them in ways that enable their importance and permanent validity to emerge, not their ephemerality and unimportance. The so-called 'canon' of English literature, which is an informal collection of works felt to be 'scriptural' in the literary world but which is not 'closed' in the hard sense, contains books which in the English-speaking world there is a taboo against reading as trivial. It is not acceptable to think that Shakespeare is deeply uninteresting, that he wrote on silly and boring themes, that his plots are inconsequential. And if such thoughts do strike the reader, the 'canonical' status of Shakespeare usually eliminates them before they can gain a hold. Dislocations of plot become clues to deeper unities, long and tedious speeches are seen as brilliant characterization. Shakespeare's authority lays on the reader the hermeneutical imperative: Read this play as important.

Now there is no need, in either the literary or the biblical sphere, to embrace a total 'reader-response' theory[4] according to which readers contribute everything to textual meaning and the texts themselves nothing. Few reader-response critics go quite that far anyway, and experience of either canon – the literary or the biblical – would be felt by most readers, unless they are familiar with and covinced by the ideas of postmodernism, to support the view that some books 'really' are more distinguished than others. There is a difference between (to put it no higher) competent and incompetent writing, themes that matter and themes that are purely trivial, *Hamlet* and *Batman*, the Epistle to the Romans and the 'Epistle to the Laodiceans'. Nevertheless, an experienced reader of the Bible or of English literature knows that some of the books concerned are better than others, and that 'canonical' status does give 'canonical' books an (unfair?) advantage. We give them the benefit of the doubt; we assume that their 'message' is worth hearing. We are willing to be surprised, to find the text less profound than we expected, just as, conversely, we are open to finding profundity in books that are not 'canonical'. But for much of the time our sense that the books in the canon are full of depth and significance is not the result of inspection with an open or neutral mind, so much as the confirmation of expectations created by the tradition that declares these works 'canonical'. This tradition gives us the hermeneutical rule: Read this book as profound. In the process we find ourselves having to use special techniques that are not needed for everyday writing in order to extract a sufficiently edifying message. One of these techniques is 'allegory', seen in the present example in the treatment of a straightforward rule about farming as containing insights into a deeper truth about human life. An example on a much larger scale would be the Song of Songs, where both Jewish and Christian assumptions about what sort of material could be imagined as appearing in a holy book have constrained interpreters to read the book as an allegory. We should like to know whether its 'canonization' caused it to be read allegorically, or whether allegorization made it possible for it to be canonized, but I doubt if we shall. Even among 'historical-critical' interpreters it remains very rare for serious allegations of triviality to be made against biblical books: Wellhausen's lampooning of Chronicles has had very few imitators.[5]

How soon were New Testament writings treated as non-trivial, in the sense just discussed? From the earliest time for which we have records, sayings of Jesus in particular are treated as oracles, from which every possible ounce of meaning is to be extracted, though (as we have seen) the sayings were seldom remembered with their gospel contexts, any more than they are today. The narrative in the Gospels is from early times regarded as more 'ephemeral' than the sayings. Nevertheless, it is impossible to reconstruct a time when the Gospels were used and yet were not accorded 'canonical' status, in the sense being used here. If we use the assumption of non-triviality as a test of canonicity, the Gospels pass it as early as we can trace them.

Paul is an interesting case, just because many of his letters have a clear 'occasional' status, as replies to particular queries or concerns. Philemon, the most 'ephemeral' of all, might serve as the best test case, though we know (despite Knox) too little about its early status. For 1 Corinthians we have the evidence of 1 Clement, for which the specific issues on which Paul addressed the Corinthians in his day can be generalized to form the basis of an 'official' text with which Clement can rebuke their descendants.[6] At all events, if we treat the rule 'Read this text as important and non-trivial' as a test of scriptural status, then (like the statistics of citation investigated by Stuhlhofer) it gives us a very early date for the authoritative status of much of the New Testament. Allegorization of the Gospels in the strict sense arrives later on the scene, but is in full flight in Clement of Alexandria and Origen.

2. Contemporary relevance is clearly related to non-ephemerality: a non-ephemeral work is one relevant to every generation, to all people at all times. This universal relevance was certainly assumed to be present in all scriptural books. It can be seen in the way that the historical books of the Old Testament were treated essentially as collections of *exempla* – stories with a moral. Biblical characters were seen as typical of various human virtues or vices. 'When this community preserved and maintained the ancient narrative tradition of the history of Israel along with [the Law], it was understood as a collection of historical examples of the attitude of man to the law and its consequences.'[7] Chronicles takes the tendency further:

as the prophet Azariah ben Oded says to Asa (2 Chron. 15.2–5), 'The Lord is with you, while you are with him. If you seek him, he will be found by you. . . . For a long time Israel was without the true God, and without a teaching priest, and without law; but when in their distress they turned to the Lord, the God of Israel, and sought him, he found by them.' This tradition of seeing Israel's history as a collection of examples of good and bad conduct was well established in Second Temple Judaism.[8] It is an interpretative approach that seems to arise naturally once stories from the past (originally perhaps told for their uniqueness!) come to be regarded as 'Scripture' and so acquire a universal character.

Josephus offers many examples of this way of reading biblical books. For him, we read them because they have something to teach us in our present situation. There are surprises in Josephus' choice of edifying examples: a favourite of his is the witch of Endor, whom he presents as an example of generosity and unselfishness for us to imitate.[9]

Thus the imperative, 'Read these works as relevant to your own situation,' can generate a moralizing approach based on biblical narratives. It can also encourage the reader to find statements about how God typically acts. The 'Deuteronomistic History' and the work of the Chronicler were read as showing not only how Israel ought to act, but also how God himself will act in response: 'when in their distress they turned to the LORD . . . he was found by them' (2 Chron. 15.4). The character of God, as both gracious and terrible, can be deduced both from the biblical narratives and from the prophecies. It is not an option (see 1, above) to think that the biblical stories set out how God *acted* in the past but not how he *acts* now. The God of Scripture is the God with whom Israel has to deal in the present.

One common implication thought to be present in the holy books was some kind of divine scheme for history. The prophetic books were not read as concerned with the time in which each prophet lived, but with history as a whole and especially with the future as it lay before readers of each generation. Again, one might say that any book which is read in this way is at least incipiently canonical or scriptural.[10]

There is a more specific way of reading books as relevant to one's own day, and that is to see them as setting out a divine plan for history whose fulfilment will be in the very near future – the 'charismatic exegesis'[11] found in both the Qumran sect and among early Christians. Paul is reading Scripture in this way when he interprets Isaiah's 'acceptable time' and 'day of salvation' (Isa. 49.8) as references to the time he was living in himself: 'Behold, now is the acceptable time; behold, now is the day of salvation' (2 Cor. 6.2). Here, even more, the presence of such exegesis demonstrates the status that the book being interpreted must have had. The more 'strained' the exegesis, the higher the status: no one would trouble to extract improbable meanings from a text, unless they felt that that text was a given for them. I have written extensively elsewhere on charismatic exegesis and the interpretation of prophecy as relevant to the reader's own day, and will say no more here.[12]

Were the New Testament books interpreted in these ways in the early Church? The more specific interpretation, according to which the climax of divine salvation would come in the reader's own day, is certainly found in Justin and in Irenaeus, and wherever there was millenarian thought among early Christians.[13] The text being interpreted is often Revelation, but the 'apocalyptic' sections of the Gospels are also important, as are Pauline texts such as 1 and 2 Thessalonians. The more generalized style of reading scriptural texts, in which they are assumed to be relevant to this generation because they are believed to be relevant to every generation, is present wherever the sayings of Jesus are quoted. Once again early Christian writers seem to take it for granted that what Jesus said will always have a bearing on present problems, aspirations, conflicts, and hopes: these sayings are 'canonical' for them.

3. All reading operates with an assumption of consistency. One assumes, charitably, that authors do not contradict themselves, and holds on to this assumption until clear evidence makes it impossible to hold any longer. Generally speaking, the higher the prestige of what we are reading, the less willing we are to suppose that it can contain inconsistencies. Reading a holiday postcard, I am neither very surprised nor particularly worried by inconsistencies, though even there I do not start by expecting them. In official documents as in 'high' literature inconsistency worries me, and calls in question the skill of the writer, unless it can be 'naturalized' as a special part of the literary effect. In an Act of Parliament or a scriptural book the presumption of consistency is so high that I will be very loath to accept that apparent contradictions are

really there. In such texts there is another hermeneutical imperative: Read this work as self-consistent. And if one is unable to do
so, then the authority of the document as a whole is called in question.

The allegation that Christian texts contained inconsistencies
was a standard piece of polemic in antiquiety. One of the objections Celsus raises to Christianity in Origen's *contra Celsum* is that
Christian texts are inconsistent with each other.[14] Josephus had
made just the same allegation against the Greeks in *contra Apionem*.[15] Demonstrating that the Scriptures of one's own community are in fact consistent becomes critical for the plausibility of
its religious culture. And again, the less convincing the attempted
demonstration, the greater must be the writer's commitment to
the Scriptures he is defending.

At this point we are not so much concerned with allegations that
books are inconsistent with *each other* – that will concern us below –
but with the suggestion that a given book is internally inconsistent.
It was not only criticism from outside that might force a community to be worried about the inconsistency of a text. The very careful
reading to which religious believers were committed meant that
they above all were likely to notice any inconsistencies there
might be, and to feel the need of a resolution. An example would
be the rabbinic discussion of possible inconsistencies in Proverbs.[16]
It is not known what the alleged inconsistencies were, but some
think one may have been 26.4–5: 'Answer not a fool according to
his folly, lest you be like him yourself. Answer a fool according to
his folly, lest he be wise in his own eyes.' It is said that the contradictions were duly resolved, and a suggestion that the book should
be *gnz* ('stored away') was overcome.

We might interpret this as meaning that the real self-consistency
of Proverbs was successfully shown. Modern readers would probably not perceive 26.4–5 as contradictory in the first place, since
the two opposed proverbs add up to a higher truth to do with the
difficulty of choosing the right action, the problem in dealing with
a 'fool'. The rabbinic solution, which commends itself little to us,
is that the first proverb is to do with those who speak folly about
the law, the second with those who speak folly in secular matters.

But we might also interpret this debate as the application of the
hermeneutical imperative: Read scriptural books as self-consistent. Once a book is holy, there is no possibility that it will really
contradict itself, and the exegete's task is to help others to see that

this is so. If this second interpretation of the rabbinic discussion is correct, then the alleged disputes over the inconsistencies of Proverbs may have been shadow-boxing. It seems quite unlikely that there was a real proposal, in early rabbinic Judaism, to 'decanonize' Proverbs – a work by Solomon. The 'dispute' may well be merely a way of showing how consistent the book is. It is very common in rabbinic literature for one voice to raise some entirely artificial objection to a text in Scripture, and for other voices to experiment with various ways of resolving it. That it will be resolved is a given for all the participants in the discussion: the consistency of the text is not an open question. But there was (and is) much pleasure to be had in seeing the skill of the debate, something like solving a difficult crossword or a chess problem.

When did a rubric of consistency begin to apply to New Testament works? It is in fact hard to think of clear inconsistencies within any of the books of the New Testament, so that there is not much scope for the puzzle-solving mentality. From early times, however, Christian writers found *mysteries* there, and of course there are passages which advertise themselves as such: most of Revelation, 2 Corinthians 12, and sayings in the Gospels such as Matthew 11.25–30. Christian exegesis came, like its Jewish counterpart, to see both mysterious and inconsistent passages as alike pointing to underlying secrets, which God was willing to reveal to those who approached the text with the right kind of reverence. For Origen as for the rabbis, 'problems' in the text are really pointers to deeper meanings. He applies this to New Testament texts as to Old, and this, again, serves to confirm the status that the New Testament writings had for him. But this was already happening in earlier generations: Justin, for example, allegorizes the book of Revelation.[17] New Testament texts are thus being treated as 'canonical' from an early date, certainly before they were described as *graphē*. Indeed, there is an example of the process within the New Testament itself, where 2 Peter says that there are 'some things . . . hard to understand' in the Pauline epistles, 'which the ignorant and unstable twist to their own destruction, as they do the other scriptures' (2 Pet. 3.16). Paul is here being treated as a scriptural writer, and *hence* as speaking in riddles – not a problem, but just what you would expect from an inspired source, though of course a danger to the simple-minded.

We might recall again that there was no higher accolade the Fathers could bestow on a text than to say it was worthy of allegorical interpretation. Such a mode of exegesis, which to us looks like a somewhat shifty way out of the difficulty presented by an inconsistent or obscure text, is to them the method by which holy writings are properly and naturally read. Thus difficulties in the text become a positive recommendation of it, releasing the spring of allegorical interpretation – far better than the dry-as-dust literalism of such as Marcion, who was willing to allegorize neither Old Testament nor New. We might put it this way: a holy book was one which had no inconsistencies, not because it was an obvious and humdrum text clear to the least intelligent reader, but because its apparent difficulties could be resolved and shown to be beautiful adornments, through which mysteries were revealed to those of the right disposition.

The obvious objection to this, as it seems nowadays, is that any inconsistency, however great, can be eliminated if approached in that spirit; indeed, the worse the inconsistency, the more brightly the text containing it will shine, once polished with the allegorist's brush. A historical enquiry like the present does not have to adjudicate on that question, but only to observe that such arguments did not generally occur to the Fathers. Perhaps we might argue that they *would* have done so, if the Fathers had been trying to discover which books were holy and which not: then they might have seen the circularity they were trapped in. But they were doing nothing of the sort; they were interpreting writings that they already believed, from tradition, to be holy, and which therefore came under the hermeneutical imperative that commanded inconsistencies to be reconciled. But this in turn confirms that the Scriptures, both Old Testament and New, were for them a given.

4. Explanations of apparent difficulties and inconsistencies result in a vision of the text as full of mysteries, with many layers of meaning below the surface sense. And this is how people in our period saw sacred texts, even when they did not contain problems for the religious mind to solve. The text meant more than any naïve reader would think. This comes out especially in a tendency to atomize the text, to read meaning into elements that to us seem sub-semantic: inflections and other bound forms, unusual spellings, even letters and the shapes of letters.

The classic case of 'reading too much into' a text can be found in Galatioans 3.16, where Paul presses the expression 'and to his seed' in Genesis 12.7, arguing that 'the promises were made to Abraham and to his offspring. It does not say, "And to offsprings," referring to many; but, referring to one, "And to your offspring," which is Christ.' The singular 'his seed' (*zar'ô*) in Genesis 12.7 most naturally means 'his descendants, his line', implying many people. But Paul sees the accidental fact that Hebrew expresses 'descendants' with a singular noun, 'seed', as providential. The writer of Genesis thereby signals (whether consciously or not) that the promises to Abraham would find their fulfilment in one man, Jesus Christ.

Non-Christian Jews would naturally have disputed Paul's particular exegesis here, but the manner of argumentation is fully acceptable within a Jewish context. As I suggested in chapter 4, Jewish biblical interpretation does not characteristically assume that writers of the biblical texts had ideas which they clothed in words and transmitted to posterity. More typically, they think of the writers as recording certain words, or even certain graphic signs, which God had given them, and from which meaning was to be deduced by using the correct tools. Rather as with structuralist and post-structuralist interpretation, the words of the text do not exist to express the writer's intentions; they exist in their own right, and their meaning is whatever can be extracted from them by approved and legitimate means. Rabbinic authorities frequently exploit unusual or unexpected features of the written text to deduce meanings that would never suggest themselves to an 'innocent' reader. Jon D. Levenson gives an attractive example:

As early as Exodus 17:16, YHWH is seen as involved in a continuing war with this desert tribe [sc. Amalek], against whom he even enjoins Israel to commit genocide. Indeed, one Amoraic midrash sees in the survival of the Amalekites a blemish upon the very nature and sovereignty of God:

Rabbi Levi said in the name of Rabbi Aha bar Hanina: As long as the descendants of Amalek are in the world, neither the name [i.e. YHWH] nor the throne is complete. When the descendants of Amalek will have perished, both the name and the throne will be complete. What is the reason? 'The enemy is no more – / ruins everlasting,' etc. What is written thereafter? 'But the LORD abides for ever; / He has set up his throne for judgment.'

Here the darshan interprets the psalmist's celebration of a divine victory and the subsequent enthronement of YHWH

as yet to be. In Rabbi Aha's mind, the psalmist did not com-
memorate, he prognosticated. Specifically, he predicted the es-
chatological annihilation of the Amalekites. . . . Underlying this
curious exegesis is the unusual wording of Exodus 17:16

> He said, 'It means, "Hand upon the throne (*kēs*) of the
> LORD (*Yāh*)!" The LORD will be at war with Amalek
> throughout the ages.'

If *kēs* means 'throne', then it lacks the final letter of the ordinary
word for 'throne' (*kissē*'). Similarly, the name of YHWH here
lacks the last two consonants that it usually (but not always)
shows. Rabbi Aha interprets these apocopated terms as an indication of the unfinished quality of God's nature and his mas-
tery over the world.[18]

A complication in the case of the Hebrew Bible is the fact that it
exists, as we have seen, effectively in two versions, oral and written, and either or both can be the basis of interpretation. Interpretation of the written text (*yš 'm lmswrh*) and of the vocalized text
(*yš 'm lmqr'*) may stand side by side, indeed interpreters may exploit the differences between them.[19] Thus, for example, in
Yoma 21b (cf. Song of Songs Rabbah on 8.8) we find a comment
on Haggai 1.8, where the kethibh has *w'kbd* ('that I may appear in
my glory') but the qere has *w'kbdh*, using the 'cohortative'. The
difference, from a modern perspective, is between two options in
Hebrew for expressing a purpose clause, *w* + imperfect and *w* +
cohortative. But 'R. Samuel b. Enia said, Why has the Kethiv
w'kbd and the Keri *w'kbdh*? It is because of the five things which
made the difference between the first and second Temple'[20] – *he*
being the number five. The oral reading tradition is just as venerable as the scribal tradition of the graphic form of the text: the
Bible consists in a sense of both, and of the interplay between
them.

It is not my intention here to present a systematic description of
rabbinic exegesis, even if I could. For our present purposes the
existence of these contrived, even playful forms of exegesis
matter because of what they tell us about the text on which they
are practised. They imply that this text is thought of as nothing
like any other text. In ordinary texts the words convey the intentions of a writer through their normal grammatical and syntactic
structures, but here the meaning is hidden in the signs or sounds of
the text, studied quite without regard to the way in which texts

normally have meaning. A modern reader of rabbinic commentary is likely to feel oppressed by the enormous and excessive weight of meaning supposed to inhabit the text; half a letter in the Bible can mean more than hundreds of volumes of secular writing. Medieval Judaism developed what can be called a 'word mysticism', in which the study of the Hebrew language becomes a religious quest.[21] We cannot go into that here, but we may note some helpful comments of Gerhardsson:

> It is not possible to interpret this [sc. a fixed text yielding very diverse and colourful interpretations] in such a way as to say that some Rabbis – or some groups – understood the Divine Word as being flexible and dynamic, while others saw it as being static. . . . We find the two tendencies side by side within the same rabbinic tradition, and even in the work of a single Rabbi. . . . It is just because it is the Sacred Word, the source of endless riches, which is found in the Scriptures, that each and every syllable must be both preserved and used. These two tendencies are also psychologically associated: the perception of the text as sacred leads partly to a desire to preserve the text without corruption, and partly to a desire to appropriate all its incomparable riches. Furthermore, certainty that the sacred words of the text have in fact been preserved without distortion adds to the frankness with which the very letter of the text is drawn upon for teaching purposes.[22]

If the sacredness of a text is perceived as being a matter of its exact graphic form, rather than of its content, that will have a dramatic effect on how the content is then understood. People may continue to read, or at least to be able to read, the text as a sequence of words and sentences conveying a continuous semantic content; but they will also, and perhaps more characteristically, come to read it as a code to be deciphered. They may well do this in an atomistic way, attributing importance, as we have seen, to what we should think of as sub-semantic or non-semantic features such as the shapes of letters, the number of words, or the layout of pages. Judaism went much further down this road than Christianity, at least in antiquity; but both religions are familiar with a way of thinking about the Bible that makes it a vast cryptogram, from which meaning is extracted by methods quite different from those used in ordinary reading.[23]

Order and Consistency

Now we turn to the canon in the 'hard' sense: lists of holy books which must be revered, with the implication that no other books fall into this category. Here there is exclusion as well as inclusion, and a sense that the books listed form an ordered whole. We shall examine two aspects of the meaning of texts that are canonical in this, stronger, sense: their order, and their mutual consistency.

1. As we have seen, both Jews and Christians in antiquity took an interest in listing the books they regarded as 'canonical'. But (as the evidence of citation shows) neither Jews nor Christians seem to have used the sacred books in exactly the way their lists would lead us to expect. In the case of the Old Testament, the Pentateuch is central for both, as all lists do imply. But when we move into the 'Prophets' and the 'Writings' in Judaism, or the 'didactic' and 'prophetic' books in Christianity, the formal structure suggested by extant lists does not match the use attested by citation. Thus Philo, for example, uses Proverbs and Psalms, which at least in later Judaism are supposed to be third-rank Scripture, much more than the historical books, which belong to the second-rank 'Prophets'. Similarly, Christians showed a marked preference for Psalms and Isaiah, suggesting an effective Old Testament canon of Pentateuch, Isaiah, Psalms – even though in theory they apparently regarded all the Old Testament as of equal status. And the deuterocanonical wisdom books, Wisdom of Solomon and Ecclesiasticus, are cited much more often than Samuel or Kings, even by writers like Jerome who theoretically doubt their authority.

Nevertheless, it is at least conceivable that the formal classification of books had some effect on how they were read and understood. It would surely be widely agreed that in separating Genesis–Deuteronomy from the so-called 'Deuteronomistic History' and calling it the 'Torah', Judaism was making a hermeneutical, not merely a bibliographical, point. J. A. Sanders has argued persuasively that drawing a line between Deuteronomy and Joshua, so that the Torah ended with the death of Moses rather than with the conquest of the land or its subsequent history under the judges and kings, was intended to signal that the Jewish people is always *in via*, on the way to the Promised Land yet never able to possess and enjoy it.[24] It would thus express the theology of the Second Temple period, in which Diaspora existence came to be seen as the norm and occupation of the Land as the exception. We could see this as expressed in Jewish liturgy at Simḥat-Torah, when the last pericope of Deuteronomy is followed immediately by the first pericope of Genesis, closing the circle and leaving the congregation, like Moses, still in the Plains of Moab, in an alien land. We might say that what is *not* read (Joshua) is as eloquent as what is read: that the community possesses an account of the conquest but does not read it liturgically is one of the most important facts we need to know to understand the reading of the Pentateuch. Sanders' hypothesis cannot really be proved, but it has many attractions.

The same could be said of one of the most interesting Christian decisions about the structure of the New Testament, the division of Luke-Acts, which made the first volume a 'Gospel' and the second not. In dividing between Deuteronomy and Joshua, Jews were directing the reader of the books defined as 'Torah' to turn first to them as the highest authority, and this certainly took effect. The great physical difference between a Torah scroll and the scrolls or (eventually) codices used for other scriptural books marked them out as belonging in different categories, and had an effect on their interpretation and thus on the meaning they were perceived as having. The same may be said, *mutatis mutandis*, of the decision about Luke-Acts within Christianity. As already noted, in the patristic era, Acts never approached a level of citation even commensurate with its size, whereas Luke, like the other Gospels, is cited several times as often as its size would predict. Acts may have suffered as the first book in the section which otherwise contains the 'Catholic' epistles, a much under-used resource in the early Church. At any rate we can safely say that the classification of books into sections or divisions of the canon was at least partially functional: it really did matter whether a Jewish book was or was not part of the Torah, whether a Christian book was or was not one of the Gospels.

That the same importance was attached to the *order* in which the books were arranged *within* categories such as 'Torah', 'Prophets', 'Gospels', and 'Epistles' is less certain. At least some rabbinic and Christian listings of books seem to be based on nothing more significant than length, which surely implies that the order has no hermeneutical implications. This certainly appears to be the basis for the order of the Pauline epistles in many manuscripts and, indeed, in the now current order – though there are a few additional complications such as the insertion of Ephesians after the shorter Galatians, and the separation of Paul's letters to individuals into a section of their own.[25] Thus the fact that Paul's correspondence has been turned into an ordered corpus is important, but the fact that (for example) the Corinthian letters come before those to Thessalonica is not. On the whole, the suggestion that the Pauline letters were in an identical and significant order from their first collection has not commended itself anyway.

Our earliest evidence for a fixed order in the Hebrew Bible is a passage in Baba Bathra 14b:

> Our rabbis taught: The order of the Prophets is, Joshua, Judges, Samuel, Kings, Jeremiah, Ezekiel, Isaiah, and the Twelve Minor Prophets. Let us examine this. Hosea came first, as it is written [Hos. 1.2]: God spoke first to Hosea. But did God speak first to Hosea? Were there not many prophets between Moses and Hosea? R. Johanan, however, has explained that he was the first of the four prophets who prophesied at that period, namely, Hosea, Isaiah, Amos, and Micah. Should not then Hosea come first? – since his prophecy is written along with those of Haggai, Zechariah, and Malachi, he is reckoned with them. But why should he not be written separately and placed first? – Since his book is so small, it might be lost. Let us see again. Isaiah was prior to Jeremiah and Ezekiel. Then why should not Isaiah be placed first? – Because the book of Kings ends with a record of destruction and Jeremiah speaks throughout of destruction and Ezekiel commences with destruction and ends with consolation and Isaiah is full of consolation; therefore we put destruction next to destruction and consolation next to consolation.[26]

Since the rabbis are not thinking of a codex, or a scroll so long as to contain the whole of the Prophets (a practical impossibility), the 'order' of the Prophets here cannot mean their order in a continuous book; though it may (as Nahum Sarna has suggested) be meant to constrain the locations in which the separate scrolls are stored in a book room.[27] More likely it is something like a mnemonic order, the order in which one ought to list the books when learning about them at school. The authorities cited are labouring hard to find some hermeneutical importance in it, but it is plain that they are struggling with something they did not themselves invent and for which they do not know the true reason. Ludwig Blau maintained that the strange order of the Prophets in this talmudic passage (where Jeremiah precedes Isaiah rather than coming second as in our printed Hebrew Bibles) is based simply on length:[28] the prophetic books are listed in order of size. For the Writings, on the other hand, the talmudic order is apparently, in intention, chronological: Ruth (pre-Davidic), Psalms (Davidic), Job, Proverbs, Ecclesiastes, Song of Songs (Solomonic), Lamentations, Daniel (exilic), Esther, Ezra-Nehemiah, Chronicles (post-exilic). But in any case no exegetical consequences seem to be drawn from the order. Ruth is not read or understood any differently when it comes first than when it comes in some other position. One possible exception is Malachi, invariably placed last in the Prophets. Here Joseph Blenkinsopp has argued that its last chapters are too appropriate to the end of the prophetic corpus to have arrived there by accident: Elijah and Moses appear together, Law and Prophecy, to prepare the way for the great Day of the Lord.[29] Especially if Malachi is not an original book of prophecy at all, but a supplement to Zechariah, this hypothesis is very attractive.

The longest patristic discussion of the order of the Gospels is in Eusebius, *Ecclesiastical History* 3:24. He takes for granted a general agreement that John should be placed fourth, and argues that this is fitting because (a) John's Gospel is the best from a literary point of view and so forms a fitting climax and (b) it was in any case the fourth to be written. Similarly Matthew is correctly placed first as having been written first. But it is not clear that the order was thought of as significant hermeneutically. There are manuscripts which arrange the four Gospels in a different order.[30] Irenaeus equates the four evangelists with the four beasts of Revelation, and this might seem to imply an order Mark–Luke–Matthew–John (lion–bull–man–eagle).[31] Similarly, in the case of the epistles the order does not seem to have been regarded as theologically important; though in the Middle Ages we meet, for example, the suggestion that Romans stands first because it was written to combat the root of all sins, pride.[32]

There are books within the biblical canon which are themselves collections, obvious cases being Psalms and Proverbs. No one has yet succeeded in showing that the order of the Proverbs is significant, though it cannot be said that many people have tried.[33] With the Psalms there are many theories about the reasons behind the order, but they do not generally assume that the compilers had a 'message' to impart through the ordering. (An exception is Brevard Childs' very interesting suggestion that Psalms 1 and 2, widely regarded as a later preface to the Psalter, are placed where they are to ensure that people will read the Psalms as having two major themes, the Torah (Ps. 1) and the Messiah (Ps. 2).[34])

Against our usual assumption that most Old Testament literature was appropriated by reading aloud and hearing, it should be noted that wisdom literature, which is learned literature, may sometimes have been ordered by sight. Sumerian proverbs were collected according to their first sign which, since Sumerian is not alphabetic, would give them a rational order only to the learned reader.[35] For an illiterate hearer their order would have appeared random. The Old Testament is rich in acrostic poetry, which can be appreciated without advanced literacy but does perhaps presuppose a fairly well-read audience. But the 'sentence literature' in the biblical book of Proverbs does not appear to be arranged on alphabetic lines, and no one has yet found more than haphazard thematic arrangements within it. It is in fact easy for a modern reader, used to carefully produced books in codex form, to exaggerate the importance of the order of texts to the ancient reader. Even if the order of chapters in a continuous history matters, the same is not necessarily true of the order of aphorisms in Proverbs.

Still less is it likely to be true of, say, the order of the Hagiographa (which varies even in printed editions)[36] or the order of Paul's epistles; and least of all will it be true of the order of the whole Old or New Testament. The New Testament, as mentioned in chapter 1, began life as four collections (Gospels, Paul, Acts + Catholic epistles, Revelation) in its earliest recensions; the Hebrew Scriptures are already threefold when we first find them as a finished collection. Reading interpretative significance into the joins *between* the sections is thus particularly hazardous, as is the attempt to find a thematic unity in the whole Hebrew Bible or even the whole Christian Bible. Certainly it is wise to avoid asking about the 'intentions' of the final redactors, and better to allow for a great deal of accident and chance in the process that gave us these collections.

2. Commenting on two incompatible programmes about Colum-

bus, screened in 1992 for the quincentenary of his voyage to America, Lynne Truss, the television reviewer of *The Times*, wrote:

> One of the perverse things about television is that somehow you expect it to remember what it has already said, which it doesn't. Like the Bible, it is a mishmash originating from all over the place, yet, also like the Bible, it raises expectations of internal consistency because it claims so much authority.[37]

The Bible in any of the forms it is encountered in the modern world gives out the strongest possible signals of unity, coherence, and closure. All the books have the same typography, the same style of translation, a consistent pagination, and a fixed order: features that arouse strong expectations that the contents will be a single 'work'. One of the first and most obvious effects of historical criticism is that it disappoints all such expectations. The disappointment is often felt quite acutely by students beginning the study of the Bible, but until recently they were usually told that the more fragmentary understanding of the Bible that resulted was truer to its contents than the illusory unity projected by our typographical conventions; and truth, even if disappointing, is always better than illusion, however attractive.

One of the most remarkable developments in biblical studies over the last twenty-five years has been a steady reversal of this tendency. On the literary side there has been the rise of movements opposed to reconstruction and textual history and in favour of interpreting 'the text, the whole text, and nothing but the text'. This was apparent in the formalism of 'the New Criticism' and of Russian formalism, in structuralism and in some kinds of post-structuralism, and in readings driven by no particular theory but standing in the Anglo-Saxon tradition of aesthetic, non-'scientific' literary criticism.[38] On the theological side there are two related but distinct styles of 'canonical' approach: Brevard Childs' 'canonical method'[39] and J. A. Sanders' 'canonical criticism'.[40] Childs, and to a lesser degree Sanders, deny any literary influence on their work, which they see as a thoroughly theological attempt to rehabilitate the actual text canonized by Jews and Christians against the attempts of historical critics to get 'behind' it.

Nevertheless most of their readers have seen significant parallels with literary criticism, even if not any direct influence. The common ground is a belief that the meaning of biblical texts is to be discerned by studying them as they stand, rather than by fragmenting them in the interests of reconstructing earlier stages: a 'holistic' or 'final form' exegesis is the only proper exegesis. But it is true that the rationale for this hermeneutical move is different in the two cases. Literary critics such as Northrop Frye[41] or Frank Kermode[42] insist on reading the Bible as it stands because that is how they would approach any other text; Childs and Sanders, because the 'final form' is the Bible as the Church and synagogue have received it, and it is only at this 'final' level that it is a *religious* text for either Jews or Christians.

The net result, however, can look rather similar, and there seems no reason why one should not point this out, provided one is clear about the difference in motivation.[43] This present convergence of biblical and literary scholars on a holistic interpretation of the Bible just as we now find it is not very surprising, however much we need to distinguish the two movements in principle.

The essential point of agreement between secular and biblical critics of a 'canonical' turn of mind is the unity or coherence of all the texts that make up Scripture: the sense that they constitute not just a collection but, in the technical sense, a 'work'. The implication of mutual consistency means that the canon, for this way of thinking, generates another 'hermeneutical imperative': Read all these books as chapters in a single work. For the 'canonical' mind, the meaning of each book is as strongly determined by its juxtaposition with the other books of the canon as is the meaning of individual chapters within a single work by their juxtaposition with each other. Once the text is seen in this way, really significant implications follow for what it can mean.

Thus more important hermeneutically than the *order* of the books is the fact that they form a *collection*. In this sense it is true to say, in Harry Gamble's words, that 'the canon [itself] is a locus of meaning'.[44] This is easy to illustrate from the canon of the Gospels.

The fourfold Gospel canon, however it was arranged, eventually forced people to read each of the Gospels as a version of the life of Jesus, not the definitive account of it; and this produced what may be called a 'kerygmatic' reading:

The collection of four Gospels ... represents a compromise which the ancient church devised to mediate between the idea of a single, self-consistent, theologically adequate gospel and the actual availability of many gospel-type documents. The collection aims at an inclusive yet not exhaustive witness to the Christ event. ... In effect, the collection introduces a principle of mutual correction and limitation whereby each Gospel is deprived of pre-eminence or complete validity. ... As a collection ... the Gospels stand in a creative tension with each other: instead of four Gospels, there is a fourfold Gospel. It seems clear, furthermore, that at or near the inception of this collection its form was taken to be an essential correlate of its proper understanding ..., such that theological meaning and authority were vested in the collection rather than in the single documents taken by themselves. Thus, the collection, by its very form, provides a critical principle for its interpretation.[45]

Similarly, the unification of Paul's letters to form a *corpus Paulinum* had the effect of departicularizing Paul's message to each individual church or person. We find this interpretation in the Muratorian Fragment, which assimilates Paul's seven letters to the seven letters in Revelation, and says,

the blessed apostle Paul himself, following the example of his predecessor John, wrote only to seven churches by name ... it is evident that one church is spread throughout the whole world. For John also, although in the Apocalypse he wrote to seven churches, nevertheless speaks to all.[46]

Even at the textual level there is evidence of a tendency to reduce the specificity of the addressees in Romans and 1 Corinthians, and Ephesians appears in any case to be a kind of encyclical.[47] However the corpus was formed, it is clear that its existence as a finished whole was felt to mitigate considerably what N. A. Dahl described as the 'problem of the particularity' of the Pauline epistles taken individually.[48] It encouraged a hermeneutic in which Paul's rulings on local issues were generalized so as to be relevant in all times and places. As Tertullian noted, Ephesians was called by some (including Marcion) 'Laodiceans'; but 'the titles do not matter, since in writing to any particular people the apostle was writing to all'.[49]

So far from the order of books in the collection being significant for interpretation, the growth of a unified Bible seems on the whole to have made it largely a matter of indifference. An assumption of general applicability is probably almost a defining condition of the 'scriptural' status of books in any religion; and alongside this there is in Christianity (as in Judaism) a general acceptance of the principle stated frequently in rabbinic literature: 'there is no before or after in the Torah'.[50] Through this dictum Jewish tradition seems to discourage the quest for the 'meaning' of the way the Bible is arranged. The functional significance of this formula is that a text from any book may be used to illuminate any other, irrespective of the relative placings of the books in question within the canon. (By 'Torah' is meant here, as often, 'Scripture' rather than just the Pentateuch.) Narratives about the past can be applied to the future, future predictions can resolve puzzles about the past. We find what Levenson describes as 'the literary simultaneity of Scripture'.[51] All of the text is equally true at the same time; as Levenson observes, 'The authorless text presupposed by a synchronic, or holistic, mode of analysis has certain affinities with the divinely authored text of premodern Jewish tradition.'

Thus interpretation of scriptural texts tends to be atomistic. The equalized 'scriptural' status conferred on each text by its inclusion in a 'canon' of sacred writings tends progressively to destroy its individual integrity and to weaken the reader's sense of it as a literary work with a beginning, middle, and end. One sees this in cases such as the 'book of the Twelve' in the Hebrew Bible, where it matters as much (or as little) that Joel 2 comes before Amos 1 as that Amos 1 comes before Amos 2: the book of the Twelve is a seamless fabric and it hardly matters whereabouts a text is taken from.

This is not to deny that commentators may choose to expound a text sequentially; but in so far as each book is theologically seen as a section from a longer work – 'the Bible' – it is relatively unusual to find attention paid to the particularity or unique internal structure of any individual book. Because they are Scripture, all the books in the canon must be heard as speaking with one voice or, at least, as consistent with each other. As Leipoldt and Morenz put it, 'Anyone who thinks about holy scriptures in a believing frame of mind will see and grasp them as a unified whole. Revelations of the deity must by their nature be different from human utterances, and must be free from contradictions in their content.'[52]

How might these considerations relate to today's discussion of canonical or holistic interpretation? It is not easy to say. Our purpose has been strictly historical: to describe some aspects of the interpretation of Scripture around the beginning of our era, not to use this either to justify or to question the work of exegetes now. In any case, as one might expect, the relation of modern to ancient exegesis tends to be oblique, even when superficially it seems the same. Some ancient exegesis, especially the rabbinic exegesis described by Levenson, looks uncannily like modern 'final form' or 'canonical' exegesis. The Bible certainly was perceived as a single book by the end of the patristic era, in both Judaism and Christianity. Its internal consistency was assumed to be total: if one book differed from another (as with the Gospels) there was a strong hermeneutical imperative to find an accommodation, perhaps by relativizing both (or all four) accounts so as to make them tell compatible parts of a more complicated story. There was no thought of 'progressive revelation', nor even much willingness to think of gradations of authority among the different books. Where these were assumed, as between the Torah and the other books in Judaism or between the Gospels and the rest of the New Testament in Christianity, it seems never to have resulted in the lesser books being actually corrected or conradicted.

Yet on the other hand the Bible was not read as a 'work' in the modern sense, as though it had a structure that yielded a continuous and ordered meaning – as, for example, in interpretations such as that of Northrop Frye in *The Great Code*.[53] It was perceived as something closer to a vast collection of (divine) aphorisms, rather as if the whole book were like the central sections of the book of Proverbs.

On the whole, then, we should conclude that the canonical *status* of books did make a considerable difference to their interpretation. They belonged in an official collection, and so were assumed not to contradict each other but to be mutually illuminating. But their canonical *order* is only a minor theme, where indeed it matters at all. We may if we wish make exegetical capital out of the fact that (for example) the Prophets precede the Writings in the Hebrew Bible but follow them in the Christian Bible,[54] or that Romans stands at the head of the Pauline corpus, or that John is presented in the canon as the last Gospel; but there is not much evidence that people in antiquity anticipated such thoughts. Normally it becomes necessary to fall back, not on empirical evidence of ancient exegesis, but on a close reading of the texts which tries to show what any careful reader would be bound to get (and, so the argument runs, is bound to have got) out of them. Sometimes these intuitions are very appealing – as for example the idea that the Psalter has been edited so that it begins with the Law and the Messiah as the two themes the reader should look out for; or as with Sanders' theory about the shape of the Pentateuch. But it is hardly ever possible to feel confident that ancient readers would have seen things in this way, especially as our actual historical evidence so often shows us atomistic interpretation of verses and passages, not to mention (in Christian writers) incorrect attribution of texts and conflation of material from more than one book. On the whole I believe canonical and synchronic readings need to be justified in their own right, as modern methods of exegesis, and not give hostages to fortune by claiming ancient precedent.

Conclusion

Scripture is a human activity ... No doubt, their scripture to a
mighty extent makes a people what they are. Yet one must not
lose sight of the point that it is the people who make it, keep
making it, scripture.

Wilfred Cantwell Smith, *What is Scripture? A Comparative
Approach*, London 1993, pp. 18–19.

THIS BOOK HAS not been intended as a systematic treatment of the
history of the biblical canon (of either Testament), in the manner
of Beckwith or von Campenhausen. My concern throughout has
been with questions which comprehensive histories all too easily
overlook, such as what we mean by a 'canon' and how the books
in it are used by religious believers. On the other hand its concerns
are primarily historical – it is not meant to contribute, except perhaps indirectly, to current debates about 'canonical criticism' as
the proper approach for Christians today. The five chapters are
essays on related themes, but not stages in a continuous argument
– though I hope that the book's leading ideas will be found coherent. My chief aim has been to try and contribute to two areas that
are important for anyone who wishes to use the word 'canon' in
speaking of the Bible.

1. The first is the question of terminology. A lack of agreement
about the use of terms bedevils many areas of study in the human-
ities, and my impression is that this is true to a particularly great
extent in biblical studies. It hardly matters how the word 'canon' is
used, if only we can agree about it; but there is no more consensus
now than there was a hundred years ago – perhaps, indeed, less. I
have tried to defend a usage which Sundberg was, to my knowledge, the first to introduce, in which a distinction is drawn between the 'Scripture' which results from the growth of writings
perceived as holy, and the 'canon' which represents official

decisions to exclude from Scripture works deemed unsuitable. In my view this distinction can greatly clarify our thinking about both the Old and the New Testament.

At the same time, we need to be on our guard against the danger of anachronism in thinking that either concept was clearly in the minds of early rabbinic or patristic writers. Any discussion which starts by assuming that there was always something called 'the canon', and that the question is only when and how it came to be delineated, is doomed to anachronism from the outset. One might think that this would result in ascribing the acceptance of this or that book as Scripture to too early a date, but strangely enough the opposite can also be the case. For example, the continuing widespread belief that in Judaism a book that 'defiles the hands' means a 'canonical' book leads to the conclusion that certain books (Ecclesiastes, Song of Songs, Esther) must have arrived late in the Old Testament 'canon', since people were still arguing about whether they 'defiled the hands' in the late first century AD. But in fact these books were probably well established as Scripture at a much earlier date than this. Our own substantive conclusions about the scriptural status of Old Testament books have thus tended in a conservative direction, in some ways.

Trying to be clear about the necessary terminology has also led us into a sharper distinction than is usual between the 'canonization' of the Old Testament and that of the New. The normal consensus sees both corpora as having followed the same pattern: growth, with gradually increasing authority; an official place in the canon; finally the erection of a wall designed to keep out other books. Yet we have seen that most of the New Testament acquired an immense prestige almost from the beginning, and threatened to eclipse the Old Testament in the minds of many Christian writers. But we have urged that it is confusing to call this the 'canonization' of the New Testament. For, first, the New Testament books were not in the beginning called Scripture, *graphē*, even though they were in some ways more important for Christians than the books that were Scripture (the Old Testament). And secondly, their status did not imply textual fixity. They were often regarded more as the basis for an extemporization of the gospel message than as writings fixed, like the Jewish Scriptures, in a precise graphic form. Thus it would be reasonable to say that the New Testament books were 'canonized' almost as soon as written, if by 'canonization' we mean 'attribution of importance';

but quite wrong if we mean 'acceptance as a sacred text'. It does not matter which we mean, provided that we do not try to mean both at the same time. The term 'canon' is now a modern English term, and critics should use it as they please, but should not mistake defining one's terms with making empirical statements about the past.

The empirical point I have tried to make is that the books of the New Testament had a high status from very early times, especially in the Gentile churches – possibly higher, but certainly different in kind, from that possessed by the Old Testament for either Christians or Jews.

I hope that the terminological discussions may have helped to throw some light on the importance or otherwise of Marcion in the formation of the New Testament. I believe that Marcion's importance probably lies chiefly in the way the reactions to him forced the Church to be unequivocal in its continued acceptance of the Old Testament (just as patristic sources suggest). Where the status of the New Testament is concerned, he represented a reactionary, rather than an innovative, stream of thought. Everyone knows that Marcion's 'canon' consisted of Gospel (Luke) + Apostle (Paul); but not enough thought has been given to the word 'canon' itself, and whether it is an appropriate way to describe what Marcion promulgated.

2. My second aim has been to open up the question what people did with the 'canon' in the ancient world, and what kinds of meaning they looked for in it. Paradoxically, it emerges that some uses of Scripture barely treated it as containing 'meaning' at all, but saw it more as a holy object or talisman. For some streams in Judaism, a book is holy if it contains the name of God – regardless of its 'content' – and profane if it does not. But 'holiness' in this sense is not conterminous with 'canonicity'. On the other hand, sacred texts are likely to contain a great excess of meaning, such that one can never come to the end of it even by using more and more ingenious interpretative tools. The text's meaning is inexhaustible.

From our perspective, however, this is very like saying that it has no meaning at all, since the 'plain sense' that an 'ordinary' reader would extract may well have nothing to do with the meaning which ancient readers valued it for. In oscillating between being a holy object, opaque and inert from the sheer weight of its sanctity, and being almost a living person, blinding us with the coruscations of its infinite meanings, Scripture was seldom the mere 'book' whose meaning we extract by the ordinary procedures of modern 'critical' reading. Such reading sees the Bible as written by one human being (or more) to carry a meaning to other human beings. I am proposing that we should be aware that that is *not* how Scripture seemed to many people in the period we have been studying. I have in all this presented Jewish and Christian readings of Scripture as strange, stranger (to my mind) than students of the Bible commonly recognize. But it is of course open to readers to say that such ways of handling the text seem to them perfectly normal. A postmodern account of the meaning of texts sees 'critical' reading as the oddity, and the multi-layered style of traditional Jewish and Christian exegesis as entirely unproblematic. I am not legislating for what one is or is not allowed to find normal, only saying that to me these interpretations seem strange, and I believe that some others will also find them so. It can hardly be doubted that many people who value the Bible do not know that it was once read in the ways I have been outlining, would be surprised to learn that it was, and would be disturbed by the suggestion that they should read it like that themselves.

The description of rabbinic and patristic exegesis has not, however, been undertaken for its own sake. There are many studies of these matters, and I have merely sketched a few main principles. The purpose has been, again, to throw light on the canon – to discover what Jews or Christians must have understood these texts to be, if they interpreted them in such ways. The further exegesis of the Bible differs from that of ordinary books, the greater must be the Bible's prestige and its elevation above more ephemeral writings. Our excursion into early biblical interpretation has thus helped to confirm the status both Old and New Testaments had in the first few centuries, while at the same time highlighting that the New Testament was not treated in quite the same way as the Old until well into the patristic age. The memory of the primitive idea that the New Testament was not a holy writing, but something more like a record, persisted, and it was not usually allegorized, for example, in the time of the Apostolic Fathers or the Apologists. Paradoxically again, however, this was partly because it was so important as a historical source: its non-allegorization is not a mark of lower *status* than the Old Testament, but of a perceived difference in *genre*.

How far should the canon be a context for our own interpretation of the Bible? We have found, not surprisingly, that a historical enquiry into the origins of the Bible does not answer this question for us. The most it can do is to indicate how far a 'canonical criticism' resembles the way in which Scripture was read in the ancient world, in the early Church and in Second Temple and early rabbinic Judaism. There clearly are important resemblances. For example, the concern to interpret sacred books as internally consistent, and as consistent with each other, is a constant concern of today's canonical readings, and it was a concern in the period we have studied.

On the other hand, there are also important differences. Canonical criticism has little in common with the early Christians who felt that the exact form of the Gospels did not matter very much, provided 'the gospel' was transmitted, and for whom the New Testament writings were so important precisely because they were not 'ancient Scripture' but a record of recent events.

The shape and order of the canon, though discussed in part by the rabbis and the Fathers, were of much less interest then than they appear to be in the work of canonical critics. The sense of Scripture as a single 'work' was necessarily fainter, in a world where the holy books existed as individual scrolls, or at best as separate collections in codices that did not contain the whole Bible. The interpretative methods used sometimes resemble canonical criticism in that they asked primarily about the meaning of the books in their present form, innocent of the history of composition: yet they were also very often highly atomistic, and evinced little concern for the flow of argument in a book, or its 'plot'. In extreme cases the quest for the text's meaning imputed significance to features that any modern reader, including a canonical critic, is likely to regard as sub-semantic.

In so far as canonical or 'final form' exegesis claims to be restoring the exegetical approach of ancient Judaism or the early Church, our discussion thus suggests that it is only partially successful. But of course such approaches may claim nothing of the kind; they may be avowedly Christian (or Jewish, or secular) styles of interpretation with their own logic. In that case nothing in the historical enquiry we have undertaken can legitimately lead to a verdict on them, favourable or unfavourable. My concern here has not been primarily to contribute to the discussion of this question, but simply to introduce the reader to some fascinating questions about the ancient reception and perception of the books that now make up our Bible, and to marvel at the variety of things human beings have done with these remarkable texts.

NOTES

Chapter 1

1 Christopher Wordsworth, *On the Canon of the Scriptures of the Old and New Testament*, London 1848. Wordsworth's excerpts include (among others) the following classic texts:

Justin Martyr, *Cohortatio ad Graecos* 13
Melito of Sardis, *apud* Eusebius, *Ecclesiastical History* 4:26
The *Muratorian Fragment*
Tertullian, *De cultu feminarum* 1:3
Eusebius of Caesarea, *Ecclesiastical History* 3:25
Athanasius, *Festal Letter* 39
Cyril of Jerusalem, *Catacheses* 4:33–6
Hilary of Poitiers, *Prologus in Libros Psalmorum* 15
Epiphanius, *Adversus Haereses* 5 and 76
   De Mensuris et Ponderibus
Council of Laodicea, Canons 59 and 60
Rufinus, *Expositio in Symbolum Apostolorum*
Philastrius, *De Haeresibus* 40
Amphilochius, *Iambi ad Seleucum*
Gregory Nazianzen, *Carmen* 33
Jerome, *Prologus Galeatus*
   Prologus in Jeremiam
     in libros Salomonis, Chromatio et Heliodoro
     in Danielem Prophetam
     in Ezram
     in Librum Tobiae
     n Librum Judith
   Epistola 50 *ad Paulinum*
   Commentaria in Matthaeum, prooemium
   De Viris Illustribus 5 and 59
   Epistola ad Dardanum 2
   Commentaria in Isaiae Prophetiam 3:6
   Prologus 7 *in Epistolarum Canonem*
Council of Hippo, Canon 38
Council of Carthage, Canon 47
Augustine, *De Doctrina Christiana* 2:3:1

2 Bruce M. Metzger, *The Canon of the New Testament: Its Origin, Development, and Significance*, Oxford 1987.

3 There is a useful discussion of the tendency of scholars to be at cross purposes in theorizing about the New Testament canon in U. Swarat, 'Das Werden des neutestamentlichen Kanons', in

G. Maier (ed.), *Der Kanon der Bibel*, Giessen 1990, pp. 25–51, esp. p. 35. (Swarat's own aim is to rehabilitate the work of Theodor Zahn, discussed below.)

4 Theodor Zahn, *Geschichte des neutestamentlichen Kanons*, 2 vols, Leipzig 1888–92.

5 Brooke Foss Westcott, *A General Survey of the History of the Canon of the New Testament*, London 1885.

6 Metzger, *Canon*, p. 21.

7 On this question see Metger, *Canon*, pp. 260, 297–9, and Harry Y. Gamble, 'The Redaction of the Pauline Letters and the Formation of the Pauline Corpus', *HThR* 94 (1975), pp. 403–18. Gamble criticizes W. Schmithals, 'On the Composition and Earliest Collection of the Major Epistles of Paul', in J. E. Steely (ed.), *Paul and the Gnostics*, Nashville 1972 (= *ZNW* 51 (1960), pp. 225–45), who thinks the collection was anti-gnostic in intention.

8 See, for example, J. N. Sanders, *The Fourth Gospel in the Early Church*, Cambridge 1943, pp. 27–31. This theory is rejected by Metzger, *Canon*, pp. 146–7, in dependence on E. F. Osborn, *Justin Martyr* (Beiträge zur historischen Theologie 47), Tübingen 1973.

9 On the Tübingen School see H. Harris, *The Tübingen School*, Oxford 1975; W. G. Kümmel, *Das neue Testament: Geschichte der Erforschung seiner Probleme*, Freiburg 1970; ET *The New Testament: The History of the Investigation of its Problems*, London 1973; and R. C. Morgan, art. 'Tübingen School' in R. J. Coggins and J. L. Houlden (eds), *A Dictionary of Biblical Interpretation*, London 1990, pp.710–13.

10 See T. Zahn, *Ignatius von Antiochien*, Gotha 1873.

11 Adolf von Harnack, *The Origin of the New Testament and the Most Important Consequences of the New Creation*, London 1925.

12 Many important examples are discussed in Isidor Frank, *Der Sinn der Kanonbildung* (Freiburger Theologische Studien 90), Freiburg 1971.

13 Albert C. Sundberg, 'Towards a Revised History of the New Testament Canon', *Studia Evangelica* IV (TU 102), Berlin 1968, pp. 452–61.

14 See W. C. van Unnik, 'De la règle μήτε προσθεῖναι μήτε ἀφελεῖν dans l'histoire du canon', *Vigiliae Christianae* 3 (1949), pp. 1–36.

15 R. M. Grant, *Heresy and Criticism: The Search for Authenticity in Early Christian Literature*, Louisville 1993, pp. 7–8.

16 See the judicious discussion by Metzger, *Canon*, pp. 98–9.

17 Hans von Campenhausen, *Die Entstehung der christlichen Bibel* (BHTh 39), Tübingen 1968; ET *The Formation of the Christian Bible*, London 1972.

18 Cf. also Frank, *Kanonbildung*.

19 Harry Y. Gamble, *The New Testament Canon: Its Making and Meaning*, Philadelphia 1985, pp. 63–5.

20 Metzger, *Canon*, pp. 99–106. See the further discussion of Montanism below, pp. 8–9 and 60.

21 A. C. Sundberg, *The Old Testament of the Early Church*, Cambridge,

Mass. and London 1964; 'Canon of the NT', *Interpreter's Dictionary of the Bible* Supplement, Nashville 1976, pp. 136–40; and see note 13 above.

22 Metzger, *Canon*, p. 282.

23 Sundberg, *Old Testament*, p. 102.

24 Geoffrey M. Hahneman, *The Muratorian Fragment and the Development of the Canon*, Oxford 1992. Sundberg's own argument can be found in his 'Muratorian Fragment', *IDB* Supplement, Nashville 1976, pp. 609–10.

25 Sundberg, 'Towards a Revised History', p. 453.

26 Sundberg, 'Canon of the NT', p. 137.

27 Harnack, *Origin*, p. xvi.

28 Sundberg, 'Canon of the NT'. Cf. L. M. McDonald, *The Formation of the Christian Bible*, Nashville 1988, for the point that citation of a work does not in itself prove its 'scriptural' status.

29 Metzger, *Canon*, pp. 289–93.

30 R. M. Grant, *Heresy and Criticism*, p. 32, questions the existence of a 'pagan canon' – see also note 62 below.

31 See chapter 5 below.

32 Metzger, *Canon*, p. 24.

33 John Barton, *Oracles of God: Perceptions of Ancient Prophecy in Israel after the Exile*, London 1986, New York 1988, pp. 13–95.

34 S. Z. Leiman, *The Canonization of Hebrew Scripture: The Talmudic and Midrashic Evidence*, Hamden, Conn., 1976, p. 14. See the discussion in R. T. Beckwith, *The Old Testament Canon of the New Testament Church and its Background in Early Judaism*, London 1985, summarized by him in 'Formation of the Hebrew Bible', in M. J. Mulder (ed.), *Mikra: Text, Translation, Reading and Interpretation of the Hebrew Bible in Ancient Judaism and Early Christianity*, Assen/Maastricht and Philadelphia 1988, pp. 87–135. Beckwith follows Leiman quite closely.

35 A. C. Sundberg, 'The "Old Testament": A Christian Canon', *CBQ* 30 (1968), pp. 143–55 – the quotation is from p. 147.

36 Franz Stuhlhofer, *Der Gebrauch der Bibel von Jesus bis Euseb: eine statistiche Untersuchung zur Kanongeschichte*, Wuppertal 1988.

37 'Wie bei allen Prozessen, die mit einem Ergebnis endeten, das auch in der Gegenwart noch Gültigkeit hat, stehen wir als Historiker in der Gefahr, zu stark gegenwartsbezogen zu urteilen. Diese Gefahr ist von der Geschichte der Naturwissenschaften, aber auch z.B. von der Geschichte des Papsttums her bekannt. Man neigt dazu, gegenwärtige Zustände oder Ansichten in frühere Zeiten zurückzuprojizieren; und selbst wenn man erkennt, daß der heutige Zustand damals nicht verwirklicht war, ist man einseitig auf die Frage fixiert, wieweit der damalige Zustand noch vom heutigen Zustand entfernt war, bzw. wie nahe er ihm bereits war: der Naturforscher erkannte noch nicht bzw. schon, was wir heute erkennen; der damalige römische Bischof wurde noch nicht bzw. schon als Papst im heutigen Sinn anerkannt, und die Kirchenschriftsteller hatten noch nicht ganz bzw. schon unseren heutigen Kanon. Die Geschichte wird

als linearer Prozeß gesehen: Die früheren Menschen hatten bereits das gleiche Ziel wie wir heute, nur waren sie ihm noch nicht so nahe. In Wirklichkeit hatten vergangene Zeiten oft andere Fragestellungen und andere Ziele als spätere, so daß wir die Vergangenheit nicht verstehen, wenn wir historische Quellen mit modernen Denkkategorien erfassen wollen; z.B. verstehen wir die frühe Geschichte des Kanons nicht, wenn wir bei jedem Autor die Frage vor Augen haben, ob er dieses oder jenes Buch zum "Kanon", zum "NT" rechnete oder nicht – damit tragen wir eine später entstandene Zweiteilung an eine frühere Zeit heran, als ob es selbstverständlich wäre, daß man nur mit dieser Zweiteilung (möglichst klar abgegrenzter Kanon) leben konnte'; Stuhlhofer, *Gebrauch*, p. 84. (The English translation in the main text, here and elsewhere, is mine.) Cf. also N. Brox, *Der Hirt des Hermas*, Göttingen 1991, p. 58, who discusses the question whether Irenaeus thought of the *Shepherd* as 'Scripture': 'Such considerations were criticised by Overbeck (as against Harnack) with the objection that this was to start out too unthinkingly from the assumption of the existence, authority, and bounds of a New Testament biblical canon, in a period when none of these things existed in this general form' ('Solche Überlegungen wurden von Overbeck (Harnack gegenüber) mit dem Einwand kritisiert, daß hier zu unbedacht von der Existenz, Autorität und Grenze eines neutestamentlichen Bibelkanons angegangen werde für eine Zeit, zu der es das alles in dieser generellen Form noch nicht gab') – citing Overbeck in *TLZ* 30 (1878), cols 281–5, a review of O. Gebhart, A. Harnack, and T. Zahn, *Patrum apostolicorum opera*, fascicle 3, Leipzig 1877.

38 A. Harnack, *Bible Reading in the Early Church*, London and New York 1912, p. v.

39 Stuhlhofer, *Gebrauch*, p. 47. For the details of the distribution of terms among the various books of the New Testament in Origen and Eusebius see E. Hennecke, *New Testament Apocrypha*, ed. W. Schneemelcher, vol. 1, London 1963, pp. 28–42, and W. G. Kümmel, *Introduction to the New Testament*, London 1975, pp. 495–9. There is a very clear discussion in Metzger, *Canon*, pp. 203–4. The threefold division is readily apparent in Eusebius, for whom the *homolegoumena* are the Gospels, Acts, and the Pauline epistles (including Hebrews), and perhaps Revelation, the *notha* are the Acts of Paul, the Shepherd, the Apocalypse of Peter, Barnabas, the Didache, the Gospel according to the Hebrews, and perhaps (!) Revelation, while James, Jude, 2 Peter, and 2 and 3 John are *antilegomena*. It will be seen that even the threefold system does not adequately cope with Revelation, which perhaps ought to be completely accepted or perhaps ought to be completely rejected, and yet is not an *antilegomenon* either.

40 On the whole manuscripts of the New Testament join Acts with the Catholic epistles to form a collection called 'Praxapostolos'; the arrangement in which Acts follows the Gospels and is followed by the

Pauline letters appears to be late. See D. Trobisch, 'Die Endredaktion des Neuen Testaments: Eine Untersuchung zur Entstehung der christlichen Bibel' (Habilitationsschrift, Heidelberg 1994), p. 39. I am grateful to Dr Trobisch for making this available to me. See the further discussion in chapter 5 below.

41 The evidence from citation may be in some measure confirmed by the number of extant manuscripts of different parts of the New Testament: 2328 of the Gospels, 779 of Paul, 655 of Acts + Catholic epistles, and 287 of Revelation (figures from Trobisch, 'Endredaktion', citing B. and K. Aland, *Der Text des Neuen Testaments: Einführung in die wissenschaftlichen Ausgaben sowie in Theorie und Praxis der modernen Textkritik*, 2nd edn, Stuttgart 1989).

42 There were indeed disagreements, especially in Rome, about the status of the Fourth Gospel, which Justin, for example, does not quote (or quotes only once). W. L. Peterson, *Tatian's Diatessaron: Its Creation, Dissemination, Significance, and History in Scholarship* (*Vigiliae Christianae* Supplement 25), Leiden 1994, writes, 'Almost all histories of the canon fail to note that John was either rejected or accepted only with reservations in the West – especially in Rome – during the first Christian centuries.' But this seems to be an exaggeration of the evidence, given the extensive quotations from John in many early Christian writers. Justin is the exception rather than the rule. Cf. Stuhlhofer, *Gebrauch*, pp. 91–8, for citation statistics.

43 C. H. Dodd, *The Present Task in New Testament Studies*, Cambridge 1936, pp. 34–5.

44 Metzger, *Canon*, p. 145.

45 Stuhlhofer, *Gebrauch*, p. 67.

46 'Jedenfalls erkennen wir hier ein Paradoxon: Die frühe Kirche zitierte das AT als "Schrift", hatte es aber anfangs nur bruchstückhaft; dagegen hatte sie das NT großenteils und benutzte es auch viel stärker, ohne es schon als "Schrift" zu zitieren' (Stuhlhofer, *Gebrauch*, p. 68).

47 'Zwischen einer Mehrklassigkeit und einem eindeutigen Kanon (= Zweiklassigkeit, Entweder-oder) gibt es immer eine Spannung. Nehmen wir an, es herrscht gerade Mehrklassigkeit, z.B. 3 Klassen, wobei die mittlere Klasse aus Büchern bestehen kann, die nicht öffentlich in der Kirche, aber privat gelesen werden dürfen. Aber das ist ein labiler Zustand, denn entweder ist das Buch gut – warum soll es dann nicht in der Kirche gelesen werden? Oder es ist schlecht – warum soll es dann überhaupt privat gelesen werden? Dieser labiler Zustand wird leicht in die eine oder andere Richtung umkippen. . . . Wenn dagegen gerade Zweiklassigkeit herrscht: *Faktisch* werden doch einige Bücher wichtiger genommen als andere, vielleicht als dogmatisch ergiebigere oder verständlichere oder das für wichtig Erachtete besser zum Ausdruck bringende Bücher (Luther: "was Christum treibet"), so daß letztlich auch innerhalb des "Kanons" Abstufungen herrschen' (Stuhlhofer, *Gebrauch*, p. 29).

48 See Stuhlhofer, *Gebrauch*, p. 56, for references to secondary litera-
    ture supporting a threefold division of Scripture in the early
    Church; and compare note 39 above.
49 Barton, *Oracles*, esp. pp. 35–95.
50 Barton, *Oracles*, pp. 77–8; cf. Stuhlhofer, *Gebrauch*, p. 68.
51 There are cases where the formula is used, e.g. Barnabas 4, which
    quotes the saying *polloi klētoi, oligoi de eklektoi*. Some think this a quo-
    tation from IV Ezra 8.3, but it may equally well be a reference to
    Matt. 22.14; see the discussion by P. F. Beatrice, 'Une citation de
    l'Évangile de Matthieu dans l'Épître de Barnabé', in J. M. Severin
    (ed.), *The New Testament in Early Christianity (La réception des écrits
    néotestamentaires dans le christianisme primitif)* (BETL 86), Leuven
    1989, pp. 231–45.
52 Theophilus, *Ad Autolycum* 3:12; see R. M. Grant (ed. and tr.), *Theo-
    philus of Antioch Ad Autolycum*, Oxford 1970.
53 On John as intentionally 'scriptural' see von Campenhausen, *For-
    matio i*, pp. 53–4. J. Leipoldt and S. Morenz, *Heilige Schriften, Beo-
    bachtungen zur Religionsgeschichte der antiken Mittelmeerwelt*, Leipzig
    1953, p. 152, interestingly suggest that since John was written so
    as to invite allegorical interpretation (as many scholars would
    agree), it was probably intended to be taken as 'Scripture' – since
    interpretability by allegory is one of the marks of a 'scriptural'
    book. On this, see further chapters 2 and 5 below.
54 See, for exmaple, B. W. Bacon, *Studies in Matthew*, London 1930; K.
    Stendahl, *The School of St Matthew and its Use of the Old Testament*, 2nd
    edn, Philadelphia 1968; and the discussion in M. D. Goulder, *Mid-
    rash and Lection in Matthew*, London 1974.
55 There are illuminating medieval parallels discussed by A. J. Minnis,
    *Medieval Theory of Authorship: Scholastic Literary Attitudes in the Later
    Middle Ages*, Aldershot 1988; for example, by allegorizing his own
    poem 'Voi che'ntendono' in the *Convivio*, Dante was giving it a kind
    of 'scriptural' status and distancing it from himself as its human
    author (p. xiii). Leipoldt and Morenz, *Heilige Schriften*, p. 7, suggest
    that Matthew, John, and Revelation were probably written for
    quasi-scriptural use and status, but that other New Testament
    books on the whole were not. Cf. also note 53 above. These ques-
    tions are relevant to the assessment of Marcion's treatment of the
    Gospels – see chapter 2 below.
56 C. H. Roberts and T. C. Skeat, *The Birth of the Codex*, London 1987,
    an extensive reworking of C. H. Roberts, 'The Codex', *Proceedings of
    the British Academy* 40 (1954), pp. 169–204. See also chapter 4 below.
57 Though it should be noted that Christian papyri of the Old Testa-
    ment are also commonly in codex form, and also use the *nomina sacra*.
58 Cf. Trobisch, 'Endredaktion'; also his popular book *Paul's Letter
    Collection: Tracing the Origins*, Minneapolis 1994.
59 Origen, *Homilies on Hebrews*.
60 Eusebius, *Ecclesiastical History* 6:25:11–14.

61 Josephus, *contra Apionem* 1:37–43; see my discussion in *Oracles*, pp. 26–7, 37–9.

62 Grant, *Heresy and Criticism*, chapter 2, provides an invaluable discussion of the critical quest for authenticity in documents followed by scholars in the ancient world. The critical tools they used were mostly those familiar in modern literary history and biblical scholarship: testing the consistency, plausiblity, chronology, and authorship of literary works. There is no reason to think that Christians were innovating when they asked whether this or that 'apostolic' writing was genuine, or when they drew up lists of 'authentic' and 'spurious' works. On the other hand, Grant may exaggerate the difference between the pagan literary 'canon', which he believes (though this is not uncontroversial) to have had no more formal status than the so-called 'canon' of modern English literature, and the biblical canon which 'was formal and authoritative' (p. 32). At most that is what some ecclesiastical authorities *wanted* the biblical canon to be; and even they seldom had the freedom to make it deviate far from the corpus of books customarily used in the churches.

63 'Daß so etwas wie ein "Index" existierte, bedeutet aber nicht, daß die Kirche bereits eine fest umgrenzte Anzahl von "kanonischen" Büchern gehabt hätte. Es war auch nicht notwendig; zur Abgrenzung gegen "Häretiker" genügte es im allgemeinen, deren Hauptwerk auf den Index zu setzen und gleichzeitig die Autorität der von Beginn an anerkannten Bücher (Mt, Pls, . . .) zu betonen. Damit war eine klare Abgrenzung gegen jede "häretische" Gruppe erreicht' (Stuhlhofer, *Gebrauch*, p. 77).

64 See Barton, *Oracles*, p. 59. On the Muratorian Fragment, Frank, *Kanonbildung*, p. 187, comments: 'Der Kanon des Neuen Testaments ist für den Fragmentisten zwar gegen Schriften anderer theologischer Tendenzen abgegrenzt, gegen mögliche weitere Schriften apostolischer Herkunft scheint er aber noch offen zu sein.' ('For the author of the Fragment the canon of the New Testament is certainly fenced off against writings with different theological tendencies, but it appears to be still open to admit possible further writings with an apostolic origin.')

65 John Barton, *People of the Book? The Authority of the Bible in Christianity*, London 1988.

66 Cf. note 38 above.

67 This good phrase was coined by Gamble, *New Testament Canon*, p. 79.

Chapter 2

1 For a recent reassessment of Marcion, see R. J. Hoffman, *Marcion: On the Restitution of Christianity. An Essay on the Development of Radical Paulinist Theology in the Second Century*, Chico, Calif. 1984.

2 'Das katholische NT hat die Marcionitische Bibel geschlagen; aber dieses NT ist eine antimarcionitische Schöpfung auf Marcioni-

tischer Grundlage', Adolf von Harnack, *Marcion: Das Evangelium vom fremden Gott (Eine Monographie zur Geschichte der Grundlegung der katholischen Kirche)*, TU 45, Leipzig 1921, p. 357*.

3 von Campenhausen, *Formation*, p. 148.

4 Metzger, *Canon*, p. 99, referring to Robert M. Grant, *The Formation of the New Testament*, New York and London 1965, p. 126.

5 C. H. Cosgrove, 'Justin Martyr and the Emerging Christian Canon: Observations on the Purpose and Destination of the Dialogue with Trypho', *Vigiliae Christianae* 36 (1982), pp. 209–32; the quotation is from p. 226.

6 John Knox, *Marcion and the New Testament*, Chicago 1942, p.31.

7 Gamble, *New Testament Canon*, p. 60.

8 Stuhlhofer, *Gebrauch*, pp. 73–6.

9 See Origen, *Epistle to Africanus* 4; Prologue to *Commentary on the Song of Songs*.

10 Frank, *Kanonbildung*.

11 Though a case is made out by D. G. Meade, *Pseudonymity and Canon: An Investigation into the Relationship of Authorship and Authority in Jewish and Earliest Christian Traditions*, Grand Rapids 1986, esp. p. 204.

12 In fact the Fragment reads *nuperrim e(t) temporibus nostris*, but see the discussion in Hahneman, *Muratorian Fragment*, pp. 27–30, 51–3.

13 See above, p. 27.

14 Knox already suggests what Stuhlhofer's statistics tend to confirm, that 'there were many churches, even as late as A.D. 150, where the Jewish Scriptures were little, if any, used.'

15 Cf. J. Leipoldt, *Geschichte des neutestamentlichen Kanons*, Leipzig 1907, vol I, p. 192 (cited in Knox, *Marcion*, p. 20): 'He did not regard Paul's letters as Holy Scripture, any more than the Gospel of Luke, but only as a particularly valuable historical source; for Marcion eliminated difficulties which offended him by changing the text, not by allegorical interpretation, in Paul's epistles too' ('Wie das Lukasevangelium galten ihm auch die Paulusbriefe nicht als Heilige Schrift, sondern nur als eine besonders wertvolle Geschichtsquelle; denn auch in den Paulusbriefen beseitigte Marcion Schwierigkeiten, die ihm aufstiessen, nicht durch allegorische Deutung, sondern durch Textänderung.')

16 For example, Barnabas 4:14b probably cites Matthew with *hōs gegraptai*, and Theophilus, *AdAutolycum* 2:36, refers to John as *graphē*.

17 Young Kyu Kim, 'Palaeographical Dating of P[46] to the Late First Century', *Biblica* 69 (1988), pp. 248–57. I am grateful to Professor Kevin Cathcart for drawing my attention to this.

18 J. J. Clabeaux, *A Lost Edition of Paul: A Reassessment of the Pauline Corpus attested by Marcion (CBQ* MS 21), Washington DC 1989.

19 'Wenn wir an die zahlreichen Kontinuitäten hinsichtlich des frühchristlichen Gebrauchs ntl. Bücher zurückdenken, sind wir beeindrückt von der "tiefen Stille, unter welcher für die betrachtende Nachwelt der Kanon zustandekommt" (Franz Overbeck S. 71).

Es ist eine Geschichte ohne alle Revolutionen; das Wesentliche ist von Beginn an gegeben, die geringfügigen Änderungen geschehen so allmählich, daß sie niemandem auffallen' (Stuhlhofer, *Gebrauch*, p. 75; the reference to Overbeck is to F. Overbeck, *Zur Geschichte des Kanons*, Chemnitz 1880, repr. Darmstadt 1965).

20 Knox, *Marcion*, p. 7 and p. 20.

21 This is in sharp contrast with the doctrine of 'false pericopes' which we find in the Clementines, where Old Testament material is to be deleted if it conflicts with the gnostic teaching of the author – cf. *Clementine Homilies* 2:52, where it is denied that Adam was really a transgressor, or Noah a drunkard, or Abraham and Jacob polygamists, or Moses a murderer instructed by an idol-priest, all of which are asserted by the Old Testament in the form it now has; see also 3:17. Compare von Campenhausen, *Formation*, p. 79.

22 'Man wußte, was diese Botschaft war, und die Frage, woher man das wußte, stellte sich nicht. Die Kirche in ihrer Gesamtheit kannte das Geschehene und kannte auch dessen Bedeutung, weil es immer wieder erzählt und verkündigt wurde': Ellen Flesseman-van Leer, 'Prinzipien der Sammlung und Ausscheidung bei der Bildung des Kanons', *ZThK* 61 (1964), pp. 404–20; the quotation is from p. 405.

23 The general consensus is that Tertullian and Eusebius are to be believed when they say that Luke formed the basis of Marcion's Gospel, and it is hard to see how Tertullian's section-by-section commentary makes any sense unless it did. The consensus has been questioned by D. S. Williams, 'Reconsidering Marcion's Gospel', *JBL* 108 (1989), pp. 477–96, but on dubious grounds – for example, he says that Tertullian criticizes Marcion for having omitted from the Gospel passages that are not in Luke anway. But Tertullian does not grant Marcion's hypothesis that Luke *ought* to be the basic text, and was, on his own terms, perfectly entitled to complain that Marcan or Matthaean passages were not in Marcion's one canonical Gospel. The consensus naturally does not imply that Marcion's Gospel was based on precisely 'our' text of Luke. Knox (*Marcion*, pp. 77–113) argues persuasively that it was a 'proto-Luke', lacking the infancy narratives.

24 'Man darf höchstens sagen, daß, was Lukas und Matthäus sich gegenüber Q und Markus an einzelnen Stellen erlaubt haben, das hat M. zum Prinzip seiner Kritik erhoben' (Harnack, *Marcion*, pp. 64–5).

25 Helmut Merkel, *Die Pluralität der Evangelien als theologisches und exegetisches Problem in der Alten Kirche* (Traditio Christiana III), Berne 1978; see also his *Die Widersprüche zwischen den Evangelien* (WUNT 13), Tübingen 1971.

26 'Auch er fußt auf einer gegebenen urkundlichen Unterlage, den drei ersten Evangelien, und schaltet mit dieser Unterlage aufs freieste, läßt fort, stellt um und corrigiert im einzelnen wie M. Auch er unterwirft den gesamten Stoff einer negativen und producierenden dogmatischen Kritik; er verfährt aber dabei weit kühner als M.,

indem er nicht nur lange Reden entwirft, sondern wahrscheinlich auch ganz neue geschichtliche Situationen erfindet' (Harnack, *Marcion*, p. 67).

27 Helmut Koester considers that Justin probably used, or even produced, a harmony of Matthew and Luke; he treated this as 'the *one* inclusive new Gospel' which would supplant Matthew and Luke (and perhaps Mark). See H. Koester, *The Text of the Synoptic Gospels in the Second Century: Origins, Recensions, Text, and Transmission*, Notre Dame and London 1989, pp. 19–37; the section on Justin is on pp. 28–37, and depends on A. Bellinzoni, *The Sayings of Jesus in the Writings of Justin Martyr* (*NT* Suppl. 17), Leiden 1967.

28 On Tatian see Metzger, *Canon*, pp. 114–17, and *The Early Versions of the New Testament: Their Origin, Transmission, and Limitations*, Oxford 1977, pp. 10–36; T. Baarda, 'Factors in the Harmonization of the Gospels, especially in the Diatessaron of Tatian', in W. L. Petersen (ed.), *Gospel Traditions in the Second Century: Origins, Recensions, Text, and Transmission* (Christianity and Judaism in Antiquity 3), London 1989, pp. 133–56; *Essays on the Diatessaron*, Kampen 1994; and Petersen, *Tatian's Diatessaron*.

29 'Tatian betrachtet... wohl wie Justin die Evangelien als historische Berichte von einem Leben Jesu, unter diesem historischen Aspekt mußte er sich aber natürlich an den sich oft widersprechenden Aussagen der Evangelien stoßen' (Frank, *Kanonbildung*, p. 140). Metzger, on the other hand, argues that 'the *Diatessaron* supplies proof that all four Gospels were regarded as authoritative, otherwise it is unlikely that Tatian would have dared to combine them in one gospel account' (*Canon*, p. 115). But the logic of this is puzzling. Might one not equally, or better, argue that *none* of the Gospels can have been regarded as authoritative, otherwise it is unlikely that he would have dared to destroy them all so as to make his own version? This at once raises the question what *kind* of authority they – and the eventual *Diatessaron* – possessed, as Scripture or as 'archives': see the detailed discussion in chapter 3 below.

30 'A remarkable cento which reminds one of filigree work', Metzger, *Early Versions*, p. 12.

31 See Theodoret, *haereticarum fabularum compendium* 1:20, *de Tatiano* (*PG* 83:372). Theodoret relates that he gathered up all the books he could find containing the *Diatessaron*, and replaced them with books of the Gospels.

32 See the summary in Metzger, *Canon*, pp. 49–50.

33 Stendahl, *School* – see chapter 1, note 54 above.

34 Harnack, *Origin*, p. 170.

35 Harnack, *Marcion*, p. 70.

36 'Das Evangelium und Apostolikon M.s waren ja auch in ihren Absichten nur halbverständlich, wenn ihnen nicht die Erklärung zur Seite trat, welche die Antithesen boten; sie mußten daher von Anfang an diese begleiten' (Harnack, *Marcion*, pp. 70–1).

37 'Endlich sollte das Werk nicht nur eine literarische Zugabe ("dos")

zum Evangelium und eine Versicherung ("patrocinium") für dasselbe sein, sondern auch ein *für die Gemeinde maßgebendes Werk, also ihr symbolisches Buch*' (Harnack, *Marcion*, p. 70).

38 Harnack, *Origin*, p. 170.

39 Origen attests this in his *Commentary on Matthew* 15:3.

40 Origen, *contra Celsum*, 1:20. See H. Chadwick, *Origen: Contra Celsum*, Cambridge 1953, 2nd edn 1965.

41 *contra Celsum*, 1:23.

42 *contra Celsum* 4:51. A belief that allegory is necessary or desirable in Christian biblical interpretation continues to be held today: see, from two very different philosophical standpoints, Andrew Louth, *Discerning the Mystery*, Oxford 1983, and Richard Swinburne, *Revelation*, Oxford 1992. It seemed quite normal to many exegetes down to the Enlightenment and beyond. Stephen Prickett makes the point that it spilled over from the Bible on to secular literature in the Middle Ages: 'The allegorical levels of *The Divine Comedy* or *The Romance of the Rose* are not in any way optional additions to the basic story; they are a normal and integral part of what literature was expected to be' (S. Prickett (ed.), *Reading the Text*, Basil Blackwell 1991, p. 2). My purpose here is not at all to argue in favour of allegorical interpretation, but simply to register that it once seemed the most natural way of reading serious literature – people did not feel they had to justify it by showing that literal interpretation was inadequate for a particular work. The opposite was the case: to insist on reading 'literally' a text that one claimed as serious rather than ephemeral would have seemed to many readers in the past simply perverse. Cf. Menachem Haran, 'Midrashic and Literal Exegesis and the Critical Method in Biblical Research', in S. Japhet (ed.), *Studies in Bible* (Scripta Hierosolymita 31), Jerusalem 1986, pp. 19–48: 'It was probably regarded as most natural that God's message, bound in words and recorded in the Book, should hold a deeper significance than the mere literal drift arising from the text as it is' (p. 28).

43 Leipoldt and Morenz, *Heilige Schriften*.

44 See the discussion in P. F. Bradshaw, *Daily Prayer in the Early Church* (Alcuin Club Collection 63), London 1981, pp. 19–20; also C. Perrot, 'The Reading of the Bible in the Ancient Synagogue', in M. J. Mulder (ed.), *Mikra*, chapter 4 (pp. 137–59).

45 *ne si in exordio legerit, sub carnalibus verbis spiritalium nuptiarum epithalamium non intelligens vulneretur*: Jerome, *Epistle* 107:12; cited in Harnack, *Bible Reading*, pp. 127–8.

46 Cosgrove, 'Justin Martyr', p. 218.

47 von Campenhausen, *Formation*, p. 59.

48 Miriam Taylor, 'The Jews in the Writings of the Early Church Fathers (150–312): Men of Straw or Formidable Rivals?', D.Phil. dissertation, Oxford 1991. I am grateful to Dr Taylor for generously

allowing me to borrow this work. See also her *Anti-Judaism and Early Christian Identity: A Critique of the Scholarly Consensus* (Studia Post-Biblica 46), Leiden 1995.

49 Beatrice, 'Une citation', p. 237, with reference to the discussion of P. Vielhauer, *Geschichte der urchristlichen Literatur*, 2nd edn, Berlin 1978, pp. 599–612. See also T. Stylianopoulos, *Justin Martyr and the Mosaic Law* (SBL Dissertation series 20), Missoula, Mont. 1975.

50 von Campenhausen, *Formation*, p. 95.

51 Cosgrove, 'Justin Martyr', p. 219. It is interesting to note that Tertullian can use the same argument against Marcion in *adversus Marcionem* 2:21 and against 'the Jews' in *adversus Judaeos* 4. In both cases he is trying to show that the Old Testament legislation about the sabbath ought not to be taken literally, but points to something higher. 'The Jews' and Marcion are united in refusing to allegorize. (The substance of the argument, which is fairly convoluted, is that Joshua and the invading Israelites cannot have observed the sabbath *literally*, since they encircled Jericho every day for seven days, and any seven-day period will always include a Saturday. Thus the Jews themselves must recognize implicitly that literal sabbath-observance has to yield to higher duties, and can therefore have a fixed and permanent significance only if it is taken symbolically. This is an example of the 'condemned out of their own mouths!' style of argumentation which Tertullian so much enjoyed.)

52 For a defence of the idea that Trypho is a real person, a Hellenized Jew, see L. W. Barnard, 'The Old Testament and Judaism in the Writings of Justin Martyr', *VT* 14 (1974), pp. 395–406; see also A. von Harnack, *Judentum und Judenchristentum in Justins Dialog mit Trypho* (TU 39) Berlin 1913, pp. 47–92. Harnack thought that the Judaism being attacked in the *Dialogue* was real Judaism, not a straw man as would be argued by Cosgrove.

53 I find it hard to believe that the orthodox rejected Marcion because he was anti-Semitic, as argued by J. Massyngbaerde Ford, 'New Covenant, Jesus, and Canonization', in R. Brooks and J. J. Collins (eds), *Hebrew Bible or Old Testament?*, Notre Dame 1990, pp. 31–9: 'one can say that the Christians' defense of their Jewish heritage is found in their response to Marcion for his anti-Semitic attempt to expunge the Old Testament from the sacred books of the Christians' (p. 38). I am afraid that the early Church did little to eradicate anti-Jewish sentiment, and certainly did not defend the Old Testament for that reason. The anti-*gnostic* value of the Old Testament doctrine of creation seems far more likely to have been at the centre of their concerns, with little attention paid to the fact that the Old Testament was of Jewish provenance. As one can see from Tertullian, Christian writers at this time feel that the Jews, like Marcion, do not know how to read the Scriptures properly; once they are so read, it becomes clear that they are the Church's books rather than the Jews'. See Barbara Aland, 'Marcion: Versuch einer neuen Interpretation', *ZThK* 70 (1973), pp. 420–47, who argues that Marcion

needs to be understood against the background of gnosis, and also of Pauline teaching about the radical sinfulness of the human race. (She does not discuss Marcion's influence on the canon.)

54 W. Wrede, *Untersuchungen zum ersten Clemensbrief*, 1891, pp. 75–6; quoted in Harnack, *Bible Reading*, p. 41.

55 Cf. note 9 above.

56 Montanism's possible connection with the canon is discussed by Metzger, *Canon*, pp. 99–106, with bibliography. The related question, whether Montanist interest in the Holy Spirit is partly responsible for the many references to the Spirit in the Western text, lies beyond my competence. But so far as I can see, Montanist influence on the text of the New Testament would be compatible with either a positive or a negative answer to the question whether Montanists wanted their own oracles to be 'canonical'.

57 von Campenhausen, *Formation*, p. 227.

58 Harnack, *Origin*, pp. 179–80.

59 D. Weiss Halivni, *Peshat and Derash: Plain and Applied Meaning in Rabbinic Exegesis*, New York, 1994, argues that Jewish exegesis shows an increasing preference for the 'plain' sense (*peshat*) as time passes, so that commitment to *derash* – which bears some resemblance to allegorization – is a sign of antiquity, rather than of remoteness from the text being interpreted, as one might naively assume. The time-scale Halivni is working with, however, involves two millennia of Jewish exegesis, not the first few centuries of our era, so his arguments do not connect directly with mine; I cite them merely as an instructive parallel, a reminder that we should not assume an interest in the literal sense is more 'natural' than allegorization to readers of important religious texts. Cf. again Haran, 'Midrashic and Literal Exegesis', p. 22.

Chapter 3

1 Stuhlhofer, *Gebrauch*, p. 68: quoted above, p. 19.

2 'Man verlangt nicht selten, daß sie [scriptures] der *grauen Vorzeit* angehören. Die Menschen besonders der Alten Welt, soweit sie fromm sind, schätzen nicht das Neue ... Die Urzeit ist die Zeit der Götter und Heroen'; Leipoldt and Morenz, *Heilige Schriften*, p. 24.

3 Minnis, *Medieval Theory of Authorship*, p. 9.

4 Cf. J. A. Burrow, *Medieval Writers and their Work: Middle English Literature and its Background, 1100–1500*, Oxford 1982.

5 See above, p. 39.

6 *legi eum quidem oportet se puplicare vero in eclesia populo neque inter profetas conpletum numero neque inter apostolos in finem temporum potest*; see Hahneman, *Muratorian Fragment*, p. 7.

7 Jesus himself appears from the Gospels to have used Scripture very little – cf. Leipold and Morenz, *Heilige Schriften*, p. 7.

8 A. Jepsen, 'Kanon und Text des Alten Testaments', *TLZ* 74 (1949), cols 65–74.

9 See Sundberg, *Old Testament*. Tertullian, incidentally, talks as though this is how the Church 'selected' its Scriptures, when he discusses the book of Enoch in *de cultu feminarum* 1:3:3: *cum Enoch eadem scriptura etiam de Domino praedicarit, a nobis quidem nihil omnino reiciendum est quod pertineat ad nos. et legimus omnem scripturam aedificationi habilem divinitus inspirari. a Iudaeis postea iam videri propterea reiectam, sicut et cetera fere quae Christum sonant.*

10 H. Gese, 'Die dreifache Gestaltwerdung des Alten Testaments', in M. Klopfenstein (ed.), *Mitte der Schrift? Ein jüdisch-christliches Gespräch* (Judaica et Christiana 11), Berne 1987, pp. 299–328; *Vom Sinai zum Zion*, Munich 1974; *Zur biblischen Theologie*, Munich 1977, 2nd edn Tübingen 1983; and see the excellent discussion in Manfred Oeming, *Gesamtbiblische Theologien der Gegenwart*, Stuttgart 1985, pp. 104–19.

11 Frank Kermode, *The Genesis of Secrecy: On the Interpretation of Narrative*, Cambridge, Mass. and London 1979, p. 107.

12 Gershom Scholem, *Zur Kabbala und ihrer Symbolik*, Zurich 1960, ET *On the Kabbalah and its Symbolism*, London 1965, pp. 14–15.

13 von Campenhausen, *Formation*, p. 91.

14 Cf. Helmut Koester, *Ancient Christian Gospels: Their History and Development*, London 1990, pp. 376–7.

15 *Clementine Recognitions* 1:59: 'James the son of Alphaeus made a speech to the people in which he sought to show that Jesus was not to be believed on the grounds that the prophets had uttered predictions about him, but much rather it was to be believed that the prophets were really prophets, because Christ bears witness to them ... for it is not the lesser who bear witness to the greater, but the greater to the lesser' (*post hunc Iacobus Alfaei sermonem fecit ad populum, quo ostenderet, non ideo credendum esse Iesu, quia de eo prophetae praedixerint, sed ideo magis credendum esse prophetis, quod vere prophetae sint, quia eis Christus testimonium reddat ... decebat enim non ab inferioribus maiori, sed a maiore inferioribus fidei testimonium dari*). There are interesting parallels to these developments in nineteenth-century debates about the 'argument from prophecy', where a similar reversal sometimes occurred by which the vindication of the New Testament by the Old turned into an authentication of the Old by means of the New. In the work of William Whiston (1708) we also find the argument that Christians should correct the Old Testament, corrupted by Jewish prejudice, so that its congruence with the New may become more apparent – cf. the discussion of Justin below. There is a great deal of illuminating material on these themes in Joanna Davson, 'Critical and Conservative Treatments of Prophecy in Nineteenth-Century Britain', D.Phil. dissertation, Oxford 1991.

16 Brevard S. Childs, for example, writes: 'In the early church the question was not whether the Jewish scriptures were still canonical, but whether the claims of Jesus Christ could be sustained on the basis of scripture' (*Introduction to the Old Testament as Scripture*, London and Philadelphia 1979, pp. 41–2.) If my discussion is correct, this

attitude did occur in the early Church, but it was not the only strand in Christian thinking, which was highly complex in its relationship to the Old Testament.

17 See also Koester, *Ancient Christian Gospels*, pp. 395–402. There is also a very subtle discussion of how well-established *testimonia* caused other adjacent texts to be drawn into Christian apologetic in Barnabas Lindars, *New Testament Apologetic*, London 1961; in his view the process is already under way within the New Testament itself. Thus Jesus' use of Ps. 22.1 ('My God, my God, why hast thou forsaken me?') on the cross led Christians to take an interest in the whole Psalm, and to invent incidents such as the soldiers casting lots for his robe (John 19.23–4) in 'fulfilment' of v. 18. Justin does no more than apply the same methods in elaborating the gospel accounts.

18 Barnabas 6:11–12; see my discussion in Barton, *People of the Book?*, p. 15.

19 Very strikingly, Justin, like Theophilus and Tatian, claims to have become a Christian through reading the *Old* Testament – see Flesseman-van Leer, 'Prinzipien der Sammlung', p. 407.

20 See Harnack, *Origin*, p. 171, and the discussion in O. Gebhart, A. Harnack, and T. Zahn, *Patrum apostolicorum opera*, and Overbeck, Review in *TLZ* 30, col. 283. Overbeck argues that the *Shepherd* had to be placed in the Old Testament in the Middle Ages because it was a prophecy, and the idea that any New Testament book could be one had died out. He points out that Athanasius and Rufinus, on the other hand, clearly regard it as (potentially, though not actually) part of the New Testament. It is commonly said that the Muratorian Fragment, on the other hand, places the Wisdom of Solomon in the New Testament: cf. Hahneman, *Muratorian Fragment*, pp. 200–5. But William Horbury has argued that the listing of Wisdom follows the listing of the New Testament books because the author of the Fragment is following the practice, found also in Eusebius, Athanasius, Epiphanius, and Rufinus, of discussing 'disputed' books of both Testaments together, after the listing of both Old and New Testament books is complete. See W. Horbury, 'Wisdom of Solomon in the Muratorian Fragment', *JTS* 45 (1994), pp. 149–59.

21 Cf. *Dialogue* 48:4.

22 Flesseman-van Leer, 'Prinzipien der Sammlung', p. 407.

23 'Clemens ist augenscheinlich der Meinung, daß ein dunkler Text der γράφη zum Erweis seiner Erfüllung durch Korrektur verdeutlicht werden darf' (Frank, *Kanonbildung*, p. 24).

24 See above, chapter 2, note 21.

25 See N. A. Dahl, 'Widersprüche in der Bibel, ein altes hermeneutisches Problem', *Studia Theologica* 25 (1971), pp. 1–19.

26 See Grant, *Heresy and Criticism*, pp.90–1.

27 'Durch dieses Theologumenon ist es dem Verfasser des 2. Clemens-

briefes möglich, das Alte Testament den Juden aus der Hand zu winden und es der christlich-kirchlichen Interpretation von vornherein zu öffnen' (Frank, *Kanonbildung*, p. 96).

28 Cf. Justin, *Dialogue* 82: 'The prophetic gifts remain with us, even to the present time. And hence you ought to understand that (the gifts) formerly among your nation have been transferred to us' – a very clear case of what is nowadays sometimes called 'supersessionism'. See also the *Epistle of the Apostles*.

29 'Der apostolische Titel ist nicht die Voraussetzung, sondern der Resultat einer Prüfung, die in erster Linie nicht nach formalen, sondern nach sachlichen, sowohl historischen wie theologischen Gesichtspunkten durchgeführt wurde ... schlecht und recht mit den Mitteln, die die Wissenschaft von damals zu bieten hatte'; Hans von Campenhausen, 'Die Entstehung des Neuen Testaments', *Heidelberger Jahrbücher* 7, Berlin/Göttingen/Heidelberg 1963, pp. 1–12; repr. in E. Käsemann (ed.), *Das Neue Testament als Kanon*, Göttingen 1970, pp. 109–23. The quotation is on p. 10 (= p. 121).

30 Cf. E. P. Sanders and M. Davies, *Studying the Synoptic Gospels*, London 1989.

31 'Der Schrift gleich wertig, ja ihr sogar übergeordnet, sind die *logoi tou kuriou Iēsou*; dabei muß aber beachtet werden, daß nur den *logoi*, nicht den diese aufzeichnenden Schriften solche Autorität zukommt'; Frank, *Kanonbildung*, p. 24. Interestingly, this principle, once established, comes to be extended backwards into the Old Testament, and in '2 Clement' Old Testament quotations are frequently introduced not by *gegraptai* but by *legei* or *eipen*, the subject being *ho theos* or *ho logos prophētikos*, or more strikingly still *Christos* – cf. 2 Clem. 3:5; 13:2; 17:4. Conversely, words of Jesus (the saying 'it is no credit to you if you love those who love you') are cited with the formula *legei ho theos* in 13:4; and the provenance of such words does not matter: Matthew, Luke, and apocryphal sources are drawn on.

32 Knox, *Marcion*, p. 30.

33 *de carne Christi* 2; see Harnack, *Origin*, p. 181.

34 See Justin, *Apology* 1:66:3, 1:67:3; *Dialogue* 100–7.

35 Cosgrove, 'Justin Martyr', p. 223. See the detailed discussion in Koester, *Ancient Christian Gospels*, pp. 24–9.

36 Cosgrove, 'Justin Martyr', p. 226. On this see the important article by David Parker, 'Scripture is Tradition', *Theology* 94 (1991), pp. 11–17. Similarly, Ellen Flesseman-van Leer writes that in the first two centuries 'neither the words of Jesus which are adduced, nor the letters, are cited as really Holy Scripture. What the Lord said and did, what the apostles handed down, is absolutely true. One can even establish that their authority is equal to that of Holy Scripture. But the authority is the authority of Jesus himself, and whether or not his words were in written form is neither here nor there. The usual introductory formula for the logia: ὁ κύριος λέγει is not primarily the starting point for the development of a New Testament

Scripture; rather, it is a reference to tradition *in nuce*' ('. . . weder die
angeführten Worte Jesu noch die Briefe werden zitiert als wirklich
Heilige Schrift. Was der Herr gesagt und getan hat and was die
Apostel überliefert haben, ist absolut wahr. Man kann auch feststel-
len, daß ihre Autorität gleichwertig der der Heiligen Schrift war.
Aber die Autorität ist die Autorität Jesu selber, und ob seine
Worte geschrieben waren oder nicht, ist dabei belanglos. Die
übliche Eingangsformel der Logia: ὁ κύριος λέγει ist nicht an
erster Stelle der Ausgangspunkt für die Entwicklung einer neutestamentlichen Schrift; vielmehr ist sie ein Hinweis auf die Tradition
in nuce'); Flesseman-van Leer, 'Prinzipien der Sammlung', p. 406.

37 von Campenhausen, *Formation*, p. 202.

38 von Campenhausen, *Formation*, p. 191.

39 Peter Abelard, *Commentaria in Epistolam Pauli ad Romanos*, prol.

40 Koester, *Ancient Christian Gospels*, p. 86.

41 Koester, *Ancient Christian Gospels*, p. 159.

42 David Aune, *The New Testament in its Literary Environment*, Philadelphia 1987. See also Richard Burridge, *What are the Gospels? A Comparison with Graeco-Roman Biography* (SNTS MS 70), Cambridge
1992.

43 Eusebius, *Ecclesiastical History*, 3:24.

44 Eusebius, *Ecclesiastical History*, 6:14.

45 See, for example, the valuable discussion in A. C. Thiselton, *New
Horizons in Hermeneutics*, London 1992, pp. 471–514, which provides
a comprehensive guide to recent literary-critical approaches to the
Bible.

46 Origen, *Commentary on John*, 1:9.

47 Sundberg, 'Canon of the NT', p. 137.

48 On this see Koester, *Ancient Christian Gospels*, pp. 31–2. David
Parker, 'Scripture is Tradition', supports this interpretation from
the point of view of a textual critic. 'For at least some early Christians', he writes, 'it was more important to hand on the spirit of
Jesus' teaching than to remember the letter'; accordingly a biblical
critic who wishes to press the exact wording of a saying in the Gospels, as though Nestle-Aland simply was the New Testament, is
likely to err: 'a view based on a precise interpretation of the wording
may be shown to be an attempt to absolutize a particular post-Jesus
interpretation' (p. 15). Parker has shown how this works out in
practice in his article 'The Early Traditions of Jesus' Sayings on
Divorce', *Theology* 96 (1993), pp. 372–83.

49 See Roberts, 'The Codex', Roberts and Skeat, *The Birth of the Codex*,
and C. H. Roberts, *Manuscript, Society and Belief in Early Egypt*
(The Schweich Lectures for 1977), London 1979. Cf. also C. C.
McCown, 'Codex and Roll in the New Testament', *HThR* 34
(1941), pp. 219–50, who argues that the codex form was adopted
by Christians in Italy who were familiar with its use in business
and were not 'literary' people who would have used scrolls; for a
similar approach see also F. G. Kenyon, *Books and Readers in Ancient*

Greece and Rome, Oxford 1932, 2nd edn 1950, though he also suggests that the codex may have been attractive to Christians because it could contain the whole Bible: on this Roberts' verdict is that it could, but rarely did. On ancient book production there is an invaluable study based on references in Jerome: E. Arns, *La technique du livre d'après S. Jérome*, Paris 1953.

50 Trobisch, 'Endredaktion', pp. 30–4 and 102–19, criticizes Roberts in some detail, concentrating especially on his tendency to generalize from too little evidence. Nevertheless, the phenomena for which Roberts sought an explanation seem to be still with us.

51 K. L. Schmidt, 'Die Stellung der Evangelien in der allgemeinen Literaturgeschichte', ΕΥΧΑΡΙΣΤΗΡΙΟΝ (Gunkel Festschrift), Göttingen 1923, pp. 50–134.

52 Roberts, *Manuscript, Society and Belief*, p. 15.

53 Gamble suggests instead that the first Christian codex was a collection of the epistles of Paul, though with this too an absence of real empirical evidence makes the theory very conjectural. (See Harry Y. Gamble, 'The Pauline Corpus and the Early Christian Book', in W. S. Babcock (ed.), *Paul and the Legacies of Paul*, Dallas 1990, pp. 265–80).

54 S. Lieberman, *Hellenism in Jewish Palestine*, New York 1950, pp. 205–6.

55 Roberts and Skeat, *The Birth of the Codex*, pp. 59–60.

56 John Muddiman, 'The First-Century Crisis: Christian Origins', in S. Sutherland, J. L. Houlden, P. Clarke, and F. Hardy (eds), *The World's Religions*, London 1988, p. 104.

57 'Nicht allein im hertzen, sondern auch eusserlich die mündliche rede und buchstabeische wort im buch imer treiben und reiben, lesen und widerlesen, mit vleissigem auffmercken und nackdenken, was der heilige Geist damit meinet'; *WA* 50:659, 22–5 – cited in W. A. Graham, *Beyond the Written Word: Oral Aspects of Scripture in the History of Religion*, Cambridge 1987, p. 237.

58 Walter Ong, *Orality and Literacy*, London 1982.

59 Werner Kelber, *The Oral and the Written Gospel*, Philadelphia 1983. For a comprehensive account of orality and literacy in the ancient world see the important work by Rosalind Thomas, *Literacy and Orality in Ancient Greece*, Cambridge 1992.

60 Graham, *Beyond the Written Word*, esp. chapter 1.

61 Cf. Wilfred Cantwell Smith, *What is Scripture?*, London 1993, p. 50: 'A text might be treasured in written form yet effective in the community chiefly in oral/aural ways'.

62 Matt. 19.16–22; Mark 10.17–22; Luke 18.18–23. Koester, *Ancient Christian Gospels*, argues that since early Christian writers often omit redactional elements when quoting from the gospel-tradition, they probably had a sayings source (such as Q) rather than our Gospels. But quotation from memory is usually an equally possible explanation, especially if we are right in thinking that early writers did not *notice* the redactional differences between the different Gospels'

versions of the same story, just as most modern Christians do not notice them when the Bible is read in church. (This does not affect the question whether there was in fact a sayings source, a hypothesis which still has many defenders, perhaps more than it had twenty years ago – see J. Kloppenborg, *The Formation of Q: Trajectories in Ancient Wisdom Collections*, Philadelphia 1987, for a full discussion of such documents.) For a convincing statement of the case that early Christians sometimes quoted what they remembered of the Gospels from reading in church, rather than checking their memories against a written text, see R. E. Brown, 'The *Gospel of Peter* and Canonical Gospel Priority', *NTS* 33 (1987), pp. 321–43, esp. p. 339.

63 See M. D. Goulder, *Midrash and Lection in Matthew*, and *The Evangelists' Calendar*, London 1978. If P. F. Bradshaw is right in his *Daily Prayer in the Early Church*, pp. 19–20, there may be scant evidence for systematic Jewish liturgical reading of *any* part of the Bible early enough to provide support for lectionary theories. It could be argued, on the other hand, that Goulder's schemes are themselves the best evidence that Scripture was read in an ordered way in the synagogue, and then in the Church, because they are too good not to be true: the hypothesis that the material in the Bible has taken on its present shape accidentally is harder to believe than the alternative, lectionary-based theory. Despite the general consensus against Goulder's theories, I find this argument hard to refute. Aune, *New Testament*, p. 202, points out that rabbinic sermons, and also the divisions of the text of the Pentateuch in Philo, imply a regular system of pericopes from the first century AD at any rate; see also Philo, *Special Laws* 2:62.

64 Mark 5.21–43.

65 Cf. Leipoldt and Morenz, *Heilige Schriften*, p. 7.

66 Explicit only in the (?deutero-Pauline) Col. 4.16–17, a passage which generated the even more obviously spurious 'Letter to the Laodiceans'. But 1 Thess. 5.27 exhorts that the letter should be read to 'all the brethren'. But none of the Pauline letters except, perhaps, Philemon seems designed for an ephemeral existence. See the discussion in Aune, *New Testament*, pp. 192–3, which draws in also Rev. 1.3, 22.18, and 2 Baruch 86.1, which reads 'When you, therefore, receive this letter, read it carefully in your assemblies. And think about it in particular, however, on your fast days. And remember me by means of this letter in the same way as I remember you by means of this, and always.'

67 Eusebius, *Ecclesiastical History* 3:16.

68 J. Knox, *Philemon among the Letters of Paul*, Chicago 1935; E. Goodspeed, *The Formation of the New Testament*, Chicago 1926. See the discussion in Trobisch, 'Endredaktion', and *Paul's Letter Collection*.

69 'Es sollte dem ursprünglichen Sinn nicht Gewalt geschehen; man glaubte die Wahrheit zu heben, nicht zu entstellen'; J. Wellhausen, *Einleitung in die drei ersten Evangelien*, Berlin 1911, p. 3.

70 'Gerade die Kanonisierung forderte zur Exegese auf und damit

auch zur Kenntnisnahme von Schwierigkeiten, die bisher übergangen werden konnten. Origenes will noch den Berichtscharakter der Apostelschriften ernstnehmen; darum muß er sich um die Harmonisierung der Widersprüche bemühen. Er erkennt aber gleichzeitig die Grenzen der Harmonisierbarkeit und kommt auch von daher zu einer starken Betonung des kerygmatischen Momentes der Evangelien'; Merkel, *Die Widersprüche zwischen den Evangelien*, p. 265.

71 See Robert Morgan, 'The Hermeneutical Significance of Four Gospels', *Interpretation* 33 (1979), pp. 376–88, for a discussion of how the diversity of the four Gospels might be appropriated and used constructively in a modern dogmatic context.

72 Otto Piper, 'The Nature of the Gospel according to Justin Martyr', *JR* 41 (1961), pp. 155–68; the quotations are from p. 165.

73 *Dialogue* 78.5, 6; 88.

74 Cf. Ptolemy, *Ad Floram*, which foregrounds the words of Jesus; see Grant, *Heresy and Criticism*, p. 50.

75 Eusebius, *Ecclesiastical History* 3:39:1. See also Loveday Alexander, 'The "Living Voice": Scepticism towards the Written Word in Early Christian and in Graeco-Roman Texts', in D. J. A. Clines, S. E. Fowl, and S. E. Porter (eds), *The Bible in Three Dimensions: Essays in Celebration of Forty Years of Biblical Studies in the University of Sheffield* (JSOT Suppl. Series 87), Sheffield 1990, pp. 221–49, with a full bibliography. The idea that the living voice was superior to the dead letter was a *topos* in the ancient world, and it could be seen as polite to apologize for writing instead of teaching orally – a kind of pretentiousness, it was felt. See Clement, *Stromateis* 1:1:7:1, which refers to the lengthy book which will give the reader so many hours of work as 'just notes', *hypomnēmata*. L. Vischer, 'Die Rechtfertigung der Schriftstellerei in der alten Kirche', *TZ* 12 (1956), pp. 320–36, suggests a special Christian reason for the perceived need to apologize for writing, based on the idea that the Gospel was originally communicated by Christ in direct contact with people, and therefore that it must continue to be communicated by the living voice rather than by written words. We have seen that there is some basis for this idea. Nevertheless, the fact that a preference for orality is a *topos* of ancient literature should not be overlooked. Graham, *Beyond the Written Word*, notes that in some religious traditions and cultures oral transmission is cultivated on the grounds that it is more secure than written – contrary to modern Western assumptions. He draws on Zoroastrian and Hindu evidence here (pp. 66 and 72); see also Thomas, *Literacy and Orality*, pp. 68–73. This should be distinguished from the religious taboo against writing down mysteries, for which see Leipoldt and Morenz, *Heilige Schriften*, p. 5.

76 *Hypotyposes* 8 (and see Eusebius, *Ecclesiastical History* 2:1:4); cf. Pirqe Aboth 1:1: 'Moses received the Law from Sinai and com-

mitted it to Joshua, and Joshua to the elders, and the elders to the prophets, and the prophets committed it to the men of the Great Synagogue.'

77 Gittin 60b, Temurah 14b; cf. j.Peah II.6, 17a, j.Megillah IV.1, 74d.

78 m. Megillah 2:1.

79 Cf. Thomas, *Literacy and Orality*, p. 124, for parallels in classical Greece: 'Political speeches were supposedly never written out; forensic speeches might be, but were delivered from memory.'

80 Lieberman, *Hellenism in Jewish Palestine*, p. 207.

81 Scholem, *On the Kabbalah and its Symbolism*, pp. 67–8.

82 See chapter 1, note 54 above.

83 Erubin 54b; see Birger Gerhardsson, *Memory and Manuscript: Oral Tradition and Written Transmission in Rabbinic Judaism and Early Christianity* (Acts Seminarii Neotestamentici Upsaliensis 22), Lund and Copenhagen 1961. There is a useful discussion of the writing down of the Oral Law in J. Weingreen, 'Oral Torah and Written Record', in F. F. Bruce and E. G. Rupp (eds), *Holy Book and Holy Tradition*, Manchester 1968, pp. 54–67.

84 Gerhardsson, *Memory and Manuscript*, p. 130; see also Graham, *Beyond the Written Word*, p. 35.

85 G. Widengren, 'Tradition and Literature in Early Judaism', *Numen* 12 (1965), pp. 42–7, argues against Gerhardsson that we do not *know* whether Jewish or Christian tradition was passed on orally or in writing. This is undoubtedly true, if 'know' is taken very strictly; but some conjectures about it are more plausible than others.

86 Birger Gerhardsson, 'Oral Tradition (New Testament)', in R. J. Coggins and J. L. Houlden (eds), *A Dictionary of Biblical Interpretation*, London 1990, pp. 498–501; the quotation is from p. 500.

87 Gerhardsson, 'Oral Tradition (New Testament)', p. 500. Cf. McCown, 'Codex and Roll', p. 238: 'Each writer would feel quite free to modify, abridge, and supplement the record in conformity with other oral or written accounts that had come to notice or in the intent of vividness, brevity, missionary effectiveness, ethical need, and religious faith.'

Chapter 4

1 Thomas, *Literacy and Orality*, p. 74, referring to the following varied studies: M. T. Clanchy, *From Memory to Written Record*, London 1979; D. Cressy, 'Books as Totems in Seventeenth-Century England and New England', *Journal of Library History* 21 (1986), pp. 92–106; S. Franklin 'Literacy and Documentation in Early Medieval Russia', *Speculum* 60 (1985), pp. 1–38; and P. Burke, 'The Uses of Literacy in Early Modern Italy', in P. Burke and R. Porter (eds), *The Social History of Language*, Cambridge 1987, pp. 21–42. See now also the fascinating study of Mary Carruthers, *The Book of Memory: A Study of Memory in Medieval Culture*, Cambridge 1990.

2 A useful study of the supposed 'council' can be found in S. J. D.

Cohen, 'The Significance of Yavneh', *HUCA* 55 (1984), pp. 27–53. For a full discussion and bibliography, see Gerhard Maier, 'Der Abschluß des jüdischen Kanons und das Lehrhaus von Jabne', in G. Maier (ed.), *Der Kanon der Bibel*, Giessen 1990, pp. 1–24.

3 See especially the discussion in Beckwith, *Old Testament Canon*, pp. 71 and 278–86, and 'Formation', who regards it as more or less obvious that 'defiling the hands' is equivalent to 'being canonical'.

4 M. D. Goodman, 'Sacred Scripture and "Defiling the Hands"', *JTS* 41 (1990), pp. 99–107.

5 Goodman, 'Sacred Scripture'. According to the Mishnah, the Pharisees countered the Sadducees' objections to some of their rulings about purity by arguing that certain things were deemed contaminating in order to keep them from casual contact. Thus the bones of an animal do not confer uncleanness, yet human bones (even those of the High Priest!) do. The explanation is: 'As is our love for them, so is their uncleanness – that no man make spoons of his father or mother. He said to them, Even so the Holy Scriptures: as is our love for them, so is their uncleanness' (m. Yadaim 4:6). See the helpful discussion of this passage in Christine Schams, 'The Attitude towards Sacred and Secular Written Documents in First-Century Judaism', M. Phil. dissertation, Oxford 1993, p. 9.

6 t. Yadaim 2:12: 'The thongs and straps which one sewed on to a book, even though it is not permitted to keep them, impart defilement to hands.' m. Yadaim 3:4 rules that the blank spaces in a scroll make the hands unclean. 3:5 adds that single sheets of a scriptural scroll have the power to defile, provided they contain at least 85 letters – as many as in the passage beginning 'And whenever the ark set out, Moses said, "Arise, O Lord, and let thy enemies be scattered..."' (Num. 10:35–6), which rabbinic authorities often declare to be a book in itself.

7 James Barr, *Holy Scripture: Canon, Authority, Criticism*, Oxford and Philadelphia 1983, pp. 50–1.

8 Goodman, 'Sacred Scripture', p. 100.

9 Barton, *Oracles of God*, p. 92.

10 I have noticed that reviewers and others often misunderstand what I have written on this subject, usually by failing to note the distinction made in chapter 1 of the present book between canonization as inclusion and canonization as exclusion. To say that no books in the present Hebrew Bible were of doubtful status in the first century AD is not the same as saying that the canon was then closed, i.e. that some books had been excluded and the number of scriptural books was deemed to be complete. This misunderstanding seems to underlie some of Beckwith's criticism of my position: see R. T. Beckwith, 'A Modern Theory of the Old Testament Canon', *VT* 41 (1991), pp. 385–95. I do not see why the inclusive/exclusive point has proved so difficult to grasp, but almost all responses to Sundberg show that the misunderstanding of it has been a well-established tradition in scholarship for thirty years now.

11 Damascus Document 15: 'he should not swear by (the Name), nor by Aleph and Lamed (Elohim), nor by Aleph and Daleth (Adonai)'.

12 m. Sanhedrin 7:5.

13 That pronouncing the most holy Name of God could be blasphemy recalls Tacitus' comment on the Jews, *profana illis omnia, quae apud nos sancta* ('all the things that are holy to us are profane to them'). The care with which the Name was hedged about can be seen from Targum Jonathan on Deut. 32:3, according to which Moses learned not to utter the Name until he had dedicated his mouth with 85 letters, making 21 words (cf. note 6 above; I am grateful to Dr Gregory Glazov for calling my attention to this passage). Ecclus 23.9–10 warns against frequent utterance of the Name.

14 A modern parallel may help to make the point. The Saudi Arabian flag is never flown at half-mast, even when the king dies. This looks like unbelievable *lèse-majesté* in such a kingdom, until one learns that the flag bears words from the Qur'an ('There is no God but God, and Muhammad is the prophet of God'), including the Name of God himself, whose sanctity overrules the normal customs of human mourning rites. (See *Die Zeit* 34:17 (August 1990), p. 3. I am grateful to Mr Alex Eaglestone for detailed information about the flag.)

15 According to some authorities there were three such copies, each one containing one particular error from which it was named (*sēpher mā'ôn, sēpher zaʿʿtûtî*, and *sēpher hîʾ*; cf. L. Blau, *Studien zum althebräischen Buchwesen und zur biblischen Litteratur- und Textgeschichte*, Strasbourg 1902, pp. 97–114). Older tradition speaks of a single scroll of the Temple Court: m. Moed Katan 3:4. According to Baba Bathra 14b it was unique in having only one roller – so how it was used remains a mystery. See also S. Talmon, 'The Three Scrolls of the Law that were found in the Temple Court', *Textus* 2 (1962), pp. 14–27.

16 m. Kelim 15.

17 t. Kelim 2:5, 8.

18 It will be apparent that these reflections owe a good deal to the theories of Mary Douglas in *Purity and Danger*, London 1969.

19 Ludwig Blau, *Zur Einleitung in die Heilige Schrift*, Budapest 1894, pp. 12–16.

20 Metaphorically speaking – there is no evidence that gloves were actually used in Jewish worship. They were elsewhere: see A. Alföldi, 'Die Ausgestaltung des monarchischen Zeremoniells am römischen Kaiserhofe', *Mitteilungen des deutschen archäologischen Instituts* (Römische Abteilung) 49 (1934), pp. 1–118, who reviews the custom of presenting gifts to the emperor with covered hands. A useful reminder that Jewish customs, though in detail unique, belonged to a pattern of observances familiar in the ancient world, or else deliberately negated those customs – in either case the environment provided an interpretative framework for what was done or not done.

21 Relevant texts are discussed in Leiman, *Canonization*, pp. 72–8; cf. my *Oracles of God*, pp. 64–8.

22 See Shabbat 116a, t. Shabbat 13:5, t. Yadaim 2:13. It should be noted that Christian books, though they used *nomina sacra* for many holy words, which being contractions would not in Jewish eyes constitute 'names', sometimes transcribed the Tetragrammaton itself in Hebrew characters. This would make them *prima facie* holy texts, which is why the ruling was needed. Sometimes the divine Name is in palaeo-Hebrew script, but sometimes in square script: several patristic authors say that the Jewish name for God was *pipi* (πιπι), approximately how one would read the Tetragrammaton if one thought of the Hebrew letters as Greek letters. See, for example, Jerome *epistola* 25 *ad Marcellam: tetragrammaton . . . quod quidam non intelligentes propter elementorum similitudinem, cum in graecis libris reppererint*, πιπι *legere consueverunt* ('Some people, not understanding the tetragrammaton, when they find it in Greek books, were accustomed to read it as πιπι because of the similarity of the letters').

23 For the material published before 1960, see K. G. Kuhn, *Konkordanz zu den Qumrantexten*, Göttingen 1960, p. 85. There are in fact about five examples, in one of which *yhwdh* (Judah) may be suspected as the correct reading, and in two others some form of the verb *hyh* (to be). In D. Barthélemy and J. T. Milik, *Qumran Cave 1* (Discoveries in the Judaean Desert 1), Oxford 1955, p. 100, Barthélemy and Milik contend that 'l'emploi du Tétragrammaton n'est pas à exclure à priori d'une composition non canonique; il y en a des exemples parmi les fragments non-bibliques de 2Q et 4Q' ('The use of the Tetragrammaton cannot be excluded a priori in a non-canonical composition; there are examples among the non-biblical fragments of 2Q and 4Q'). It is however, even on the most favourable reading of doubtful places, very unusual. There is a full discussion of the devices used to avoid it in M. Delcor, 'Des diverses manières d'écrire le tétragramme sacré dans les anciens documents hébraïques', *Revue de l'histoire des religions* 147 (1955), pp. 145–73. More recent work on the Scrolls has yielded a few, but not many, examples of the Tetragrammaton in non-biblical texts. We cannot absolutize the rule against it, but it is not usual. Where it does appear, it is commonly in palaeo-Hebrew script, and more often it is indicated with dots as in the Community Rule. For a full summary of the evidence in major Qumran documents, see P. W. Skehan, 'The Divine Name at Qumran, in the Masada Scroll, and in the Septuagint', *Bulletin of the International Organization for Septuagint and Cognate Studies* 13 (1980), pp. 14–44, together with further discussion in A. Pietersma, 'Kyrios or Tetragram: A Renewed Quest for the Original LXX', in A. Pietersma and C. Cox (eds), *De Septuaginta: Studies in Honour of John William Wevers on his Sixty-Fifth Birthday*, Mississauga, Ontario 1984, pp. 85–101. A useful and up-to-date survey can be found in Emanuel Tov, *Textual Criticism of the Hebrew Bible*, Minneapolis 1992.

24 See O. Betz, 'Das Problem des "Kanons" in den Texten von Qumran', in Maier (ed.), *Kanon*, pp. 70–101, esp. p. 73. (I have been unable to consult H.-Aa. Mink, 'The Use of Scripture in the Temple Scroll and the Status of the Scroll as Law', *SJOT* 1987, pp. 20–50.)

25 The idea continued after the Middle Ages. Elias Levita comments that Hebrew is called the holy language (*ha-lashôn ha-qādôsh*) 'because the words of the Law, the Prophets, and all the holy statements were uttered therein, and because the Creator is therein called by his holy names (*niqrâ' ha-bōrê' bāh bᵉ shēmôtâw ha-qᵉdôshîm*). See C. D. Ginsburg (ed.), *The Massoreth ha-Massoreth of Elias Levita*, London 1867, p. 195.

26 Cf. m. Erubin 13a: 'R. Ishmael said, "My son, be careful in your work, for it is the work of God; if you omit a single letter, or write a letter too many, you will destroy the whole world." '

27 Joseph Gikatila, *Sha'are 'Orah* 2b; cited in Scholem, *On the Kabbalah*, p. 42.

28 Soferim 5:12.

29 Soferim 5:2–3.

30 Soferim 5:17.

31 Of course 'Solomon' may have been treated as a divine Name because by this time the interpretation of the Song as an allegory of God's love for Israel had already led to an equivalence between Solomon and God.

32 See G. Scholem, 'The Name of God and the Linguistic Theory of the Kabbalah', *Diogenes* 79–80 (1972), pp. 59–194. I am grateful to Dr Tal Goldfajn for making me aware of this article. For Christian variations on the theme of the Name of God, see B. P. Copenhaver, 'Lefèvre d'Étaples, Symphorien Champier, and the Secret Names of God', *Journal of the Warburg and Courtauld Institutes* 40 (1977), pp. 189–211. To pursue these themes further would lead us too far from the matter in hand.

33 Sotah 47a, cf. Sanhedrin 107b, and see L. Ginzberg, *Legends of the Jews* IV, Philadelphia 1982–3. See G. Scholem, *Major Trends in Jewish Mysticism*, Jerusalem 1941, p. 182.

34 Abodah Zarah 17b–18b.

35 Roberts, *Manuscript, Society and Belief*, pp. 10–40.

36 Chrysostom, Homily 72.

37 Cf. Trobisch, 'Endredaktion', p. 43.

38 I am grateful to Christine Schams for helpful conversations on this subject. The origin of the *nomina sacra* is a mystery. There may (according to Thomas, *Literacy and Orality*, p. 61) have been some anticipation of the system in Greek graffiti of the classical period, where single letters may be used to denote gods – e.g. 'A' for Athene. But the reason is entirely obscure. Real parallels to the characteristic contracted forms – XC, ΘC, etc. – seem to be lacking – so much so that U. Wilcken has argued that it was probably the innovation of a single person, 'who deliberately avoided what was customary in order to ensure the expression of the singularity of the

words' ('der gerade absichtlich das Gebräuchliche mied, um den Eindruck der Singularität dieser Worte zu sichern'); L. Mitteis and U. Wilcken (eds), *Grundzüge und Chrestomathie der Papyruskunde* I, p. xiv; cited in Trobisch, 'Endredaktion', p. 30.

39 Details of the system of *nomina sacra* are in Trobisch, 'Endredaktion'; see also Roberts, *Manuscript, Society and Belief*, pp. 26–48.

40 Barnabas 9:8.

41 Clement, *Stromateis* 6:11.

42 Cf. above, ch. 3, n. 56.

43 James Barr, 'A New Look at Kethibh-Qere', OS 21 (1981), pp. 19–37; cf. also ' "Guessing" in the Septuagint', in D. Fraenkel, U. Quast, and J. W. Wevers (eds), *Studien zur Septuaginta – Robert Hanhart zu Ehren*, Göttingen 1990, pp. 19–34.

44 On this see E. J. Revell, 'Masorah' and 'Masoretes' in *ABD* 4, pp. 592–3 and 593–4, and W. S. Morrow, 'Kethib and Qere', *ABD* 4, pp. 24–30. Both writers are in essential agreement with Barr. Barr argues that translation was also sometimes designed to be neutral in respect of interpretation, to deliver a kind of 'copy' of the original Hebrew to the reader with obscurities left obscure. Literal translation, like the KQ system, could be seen as a *refusal* to solve the puzzles of the text. See J. Barr, *The Typology of Literalism in Ancient Biblical Translation* (Nachrichten der Akademie der Wissenschaften in Göttingen I. Philologisch-historische Klasse 11), Göttingen 1979, pp. 275–325. Aquila's insistence on rendering the accusative particle *et* by Greek *sun* would similarly be an example of the desire to produce a sort of equivalent of the text, rather than what we should see as a fluent translation.

45 H. H. Schmid, *Wesen und Geschichte der Weisheit*, Berlin 1966, pp. 74–8, draws attention to the phenomenon in New Kingdom Egypt of old texts being valued *because* they were incomprehensible. 'Reading' such texts was no longer a matter of understanding them, but of decoding them, or even of being silent in the face of mystery.

46 Professor William Johnstone pointed out to me that, against this, in most places the Masoretes will have read the text much as we do, extracting a normal sense from it; incomprehensiblity is far from being the norm in the Hebrew Bible. I am sure this is both true and important. Nevertheless it seems to me that the difficult cases, rather than the easy ones, were at the source of Masoretic *theories* about the text – much as for Christian exegetes such as Origen it was the obscurities in the text that were foregrounded, in order to justify the theory of a cryptic divine message beneath the surface of the text.

47 Graham, *Beyond the Written Word*, p. 6.

48 Smith, *What is Scripture?*, pp. 234–5.

49 Graham, *Beyond the Written Word*, p. 111.

50 Graham, *Beyond the Written Word*, p. 104.

51 L. G. Kelly, *The True Interpreter: A History of Translation Theory and Practice in the West*, Oxford 1979, p. 63.

52 Burrow, *Medieval Writers*, p. 47. There is an extensive literature on the ancient tendency to read aloud, even when solitary. See Thomas, *Literacy and Orality*, p. 13: 'Solitary and silent reading were almost unknown. In both Greece and Rome written texts, particularly literary ones, were usually read aloud.' The classic study is B. M. W. Knox, 'Silent Reading in Antiquity', *Greek, Roman, and Byzantine Studies* 9 (1968), pp. 421–35; see also his 'Books and Readers in the Greek World', *Cambridge History of Classical Literature*, ed. P. E. Easterling and B. M. Walker I, 1985, p. 1–16. Still important is J. Balogh, ' "Voces paginarum": Beiträge zur Geschichte des lauten Lesens und Schreibens', *Philologus* 82 (1927), pp. 84–109 and 212–40.

53 *etsi nos non intelligimus quae de ore proferimus, illae tamen virtutes, quae nobis adsunt, intelligunt et velut carmine invitatae adesse nobis et ferre auxilium delectantur*: Leipoldt and Morenz, *Heilige Schriften*, p. 188. Smith, *What is Scripture?*, p. 156, cites a Buddhist parallel: 'Some outstanding Japanese religious leaders ... wrote some of their own works in Chinese, which were later chanted liturgically without being "understood" in the modern secular sense of that word.' Much the same could be said about the use of Latin in the Catholic Church before the Second Vatican Council, in the case of congregations who did not 'understand' it in the ordinary sense; it was sometimes defended (as 'Prayer Book English' is now) as conveying a sense of divine mystery and transcendence more important than the mere transfer of information in intelligible words. The experience of people in many religions suggests that this defence – whether or not it is convincing – is certainly not vacuous.

Chapter 5

1 Christoph Dohmen and Manfred Oeming, *Biblischer Kanon: Warum und Wozu? Eine Kanontheologie* (Quaestiones Disputatae 137), Freiburg/Basle/Vienna 1992.

2 Dohman and Oeming, *Biblischer Kanon*, p. 79.

3 On which see esp. Smith, *What is Scripture?*

4 On reader-response criticism, associated especially with the work of Wolfgang Iser, see Thiselton, *New Horizons in Hermeneutics*, pp. 515–55.

5 See Julius Wellhausen, *Prolegomena to the History of Israel*, Edinburgh 1885 (repr. as *Prolegomena to the History of Ancient Israel*, New York 1957), pp. 171–227 (from the German *Geschichte Israels I.*, Marburg 1878; 2nd edn 1883, as *Prolegomena zur Geschichte Israels*).

6 e.g. 1 Clement 47–50.

7 Martin Noth, 'The Laws in the Pentateuch: Their Assumptions and Meaning', in his *The Laws in the Pentateuch and Other Essays*, Edinburgh and London 1966, pp. 1–107; the quotation is from p. 87.

German original: *Die Gesetze im Pentateuch (ihre Voraussetzungen und ihr Sinn)* (Schriften der Königsberger Gelehrten Gesellschaft, geisteswissenschaftliche Klasse 17), Halle 1940.

8 Cf. my discussion in *Oracles of God*, pp. 154–72.

9 Josephus, *Antiquities* 6:340–2.

10 Cf. Barton, *Oracles of God*, pp. 214–34.

11 The expression is taken from David Aune, *Prophecy in Early Christianity and the Ancient Mediterranean World*, Grand Rapids 1983.

12 Barton, *Oracles of God*, pp. 179–202.

13 See Justin, *Dialogue* 81; Irenaeus, *adversus haereses* 2:31:3; 3:23:7; 4:20:2, 11; 5:26:1–3; 5:35:2.

14 Origen, *contra Celsum* book 4, esp. 1–50.

15 Josephus, *contra Apionem* 1:37–43.

16 See Shabbat 30b.

17 Cf. Justin, *Dialogue* 125.

18 J. D. Levenson, *God and the Persistence of Evil*, San Francisco and London 1988, pp. 37–8. The rabbinic quotations are from Tanḥuma *kî tēsē* 11. It should be said that some aspects of rabbinic interpretation, especially the almost playful exploitation of ambiguities in the written text, are related to the peculiarities of a consonantal writing system. It would be hard to transfer most of it to texts in a phonetic system which marked vowels, especially one so nearly perfect as the Greek alphabet. In a sense a purely consonantal text approximates more to a memory-jogger or set of rough notes, except for texts whose content is highly predictable. Modern Israeli Hebrew has reduced ambiguity by, among other things, consistent use of vowel-letters, but in the biblical text this is still chaotic. In ancient times the difficulty of reading Hebrew by contrast with Greek or Latin was commented on, and Jerome notes that the form of Hebrew letters compounds the problem: there are only twenty-two letters, yet a number of them look the same as others! Blau cites a comment of Jerome's: *ad nocturnum lumen nequaquam valeamus hebraeorum volumina relegere, quae etiam ad solis dieique fulgorem litterarum nobis parvitate saecantur* ('by night we cannot possibly read the volumes of the Hebrews, which even by day in full sunlight are obscured for us by the smallness of the letters'; reading *caecantur* for *saecantur*. I have been unable to locate this passage, which Blau ascribes to the prologue to Ezekiel, 20). Small and barely legible texts were not really meant for anyone who needed to *read* them, in the sense of working out what they meant; they were for those who knew the biblical text already and needed just a written reminder. Blau commented, 'where there was so great a knowledge of scripture, the text really served simply as an aid, like catchwords, because for every word that was actually read another ten presented themselves of their own accord' ('bei einer solch immensen Kenntniss der Schrift diente der Text eigentlich nur als Hilfsmittel, wie etwa Stichworte, denn zu jedem wirklich gelesenen Wort stellten sich andere zehn von selbst ein'; Blau, *Buchwesen*, p. 80). Many writing systems have

arisen to support memory rather than to make it possible to read previously unknown words or phrases: on this see W. C. Brice, 'The Principles of Non-Phonetic Writing', in W. Haas (ed.), *Writing without Letters*, Manchester 1976, pp. 29–44; see also James Barr, 'Reading a Script without Vowels' in the same volume, pp. 71–100: 'The reader has read the text many times before. In such a case the written (mainly consonantal) text serves as a sort of mnemonic' (p. 83).

19 See James Barr, 'Vocalization and the Analysis of Hebrew among the Ancient Translators', VTS 16 (1967), pp. 1–11, with reference to W. Bacher, *Die exegetische Terminologie der jüdischen Traditionsliteratur* I, pp. 108 and 119ff.

20 See Ginsburg (ed.), *The Massoreth ha-Massoreth of Elias Levita*, p. 111.

21 See esp. Scholem, 'The Name of God and the Linguistic Theory of the Kabbala'.

22 Gerhardsson, *Memory and Manuscipt*, pp. 40–1.

23 Perhaps the main Christian examples in modern times would be the interpretative system of the *Scofield Reference Bible*, where a doctrinal framework which is already 'known' constrains the exegesis of every verse, often producing interpretations far removed from the 'natural' sense of the text.

24 See J. A. Sanders, *Torah and Canon*, Philadelphia 1972. Proposals of the same logical type can be found in J. Blenkinsopp, *A History of Prophecy in Israel*, London 1984, pp. 116–17, on the fact that Malachi is the last of the prophets, and Smith, *What is Scripture?*, pp. 94–5: 'Among the more decisive differences between the Jewish "Bible", whatever one call it, and the Christian Old Testament is the order of the books constituting them. The two begin in the same fashion. . . . Opening with the creation of the world has given the vision of each community a cosmic context for their life and faith. . . . In contrast, the two scriptures end quite divergently. In the Jewish case their Bible closes with II Chronicles and the edict of Cyrus, "Let them go up" to Jerusalem; in the Christian case, their Old Testament closes with Malachi and the prediction of a coming messianic figure.' As is well known, there is little evidence that Chronicles formed the last book of the Hebrew Bible in ancient times, though it does now; even in the Leningrad codex, which is the 'standard' for printed Bibles, the order is in fact Chronicles, Ezra, Nehemiah. Similarly, the Christian Bible in the LXX arrangement quite commonly ends with Isaiah (possibly even better than Malachi if the next book of the Bible is to be Matthew); on the LXX arrangement in general see J. Goldingay, *Approaches to Old Testament Interpretation*, Leicester 1981, pp. 138–45, and see H. B. Swete, *An Introduction to the Old Testament in Greek*, Cambridge 1900, pp. 218ff., for details of the various LXX arrangements. Smith's point can stand as an account of the meaning that might legitimately be found in the present arrangement of Jewish and Christian Bibles. It is less clear that anyone *intended* them to have that meaning, and quite uncertain

whether anyone in antiquity so interpreted them. The question at once plunges us into the modern debate about authorial intention, texts as free-standing entities, and the status and function of the canon. My present purpose is not to suggest that purely historical evidence can give us an answer to these questions, but only to establish what the historical evidence is, and to remind the reader that it is extremely thin.

25 On the formation of the Pauline corpus see Trobisch, *Paul's Letter Collection*. Trobisch believes that a fixed order emerged very early; for the contrary view, which seems more plausible to me, see McCown, 'Codex and Roll', who points out that (for example) Marcion seems to have known ten Pauline epistles, Polycarp thirteen, and that the order varies: the Chester Beatty Paul has Romans, Hebrews, Corinthians, Ephesians, Galatians ... 'Each individual, copying for himself or his church, did what was right in his own eyes' (McCown, p. 246); cf. p. 249: 'The books themselves, their collection into codices, and their eventual canonization were all informal, spontaneous, democratic processes. They were products of the vigorous life of the early church.'

26 See my detailed discussion of this passage in Barton, *Oracles of God*, pp. 19–21.

27 N. M. Sarna, 'The Order of the Books', in C. Berlin (ed.), *Studies in Jewish Bibliography, History and Literature in Honor of I. Edward Kiev*, New York 1971, pp. 407–13.

28 Blau, *Buchwesen*, p. 59.

29 See J. Blenkinsopp, *Prophecy and Canon: A Contribution to the Study of Jewish Origins*, Notre Dame 1977.

30 See Hahneman, *Muratorian Fragment*, pp. 183–7. The order recognized by Eusebius is normal in Eastern manuscripts, but in the West other orderings were for some time preferred, particularly ones which placed the 'apostolic' Gospels (Matthew and John) first.

31 Irenaeus' order varies from passage to passage, though it is never (as Hahneman points out) the same as our order.

32 Peter Abelard, *Commentaria in Epistolam Pauli ad Romanos*, prol. He also makes the more prosaic point that Romans is addressed to the chief church.

33 The standard English-language commentary, W. McKane, *Proverbs* (OTL), London 1970, at no point even considers the possibility that the aphorisms in Proverbs might have a different meaning as part of the collection than they have when taken individually.

34 See Childs, *Introduction*, pp. 515–16.

35 I owe this information to a seminar paper by Professor R. J. Clifford.

36 Cf. L. B. Wolfenson, 'Implications of the Place of the Book of Ruth in Editions, Manuscripts, and Canon of the Old Testament', *HUCA* 1 (1924), pp. 90–129, esp. pp. 154–5.

37 *The Times*, 1 August 1992.

38 On these various currents of thought see my comments in J. Barton, *Reading the Old Testament: Method in Biblical Study*, London 1984, 2nd edn 1996.

39 See Childs, *Introduction; Biblical Theology of the Old and New Testaments*, Philadelphia 1992.

40 See Sanders, *Torah and Canon*, and the various articles collected in *From Sacred Story to Sacred Text: Canon as Paradigm*, Philadelphia 1987.

41 C. Northrop Frye, *The Great Code: The Bible and Literature*, London, Melbourne, and Henley 1982.

42 Kermode, *Genesis of Secrecy*. The volume Kermode edited with Robert Alter, *The Literary Guide to the Bible*, London 1987, applies this style of criticism to the whole Bible (Hebrew Scriptures + New Testament, excluding the Apocrypha).

43 My own attempt to do this in *Reading the Old Testament*, pp. 100–1, was rewarded with a sharp rebuke from Childs: see his *Old Testament Theology in a Canonical Context*, London 1985, p. 6: 'it is a basic misunderstanding to try to describe a canonical approach as a form of structuralism (*contra* Barton)'. I believe this is a serious misunderstanding of my position, but the question is not of primary concern here.

44 Gamble, *New Testament Canon*, p. 79.

45 Gamble, *New Testament Canon*, p. 76. For an illuminating discussion of the implications of there being four Gospels see Morgan, 'Hermeneutical Significance'. The titles of the Gospels provide a clear hermeneutical direction for the reader. They do not use the term 'Gospel' as the name of a literary genre, but instead speak of each 'Gospel' as '[the gospel] according to X'. Thus the reader is invited to think of there being one 'gospel' attested by four witnesses (see also Trobisch, 'Endredaktion', p. 54, who however considers that *euangelion* is intended as the name of a genre). Titles are in general a very strong way of constraining the interpretation of texts: cf. G. Genette, 'Structure and Function of the Title in Literature', *Critical Enquiry* 14 (1988), pp. 692–720. Genette makes the point that the 'readership' of titles is much larger than that of the books they entitle, and that a title can thus paradoxically inform more people than the book itself. Certainly the hermeneutical point here, that each of the four Gospels is to be read as *the* gospel (in one version) is conveyed much more by the titles than by the text itself. If we suppose that one of the evangelists – say Luke – intended to eliminate all other Gospels by his work, then the title appended to his book by some unknown editor thwarted his purpose more effectively in two words than any number of alterations to his text could have done. Titles can thus subvert the works to which they are appended: think of Magritte's famous picture of a pipe with the legend, 'Ceci n'est pas une pipe.'

46 Muratorian Fragment 11. 47–50, *cum ipse beatus apostolus paulus sequens prodecessoris sui Iohannis ordinem nonnisi (c)nomenati semptae eccles(e)iis scribat . . . una tamen per omnem orbem terrae ecclesia deffusa esse denoscitur.*

Et Iohannis eñi In apocalebsy licet septē eccleseis scribat tamen omnibus dicit verū.

47 See Harry Y. Gamble, *The Textual History of the Letter to the Romans* (Studies and Documents 42), Grand Rapids 1977, pp. 115–24.

48 See N. A. Dahl, 'The Particularity of the Pauline Epistles as a Problem in the Ancient Church', *Neotestamentica et Patristica* (*NT* Suppl. 6), Leiden 1962, pp. 261–71.

49 *adversus Marcionem* 5:17:1: *nihil autem de titulis interest, cum ad omnes apostolus scripserit dum ad quosdam.*

50 See Pesahim 6b, and Mekhilta on Exod. 15.9–10.

51 J. D. Levenson, 'The Eighth Principle of Judaism and the Literary Simultaneity of Scripture', *JR* 68 (1988), pp. 205–25.

52 'Wer über heilige Schriften gläubig nachdenkt, wird sie als ein einheitliches Ganzes schauen und zusammenfassen. Offenbarungen der Gottheit müssen sich ihrem Wesen nach von menschlichen Äußerungen unterscheiden und in ihrem Inhalt ohne Widerspruch sein'; Leipoldt and Morenz, *Heilige Schriften*, p. 37. This principle certainly applied to the New Testament from an early date. Gaius is said to have rejected the Fourth Gospel and Revelation on the grounds that they contradicted Paul and the Synoptic Gospels, since such contradictions were a priori impossible within inspired Scripture. Hippolytus refuted him, not by arguing that such contradictions could occur, but by 'demonstrating' that the contradictions in question were only apparent.

53 See note 41 above.

54 See J. Miles, *God: A Biography*, New York, 1995, pp. 15–19.

BIBLIOGRAPHY

Aland, B., 'Marcion: Versuch einer neuen Interpretation', *ZThK* 70 (1973), pp. 420–47.

Aland, B. and K., *Der Text des Neuen Testaments: Einführung in die wissenschaftlichen Ausgaben sowie in Theorie und Praxis der modernen Textkritik*, 2nd edn, Stuttgart 1989.

Alexander, Loveday, 'The "Living Voice": Scepticism towards the Written Word in Early Christian and in Graeco-Roman Texts', in D. J. A. Clines, S. E. Fowl, and S. E. Porter (eds), *The Bible in Three Dimensions: Essays in Celebration of Forty Years of Biblical Studies in the University of Sheffield* (*JSOT* Suppl. Series 87), Sheffield 1990, pp. 221–49.

Alföldi, A., 'Die Ausgestaltung des monarchischen Zeremoniells am römischen Kaiserhofe', *Mitteilungen des deutschen archäologischen Instituts* (Römische Abteilung) 49 (1934), pp. 1–118.

Arns, E., *La technique du livre d'après S. Jérome*, Paris 1953.

Aune, David, *The New Testament in its Literary Environment*, Philadelphia 1987.

Aune, David, *Prophecy in Early Christianity and the Ancient Mediterranean World*, Grand Rapids 1983.

Baarda, T., 'Factors in the Harmonization of the Gospels, especially in the Diatessaron of Tatian', in W. L. Petersen (ed.), *Gospel Traditions in the Second Century: Origins, Recensions, Text, and Transmission* (Christianity and Judaism in Antiquity 3), London 1989, pp. 133–56.

Baarda, T., *Essays on the Diatessaron*, Kampen 1994.

Bacher, W., *Die exegetische Terminologie der jüdischen Traditionsliteratur* I.

Bacon, B. W., *Studies in Matthew*, London 1930.

Balogh, J., ' "Voces paginarum": Beiträge zur Geschichte des lauten Lesens und Schreibens', *Philologus* 82 (1927), pp. 84–109 and 212–40.

Barnard, L. W., 'The Old Testament and Judaism in the Writings of Justin Martyr', *VT* 14 (1974), pp. 395–406.

Barr, James, ' "Guessing" in the Septuagint', in D. Fraenkel, U. Quast, and J. W. Wevers (eds), *Studien zur Septuaginta – Robert Hanhart zu Ehren*, Göttingen 1990, pp. 19–34.

Barr, James, 'A New Look at Kethibh-Qere', OS 21 (1981), pp. 19–37.

Barr, James, 'Reading a Script without Vowels', in W. Haas (ed.), *Writing without Letters*, Manchester 1976, pp. 71–100.

Barr, James, 'Vocalization and the Analysis of Hebrew among the Ancient Translators', VTS 16 (1967), pp. 1–11.

Barr, James, *Holy Scripture: Canon, Authority, Criticism*, Oxford and Philadelphia 1983.

Barr, James, *The Typology of Literalism in Ancient Biblical Translation* (Nachrichten der Akademie der Wissenschaften in Göttingen I. Philologisch-historische Klasse 11), Göttingen 1979, pp. 275–325.

Barthélemy, D., and Milik, J. T., *Qumran Cave 1* (Discoveries in the Judaean Desert 1), Oxford 1955.

Barton, John, *Oracles of God: Perceptions of Ancient Prophecy in Israel after the Exile*, London 1986, New York 1988.

Barton, John, *People of the Book? The Authority of the Bible in Christianity*, London 1988.

Barton, John, *Reading the Old Testament: Method in Biblical Study*, London 1984, 2nd edn 1996.

Beatrice, P. F., 'Une citation de l'Évangile de Matthieu dans l'Épître de Barnabé', in J. M. Severin (ed.), *The New Testament in Early Christianity (La réception des écrits néotestamentaires dans le christianisme primitif)* (BETL 86), Leuven 1989, pp. 231–45.

Beckwith, R. T., 'Formation of the Hebrew Bible', in M. J. Mulder (ed.), *Mikra: Text, Translation, Reading and Interpretation of the Hebrew Bible in Ancient Judaism and Early Christianity*, Assen/Maastricht and Philadelphia 1988, pp. 87–135.

Beckwith, R. T., 'A Modern Theory of the Old Testament Canon', *VT* 41 (1991), pp. 385–95.

Beckwith, R. T., *The Old Testament Canon of the New Testament Church and its Background in Early Judaism*, London 1985.

Bellinzoni, A., *The Sayings of Jesus in the Writings of Justin Martyr* (NT Suppl. Series 17), Leiden 1967.

Betz, O., 'Das Problem des "Kanons" in den Texten von Qumran', in G. Maier (ed.), *Der Kanon der Bibel*, Giessen 1990, pp. 70–101.

Blau, Ludwig, *Studien zum althebräischen Buchwesen und zur biblischen Litteratur- und Textgeschichte*, Strasbourg 1902.

Blau, Ludwig, *Zur Einleitung in die Heilige Schrift*, Budapest 1894.

Blenkinsopp, J., *A History of Prophecy in Israel*, London 1984.

Blenkinsopp, J., *Prophecy and Canon: A Contribution to the Study of Jewish Origins*, Notre Dame 1977.

Bradshaw, Paul F., *Daily Prayer in the Early Church* (Alcuin Club Collection 63), London 1981.

Brice, W. C., 'The Principles of Non-Phonetic Writing', in W. Haas (ed.), *Writing without Letters* (Manchester 1976), pp. 29–44.

Brown, R. E., 'The *Gospel of Peter* and Canonical Gospel Priority', *NTS* 33 (1987), pp. 321–43.

Brox, N., *Der Hirt des Hermas*, Göttingen 1991.

Burke, P., 'The Uses of Literacy in Early Modern Italy', in P. Burke and R. Porter (eds), *The Social History of Language*, Cambridge 1987.

Burridge, Richard, *What are the Gospels? A Comparison with Graeco-Roman Biography* (SNTS MS 70), Cambridge 1992.

Burrow, J. A., *Medieval Writers and their Work: Middle English Literature and its Background, 1100–1500*, Oxford 1982.

Campenhausen, Hans von, 'Die Entstehung des Neuen Testaments', *Heidelberger Jahrbücher* 7 (Berlin/Göttingen/Heidelberg 1963), pp. 1–

12; repr. in E. Käsemann (ed.), *Das Neue Testament als Kanon*, Göttingen 1970, pp. 109–23.

Campenhausen, Hans von, *Die Entstehung der christlichen Bibel* (BHTh 39), Tübingen 1968; ET *The Formation of the Christian Bible*, London 1972.

Carruthers, Mary, *The Book of Memory: A Study of Memory in Medieval Culture*, Cambridge 1990.

Chadwick, H., *Origen: Contra Celsum*, Cambridge 1953.

Childs, Brevard S., *Biblical Theology of the Old and New Testaments*, Philadelphia 1992.

Childs, Brevard S., *Introduction to the Old Testament as Scripture*, London and Philadelphia 1979.

Childs, Brevard S., *Old Testament Theology in a Canonical Context*, London 1985.

Clabeaux, J. J., *A Lost Edition of Paul: A Reassessment of the Pauline Corpus attested by Marcion* (CBQ MS 21), Washington DC 1989.

Clanchy, M. T., *From Memory to Written Record*, London 1979.

Cohen, S. J. D., 'The Significance of Yavneh', *HUCA* 55 (1984), pp. 27–53.

Copenhaver, B. P., 'Lefèvre d'Étaples, Symphorien Champier, and the Secret Names of God', *Journal of the Warburg and Courtauld Institutes* 40 (1977), pp. 189–211.

Cosgrove, C. H., 'Justin Martyr and the Emerging Christian Canon: Observations on the Purpose and Destination of the Dialogue with Trypho', *Vigiliae Christianae* 36 (1982), pp. 209–32.

Cressy, D., 'Books as Totems in Seventeenth-Century England and New England', *Journal of Library History* 21 (1986), pp. 92–106.

Dahl, Niels A., 'The Particularity of the Pauline Epistles as a Problem in the Ancient Church', *Neotestamentica et Patristica* (*NT* Suppl. series 6), Leiden 1962, pp. 261–71.

Dahl, Niels A., 'Widersprüche in der Bibel, ein altes hermeneutisches Problem', *Studia Theologica* 25 (1971), pp. 1–19.

Davson, Joanna, 'Critical and Conservative Treatments of Prophecy in Nineteenth-Century Britain', D.Phil. dissertation, Oxford 1991.

Delcor, M., 'Des diverses manières d'écrire le tétragramme sacré dans les anciens documents hébraïques', *Revue de l'histoire des religions* 147 (1955), pp. 145–73.

Dodd, C. H., *The Present Task in New Testament Studies*, Cambridge 1936.

Dohmen, Christoph and Oeming, Manfred, *Biblischer Kanon: Warum und Wozu? Eine Kanontheologie* (Quaestiones Disputatae 137), Freiburg/Basle/Vienna 1992.

Douglas, Mary, *Purity and Danger*, London 1969.

Flesseman-van Leer, Ellen, 'Prinzipien der Sammlung und Ausscheidung bei der Bildung des Kanons', *ZThK* 61 (1964), pp. 404–20.

Ford, J. Massyngbaerde, 'New Covenant, Jesus, and Canonization', in R. Brooks and J. J. Collins (eds), *Hebrew Bible or Old Testament?*, Notre Dame 1990, pp. 31–9.

Frank, Isidor, *Der Sinn der Kanonbildung* (Freiburger Theologische Studien 90), Freiburg 1971.

Franklin, S., 'Literacy and Documentation in Early Medieval Russia', *Speculum* 60 (1985), pp. 1–38.

Frye, C. Northop, *The Great Code: The Bible and Literature*, London, Melbourne and Henley 1982.

Gamble, Harry Y., 'The Pauline Corpus and the Early Christian Book', in W. S. Babcock (ed.), *Paul and the Legacies of Paul*, Dallas 1990, pp. 265–80.

Gamble, Harry Y., 'The Redaction of the Pauline Letters and the Formation of the Pauline Corpus', *HThR* 94 (1975), pp. 403–18.

Gamble, Harry Y., *The New Testament Canon: Its Making and Meaning*, Philadephia 1985.

Gamble, Harry, Y., *The Textual History of the Letter to the Romans* (Studies and Documents 42), Grand Rapids 1977.

Gebhart, O., Harnack, A. von, and Zahn, T., *Patrum Apostolicorum Opera*, Leipzig 1877.

Genette, G., 'Structure and Function of the Title in Literature', *Critical Enquiry* 14 (1988), pp. 692–720.

Gerhardsson, Birger, art. 'Oral Tradition (New Testament)', in R. J. Coggins and J. L. Houlden (eds), *A Dictionary of Biblical Interpretation*, London 1990, pp. 498–501.

Gerhardsson, Birger, *Memory and Manuscript: Oral Tradition and Written Transmission in Rabbinic Judaism and Early Christianity* (Acta Seminarii Neotestamentici Upsaliensis 22), Lund and Copenhagen 1961.

Gese, H., 'Die dreifache Gestaltwerdung des Alten Testaments', in M. Klopfenstein (ed.), *Mitte der Schrift? Ein jüdisch-christliches Gespräch* (Judaica et Christiana 11), Berne 1987, pp. 299–328.

Gese, H., *Vom Sinai zum Zion*, Munich 1974.

Gese, H., *Zur biblischen Theologie*, Munich 1977, 2nd edn Tübingen 1983.

Ginsburg, C. D. (ed.), *The Massoreth ha-Massoreth of Elias Levita*, London 1867.

Ginzberg, L., *Legends of the Jews* IV, Philadelphia 1982–3.

Goldingay, J., *Approaches to Old Testament Interpretation*, Leicester 1981.

Goodman, M. D., 'Sacred Scripture and "Defiling the Hands"', *JTS* 41 (1990), pp. 99–107.

Goodspeed, E., *The Formation of the New Testament*, Chicago 1926.

Goulder, M. D., *The Evangelists' Calendar*, London 1978.

Goulder, M. D., *Midrash and Lection in Matthew*, London 1974.

Graham, W. A., *Beyond the Written Word: Oral Aspects of Scripture in the History of Religion*, Cambridge 1987.

Grant, R. M., *The Formation of the New Testament*, New York and London 1965.

Grant, R. M., *Heresy and Criticism: The Search for Authenticity in Early Christian Literature*, Louisville, Ky. 1993.

Grant, R. M. (ed. and tr.), *Theophilus of Antioch Ad Autolycum*, Oxford 1970.

Hahneman, Geoffrey M., *The Muratorian Fragment and the Development of the Canon*, Oxford 1992.

Halivni, D. Weiss, *Peshat and Derash: Plain and Applied Meaning in Rabbinic Exegesis*, New York 1994.

Haran, Menachem, 'Midrashic and Literal Exegesis and the Critical Method in Biblical Research', in Sara Japhet (ed.), *Studies in Bible* (Scripta Hierosolymita 31), Jerusalem 1986, pp. 19–48.

Harnack, Adolf von, *Bible Reading in the Early Church*, London and New York 1912.

Harnach, Adolf von, *Judentum und Judenchristentum in Justins Dialog mit Trypho* (TU 39), Berlin 1913.

Harnack, Adolf von, *Marcion: Das Evangelium vom fremden Gott (Eine Monographie zur Geschichte der Grundlegung der katholischen Kirche)* (TU 45), Leipzig 1921.

Harnack, Adolf von, *The Origin of the New Testament and the Most Important Consequences of the New Creation*, London 1925.

Harris, H., *The Tübingen School*, Oxford 1975.

Hennecke, F., *New Testament Apocrypha*, ed. W. Schneemelcher, vol. 1, London 1963.

Hoffmann, R. J., *Marcion: On the Restitution of Christianity. An Essay on the Development of Radical Paulinist Theology in the Second Century*, Chico, Calif. 1984.

Horbury, William, 'Wisdom of Solomon in the Muratorian Fragment', *JTS* 45 (1994), pp. 149–59.

Jepsen, A., 'Kanon und Text des Alten Testaments', *TLZ* 74 (1949), cols 65–74.

Kelber, Werner, *The Oral and the Written Gospel*, Philadelphia 1983.

Kelly, L. G., *The True Interpreter: A History of Translation Theory and Practice in the West*, Oxford 1979.

Kenyon, F. G., *Books and Readers in Ancient Greece and Rome*, Oxford 1932, 2nd edn 1950.

Kermode, Frank, *The Genesis of Secrecy: On the Interpretation of Narrative*, Cambridge, Mass. and London 1979.

Kermode, F. and Alter, R., *The Literary Guide to the Bible*, London 1987.

Kim, Young Kyu, 'Palaeographical Dating of P^{46} to the Late First Century', *Biblica* 69 (1988), pp. 248–57.

Kloppenborg, J., *The Formation of Q: Trajectories in Ancient Wisdom Collections*, Philadelphia 1987.

Knox, B. M. W., 'Books and Readers in the Greek World', *Cambridge History of Classical Literature* 1, ed. P. E. Easterling and B. M. Walker, Cambridge 1985, pp. 1–16.

Knox, B. M. W., 'Silent Reading in Antiquity', *Greek, Roman, and Byzantine Studies* 9 (1968), pp. 421–35.

Knox, John, *Marcion and the New Testament*, Chicago 1942.

Knox, John, *Philemon among the Letters of Paul*, Chicago 1935.

Koester, Helmut, *Ancient Christian Gospels: Their History and Development*, London 1990.

Koester, Helmut, *The Text of the Synoptic Gospels in the Second Century:*

Origins, Recensions, Text, and Transmission, Notre Dame and London 1989.

Kuhn, K. G., *Konkordanz zu den Qumrantexten*, Göttingen 1960.

Kümmel, W. G., *Das neue Testament: Geschichte der Erforschung seiner Probleme*, Freiburg 1970; ET *The New Testament: The History of the Investigation of its Problems*, London 1973.

Kümmel, W. G., *Introduction to the New Testament*, London 1975.

Leiman, Sid Z., *The Canonization of Hebrew Scripture: The Talmudic and Midrashic Evidence*, Hamden, Conn. 1976.

Leipoldt, J., *Geschichte des neutestamentlichen Kanons*, Leipzig 1907.

Leipoldt, J. and Morenz, S., *Heilige Schriften, Beobachtungen zur Religionsgeschichte der antiken Mittelmeerwelt*, Leipzig 1953.

Levenson, J.D., 'The Eighth Principle of Judaism and the Literary Simultaneity of Scripture', *JR* 68 (1988), pp. 205–25.

Levenson, J. D., *God and the Persistence of Evil*, San Francisco and London 1988.

Lieberman, S., *Hellenism in Jewish Palestine*, New York 1950.

Lindars, Barnabas, *New Testament Apologetic*, London 1961.

Louth, Andrew, *Discerning the Mystery*, Oxford 1983.

Maier, Gerhard, 'Der Abschluß des jüdischen Kanons und das Lehrhaus von Jabne', in G. Maier (ed.), *Der Kanon der Bibel* (Giessen 1990), pp. 12–24.

Maier, G. (ed.), *Der Kanon der Bibel*, Giessen 1990.

McCown, C. C., 'Codex and Roll in the New Testament', *HThR* 34 (1941), pp. 219–50.

McDonald, L. M., *The Formation of the Christian Bible*, Nashville 1988.

McKane, W., *Proverbs* (OTL), London 1970.

Meade, D. G., *Pseudonymity and Canon: An Investigation into the Relationship of Authorship and Authority in Jewish and Earliest Christian Traditions*, Grand Rapids 1986.

Merkel, Helmut, *Die Pluralität der Evangelien als theologisches und exegetisches Problem in der Alten Kirche* (Traditio Christiana III), Berne 1978.

Merkel, Helmut, *Die Widersprüche zwischen den Evangelien* (WUNT 13), Tübingen 1971.

Metzger, Bruce M., *The Canon of the New Testament: Its Origin, Development, and Significance*, Oxford 1987.

Metzger, Bruce M., *The Early Versions of the New Testament: Their Origin, Transmission, and Limitations*, Oxford 1977.

Miles, J., *God: A Biography*, New York 1995.

Mink, H.-Aa., 'The Use of Scripture in the Temple Scroll and the Status of the Scroll as Law', *SJOT* 1987, pp. 20–50.

Minnis, A. J., *Medieval Theory of Authorship: Scholastic Literary Attitudes in the Later Middle Ages*, Aldershot 1988.

Mitteis, L. and Wilcken, U. (eds), *Grundzüge und Chrestomathie der Papyruskunde* I.

Morgan, Robert, 'The Hermeneutical Significance of Four Gospels', *Interpretation* 33 (1979), pp. 376–88.

Morgan, Robert, art. 'Tübingen School', in R. J. Coggins and J. L.

Houlden (eds), *A Dictionary of Biblical Interpretation*, London 1990, pp. 710–13.

Morrow, W. S., art. 'Kethib and Qere', *ABD* 4, pp. 24–30.

Muddiman, John B., 'The First-Century Crisis: Christian Origins', in S. Sutherland, J. L. Houlden, P. Clarke, and F. Hardy (eds), *The World's Religions*, London 1988.

Noth, Martin, *Die Gesetze im Pentateuch (ihre Voraussetzungen und ihr Sinn)* (Schriften der Königsberger Gelehrten Gesellschaft, geisteswissenschaftliche Klasse 17), Halle, 1940; ET 'The Laws in the Pentateuch: Their Assumptions and Meaning', in M. Noth, *The Laws in the Pentateuch and Other Essays*, Edinburgh and London 1966, pp. 1–107.

Oeming, Manfred, *Gesamtbiblische Theologien der Gegenwart*, Stuttgart 1985.

Ong, Walter, *Orality and Literacy*, London 1982.

Osborn, E. F., *Justin Martyr* (BHTh 47), Tübingen 1973.

Overbeck, Franz, review of O. Gebhart, A. Harnack, and T. Zahn, *Patrum apostolicorum opera*, fascicle 3 (Leipzig 1877), *TLZ* 30 (1878), cols 281–5.

Overbeck, Franz, *Zur Geschichte des Kanons*, Chemnitz 1880, repr. Darmstadt 1965.

Parker, David, 'The Early Traditions of Jesus' Sayings on Divorce', *Theology* 96 (1993), pp. 372–83.

Parker, David, 'Scripture is Tradition', *Theology* 94 (1991), pp. 11–17.

Perrot, C., 'The Reading of the Bible in the Ancient Synagogue', in M. J. Mulder (ed.), *Mikra: Text, Translation, Reading and Interpretation of the Hebrew Bible in Ancient Judaism and Early Christianity*, Assen/Maastricht and Philadelphia 1988, pp. 137–59.

Petersen, W. L., *Tatian's Diatessaron: Its Creation, Dissemination, Significance, and History in Scholarship* (*Vigilae Christianae* Supplement 25), Leiden 1994.

Pietersma, A., 'Kyrios or Tetragram: A Renewed Quest for the Original LXX', in A. Pietersma and C. Cox (eds), *De Septuaginta: Studies in Honour of John William Wevers on his Sixty-Fifth Birthday*, Mississauga, Ontario 1984, pp. 85–101.

Piper, Otto, 'The Nature of the Gospel according to Justin Martyr', *JR* 41 (1961), pp. 155–68.

Prickett, Stephen (ed.), *Reading the Text*, Oxford 1991.

Revell, E. J., artt. 'Masorah' and 'Masoretes', *ABD* 4, pp. 592–3 and 593–4.

Roberts, C. H., 'The Codex', *Proceedings of the British Academy* 40 (1954), pp. 169–204.

Roberts, C. H., *Manuscript, Society and Belief in Early Egypt* (The Schweich Lectures for 1977), London 1979.

Roberts, C. H. and Skeat, T.C., *The Birth of the Codex*, London 1987.

Sanders, E. P. and Davies, M., *Studying the Synoptic Gospels*, London 1989.

Sanders, J. A., *From Sacred Story to Sacred Text: Canon as Paradigm*, Philadelphia 1987.

Sanders, J. A., *Torah and Canon*, Philadelphia 1972.

Sanders, J. N., *The Fourth Gospel in the Early Church*, Cambridge 1943.

Sarna, N. M., 'The Order of the Books', in C. Berlin (ed.), *Studies in Jewish Bibliography, History and Literature in Honor of I. Edward Kiev*, New York 1971, pp. 407–13.

Schams, Christine, 'The Attitude towards Sacred and Secular Written Documents in First-Century Judaism', M.Phil. dissertation, Oxford 1993.

Schmid, H. H., *Wesen und Geschichte der Weisheit*, Berlin 1966.

Schmidt, K. L., 'Die Stellung der Evangelien in der allgemeinen Literaturgeschichte', *ΕΥΧΑΡΙΣΤΗΡΙΟΝ (Gunkel-Festschrift)*, Göttingen 1923.

Schmithals, W., 'On the Composition and Earliest Collections of the Major Epistles of Paul', in J. E. Steeley (ed.), *Paul and the Gnostics*, Nashville, Tenn. 1972 = *ZNW* 51 (1960), pp. 225–45.

Scholem, G. 'The Name of God and the Linguistic Theory of the Kabbalah', *Diogenes* 79–80 (1972), pp. 59–194.

Scholem, G., *Major Trends in Jewish Mysticism*, Jerusalem 1941.

Scholem, G., *Zur Kabbala und ihrer Symbolik*, Zurich 1960; ET *On the Kabbalah and its Symbolism*, London 1965.

Skehan, P. W. 'The Divine Name at Qumran, in the Masada Scroll, and in the Septuagint', *Bulletin of the International Organization for Septuagint and Cognate Studies* 13 (1980), pp. 14–44.

Smith, Wilfred Cantwell, *What is Scripture?* London 1993.

Stendahl, K., *The School of St Matthew and its Use of the Old Testament*, 2nd edn, Philadelphia 1968.

Stuhlhofer, Franz, *Der Gebrauch der Bibel von Jesus bis Euseb: eine statistische Untersuchung zur Kanongeschichte*, Wuppertal 1988.

Stylianopoulos, T., *Justin Martyr and the Mosaic Law* (SBL dissertation series 20), Missoula, Mont. 1975.

Sundberg, Albert C., art. 'Canon of the NT', *Interpreter's Dictionary of the Bible* Supplement, Nashville 1976, pp. 136–40.

Sundberg, Albert C., art. 'Muratorian Fragment', *Interpreter's Dictionary of the Bible* Supplement, Nashville 1976, pp. 609–10.

Sundberg, Albert C., 'The "Old Testament": A Christian Canon', *CBQ* 30 (1968), pp. 143–55.

Sundberg, Albert C., 'Towards a Revised History of the New Testament Canon', *Studia Evangelica* 4 (TU 102, Berlin 1968), pp. 452–61.

Sundberg, Albert C., *The Old Testament of the Early Church*, Cambridge, Mass. and London 1964.

Swarat, U., 'Das Werden des neutestamentlichen Kanons', in G. Maier (ed.), *Der Kanon der Bibel*, Giessen 1990, pp. 25–51.

Swete, H. B., *An Introduction to the Old Testament in Greek*, Cambridge 1900.

Swinburne, Richard, *Revelation*, Oxford 1992.

Talmon, S., 'The Three Scrolls of the Law that were found in the Temple Court', *Textus* 2 (1962), pp. 14–27.

Taylor, Miriam, 'The Jews in the Writings of the Early Church Fathers (150–312): Men of Straw or Formidable Rivals?', D.Phil. dissertation, Oxford 1991.

Taylor, Miriam, *Anti-Judaism and Early Christian Identity: A Critique of the Scholarly Consensus* (Studia Post-Biblica 46), Leiden 1995.

Thiselton, Anthony C., *New Horizons in Hermeneutics*, London 1992.

Thomas, Rosalind, *Literacy and Orality in Ancient Greece*, Cambridge 1992.

Tov, Emanuel, *Textual Criticism of the Hebrew Bible*, Minneapolis 1992.

Trobisch, David, 'Die Endradaktion des Neuen Testaments: eine Untersuchung zur Entstehung der christlichen Bibel', Habilitationsschrift, Heidelberg 1994.

Trobisch, David, *Paul's Letter Collection: Tracing the Origins*, Minneapolis 1994.

Unnik, W. C. van, 'De la règle $\mu\acute{\eta}\tau\epsilon$ $\pi\rho o\sigma\theta\epsilon\hat{\iota}\nu\alpha\iota$ $\mu\acute{\eta}\tau\epsilon$ $\alpha\phi\epsilon\lambda\epsilon\hat{\iota}\nu$ dans l'histoire du canon', *Vigilae Christianae* 3 (1949), pp. 1–36.

Vielhauer, P., *Geschichte der urchristlichen Literatur*, 2nd edn, Berlin 1978.

Vischer, L., 'Die Rechtfertigung der Schriftstellerei in der alten Kirche', *TZ* 12 (1956), pp. 320–36.

Weingreen, J., 'Oral Torah and Written Record', in F. F. Bruce and E. G. Rupp (eds), *Holy Book and Holy Tradition*, Manchester 1968, pp. 54–67.

Wellhausen, Julius, *Einleitung in die drei ersten Evangelien*, Berlin 1911.

Wellhausen, Julius, *Geschichte Israels I*, Marburg 1878, 2nd edn, as *Prolegomena zur Geschichte Israels* 1883; ET *Prolegomena to the History of Israel*, Edinburgh 1885; repr. as *Prolegomena to the History of Ancient Israel*, New York 1957.

Westcott, Brooke Foss, *A General Survey of the History of the Canon of the New Testament*, London 1885.

Widengren, G., 'Tradition and Literature in Early Judaism', *Numen* 12 (1965), pp. 42–7.

Williams, D. S., 'Reconsidering Marcion's Gospel', *JBL* 108 (1989), pp. 477–96.

Wolfenson, L. B., 'Implications of the Place of the Book of Ruth in Editions, Manuscripts, and Canon of the Old Testament', *HUCA* 1 (1924), pp. 90–129.

Wordsworth, Christopher, *On the Canon of the Scriptures of the Old and New Testament*, London 1848.

Wrede, W., *Untersuchungen zum ersten Clemensbrief*, 1891.

Zahn, Theodor, *Geschichte des neutestamentlichen Kanons*, 2 vols, Leipzig 1888–92.

Zahn, Theodor, *Ignatius von Antiochien*, Gotha 1873.

Index of Biblical and other Primary Sources

Index of Modern Names

Subject Index